Schools Council
Research Studies

# Record Keeping
# in Primary Schools

Philip Clift
Gaby Weiner
Edwin Wilson

Macmillan Education
London and Basingstoke

© Schools Council Publications 1981

First published 1981

Reprinted 1982

Published by
MACMILLAN EDUCATION LTD
Houndmills Basingstoke Hampshire RG21 2XS
and London

Associated companies throughout the world

Printed and bound in Great Britain
at The Pitman Press, Bath

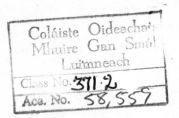
British Library Cataloguing in Publication Data

Clift, Philip
Record keeping in primary schools. – (Research
studies/Schools Council)
1. Personnel records in education – England
2. Elementary school administration – England
I. Title    II. Weiner, Gaby
III. Wilson, Edwin
651.5'042        LB2845.7

ISBN 0-333-30945-6

# Contents

# Tables, figures and example records

# Authors' note

The Schools Council project on which this report is
based began in 1976 and lasted for two years. Edwin
Wilson was seconded to the National Foundation for
Educational Research from the Berkshire local authority as research officer, responsible for its day-to-
day running. Beulah Mathew was project secretary
throughout.

### ACKNOWLEDGEMENTS

The team members wish to acknowledge their gratitude
to the primary school advisers who nominated schools,
the teachers in those schools for their patience and
hospitality, and the teachers in the working groups
set up by the project for their year-long loyalty and
hard work, done mainly after the end of the teaching
day.

  Thanks are due to all the schools and local authorities that provided examples of records, some of which
are reproduced in this book, and to the following pub-
lishers, organizations and authors, for permission to
include copyright material from the sources named:

the Macmillan Publishing Co., New York, for several
extracts from books by N.E. Gronlund: *Measurement and
Evaluation in Teaching*, copyright © 1976 Norman E.
Gronlund, and *Stating Behavioral Objectives for Class-
room Instruction*, copyright © 1970 and 1978 Norman
E. Gronlund;
the Schools Council and Oliver & Boyd, for Figs 2 and
3 and Example 5.15, from *Match and Mismatch: Raising
Questions*, by the Schools Council Progress in Learning
Science project;
Professor Michael Rutter, for Example 5.19, from his
Child Scale B;
the National Foundation for Educational Research, for
Fig. 5, from *Basic Mathematics Test B*;
the Bobbs-Merrill Co., Indianapolis, for the chart on
'Types of arithmetic habits observed in elementary
school pupils', from *Diagnostic Chart for Fundamental*

*Processes in Arithmetic*, by G.T. Buswell and L. John;
the Schools Council and Macmillan Education, for the
list of 72 aims of primary education, from *The Aims
of Primary Education: a Study of Teachers' Opinions*,
by P.M.E. Ashton *et al.*;
the Center for the Study of Evaluation, Graduate
School of Education, University of California (Los
Angeles), for the taxonomy of early childhood
education goals, from *Preschool/Kindergarten Test
Evaluations*, by R. Hoepfner *et al.*;
the Service Children's Education Authority of the
Ministry of Defence, for appendix E.

# 1 Introduction: the context of the project

Publicly funded research and development tend to
reflect the priorities of their day.  Thus, whilst
for teachers the topic of school record keeping has
a perennial quality, the lifetime of the Schools
Council project on Record Keeping in Primary Schools
has coincided with an increase in the amount of
public attention given to it.  This attention has
been characterized by concern over two main issues:
*confidentiality* and *accountability*.

Both are issues of general concern in our society
today, and the anxiety expressed probably arises to
some extent from perceptions of the 'big brother'
computer on the one hand and a sense of impotence in
the face of large institutions on the other.  Recorded information about the individual, obtained with
or without his/her co-operation, apparently available
to various persons and agencies without his/her consent when that individual does not have access as a
right, is one very real source of popular misgiving.
Institutions, governmental and commercial, with great
potential for influencing the life of the individual,
to the cost of which he/she contributes, directly or
indirectly, but which neither he/she nor an elected
representative appears to control, are another.

In schools, a curriculum designed broadly to develop certain skills is offered within an organizational
framework which implicitly endorses certain attitudes
and values.  Pupils' responses to both are assessed,
both formally and informally, and the results of this
assessment recorded.  The appropriateness of the
curriculum, both in content and context, the efficiency with which it is taught, the impartiality and
validity with which pupils' responses to it are
assessed and the accuracy with which these assessments
are recorded are all quite proper subjects for public
concern.  Where records are of doubtful accuracy,
ambiguously expressed, or lacking in important information, future teaching may be undermined to the
immediate detriment of the individual pupil and the
ultimate credibility of the education system as a

whole.

As public issues, the control of personal information and the accountability of institutions seem likely to endure.  They have political and technical
attributes.  *Who* should have access to specific information is a political question, as is who should be
held accountable, to whom and for what.  *How* to ensure
the appropriate and efficient dissemination of confidential information, and how account may most effectively be rendered, are technical questions.  Since
the issue of confidentiality of school records is
dealt with fully in chapter 8, it is not proposed to
discuss it further here.  Accountability, whilst implicit throughout this report, is not the subject of
a separate chapter and thus merits further discussion.

In the commercial world the keeping of records and
accounts is seen as a basis for sound business practice.  Outputs of goods and services are quantified
and related to inputs of manpower and finance as a
measure of efficiency.  Accounting in this sense can
be given concrete expression in terms of profitabil-
ity, payment of dividends and the return on capital
invested.  This measurement of productivity or effectiveness assumes that a system has a measurable input,
a process and a measurable output.  But '... when we
come to apply the concept to education there are no
physical units of output to be measured, and no
selling price to indicate the money value of output'.[1]
Further, this model of educational accountability
assumes that schools are in fact wholly, or at any
rate mainly, responsible for the quality of pupil they
'produce'.  Research suggests that this is not so:
'Variations in what children learn in school depend
largely on variations in what they bring to school,
not on variations in what schools offer them'.[2]

Accountability in the professions has thus to be
of a different nature.  The disparate requirements of
those with a 'right to know' (employers, supervisors,
professional organizations, the general public),
imply a wide variety of output measures.  School records serve a number of purposes (see chapter 3) and
accountability, in the educational context, has not
usually been seen in a narrow sense but rather in relation to persons who 'need to know'.  These include
parents, pupils, fellow-teachers, headteachers, education officers, advisers, educational psychologists and
others with a professional need for information.  The
kinds of information which these different persons
'need to know' are quite disparate;  hence educational
accountability takes many forms.

It appears, however, that recently the concept has

begun to be understood more often in its rather
narrower sense of bringing persons to book where there
is suspicion of inefficiency or malpractice:  'Only
those with a vested interest in concealing their own
mediocrity, it can be argued, will strive to deny
citizens the information on which they may base a rational and discriminating choice'.[3]  Recent economic
constraint in the public sector has heightened the
cost-consciousness of the general public, and has
probably much to do with the present interest in
accountability:  'If the professionals don't offer to
evaluate their own performance at all levels, then an
increasingly cost-conscious public may demand that
someone else does it for them'.[4]  This new climate,
actively fostered by bodies such as the Consumer
Council, has encouraged customers to complain when
goods and services are below their expected standard.
However, it is difficult to apply this spirit of con-
sumerism to education:  are parents or pupils the
consumers, or both?  Whose criteria are to be used in
assessing the product?

  Public discussion about 'standards' in education
featured prominently but inconclusively during the
lifetime of the project (1976-78).  According to the
1977 Green Paper which summarized the series of regional debates initiated by the Prime Minister James
Callaghan's speech on education given at Ruskin
College, Oxford in 1976:  'At the regional conferences
there was no widespread view that there had been a
serious decline in educational standards.  But elsewhere the conviction has been expressed that deterio-
ration has occurred.'[5]  The alleged fall in standards
has received considerable attention in the popular
press and in a series of 'Black Papers' on education.
Comments on the latter, such as:  '... the factual
basis of the Black Paper view is extremely weak ...
handicapped by severe philosophical confusion ... a
plea for ideological commitment to the values and
practices of a social order ... now passed',[6] indicate how far socio-political views colour the argument:  standards must be seen in the social context
of a particular time.  Since the term is used by
the general public in a rather loose way to include
many aspects of academic and personal behaviour, it
would seem difficult to come to any firm conclusions about any alleged rise or fall in standards.

  It would appear also that there is a mismatch between what some schools are providing in the way of
education and what employers expect of their employ-
ees.  This view was given cautious endorsement in the
Green Paper:  'In some schools the curriculum has been

overloaded, so that the basic skills of literacy and
numeracy, the building blocks of education, have been
neglected. A small minority of schools has simply
failed to provide an adequate education by modern
standards.'[7]  The Department of Education and Science
(DES) has set up an Assessment of Performance Unit
(APU) in order to obtain information about pupils'
performances in a more systematic way than hitherto.
The data gathered will enable a national picture to
be built up, though only after some years of data
collection will it be possible to say with any certainty whether standards of attainment are rising or
falling relative to the first monitoring results
(mathematics 1978, language 1979, science 1980, first
foreign language later.  Monitoring in personal and
social development, aesthetics and physical development are all the subject of exploratory study:  there
is no commitment at the time of writing to conduct
monitoring in these areas).

Other methods of collecting information about
pupils' performance, particularly school records, have
been much less systematic and are therefore of little
value in building up a national picture.  The value of
school records in providing information for making
decisions depends a great deal on the zeal and accuracy of persons completing them.  Doubts about the
efficiency of these records were highlighted recently
(1975-6) when one local authority, following a change
in its political composition, decided to retain
eleven-plus selection for grammar schools.  The switch
came too late to allow for the usual selection procedures and it was decided to allocate pupils to secondary schools on the basis of their school records.
This appeared to engender much consternation locally;
it was rumoured that many of the pupils' records contained minimal information and some had no entries at
all on them, apart from the pupil's name.  This incident serves as a cautionary tale for the unwary.  One
never knows when accounting of this kind, based on
school records, may be required for unexpected but
perfectly legitimate reasons.

'Standards' in relation to school record keeping
pose political and technical problems.  The problems
of rendering account in the light of changes in ways
of school organization are mainly technical.
Teachers' completion of a weekly record book has
suited the class-based teaching approach.  The teacher
was able to 'control' the progress of pupils within a
manageable range, and entries in the weekly record
book indicated what a teacher had planned and *taught*
and, by implication, what children had 'learnt'.

The Plowden Report (1967)[8] advocated a more informal approach to educating primary age pupils.  The
philosophy behind the so-called 'progressive movement'
in education was the provision of facilities which
enabled a happy and supportive *learning* atmosphere to
be created in schools.  Where a 'progressive' approach
has been adopted, the emphasis for teaching purposes
has been on individuals or small groups of pupils
rather than on a whole-class group.  The most common
terms for describing the different aspects of changes
in organization are as follows.

(1)  *Integrated day:*  Several activities, e.g.
     mathematics, writing, etc., take place at the
     same time within a classroom or area.
(2)  *Vertical or family grouping:*  Pupils from
     different age groups work together.  One of
     the benefits claimed in support of this
     approach is that older pupils understand
     better what they have learnt by explaining to
     younger pupils how things are done ('to teach
     is to understand').
(3)  *Team teaching or co-operative teaching:*  Two
     or more teachers work together (one of them
     in a co-ordinating role) and have responsibil-
     ity for organizing a large group of pupils.
     The different talents of individual teachers
     can be used more flexibly in this way.
(4)  *Open plan buildings:*  This is a rather vague
     and generalized term used to describe buil-
     dings which do not have a traditional class-
     room structure.

The need to account and keep records of the varied
experiences and activities offered to children in
place of the 'taught curriculum' of yester-year poses
many problems.  In a study of team teaching practices
in Britain, Freeman[9] quotes, in case studies, the problems teachers had encountered in keeping adequate records.  The Record Keeping project team have visited
schools where team teaching has been abandoned primarily because of the difficulties involved in monitoring and recording pupil progress.
It is not suggested that there has been a wholesale
adoption of the 'progressive' mode.  On the contrary,
such reliable evidence as exists,[10] and the experience
of the project team, suggest that there has not.
Individualization of learning within a wide range of
organizational modes is, however, in evidence throughout the primary school domain, and has implications
for record keeping practice.

A factor which re-emphasizes the need for teachers
to keep accurate and appropriate records of children's
educational progress is the increase in population
mobility which has characterized the middle years of
this century.  Families have tended to move house more
frequently since the last war for a variety of
reasons.  Recent census figures suggest that 625 000
children move house each year.  Though many of these
may not change their school, a large number of children, sufficient to populate a sizable city, will
change schools at a time other than primary/secondary
transition.[11]

Until recently this turnover of pupils in schools
was matched by turnover of their teachers.  This turnover was running at an average rate of 20% and at 25%
in some inner-city areas in 1973.  However, recent
financial constraint and the reduction in the numbers
of teachers employed by local authorities, following
the decline in pupil population (mainly in primary
schools to date), have coincided with a reduction in
teacher mobility to about 10% (in 1977).[12]  Information regarding pupils' progress can easily be lost
unless adequate records are left before taking up a
new teaching post or other employment.

Teachers in many schools give account of themselves
to their pupils' parents through the sending of reports, by holding interviews or both.  The Taylor
Report, *A New Partnership for our Schools* (1977), in
one of its recommendations concerning the governing
of schools, states:

> ... the governing body should satisfy itself that adequate
> arrangements are made to inform parents, to involve them in
> their children's progress and welfare, to enlist their
> support, and to ensure their access to the school and a
> teacher by reasonable arrangement.[13]

The partnership between school and community was also
included in the recommendations of the 1977 Green
Paper, which also gives a mention to the subject of
accountability:

> It is an essential ingredient of this partnership that
> schools should be accountable for their performance:
> accountable to the local education authority - and those
> who elect it - as part of the public system of education;
> accountable through the school governors and managers to
> the local community that they serve.[14]

These were recommendations only, however, and the
following statement, contemporary with them, was probably an accurate portrayal of the situation prior to
the 1980 Education Act: 'The teacher is normally insu-

lated from the public, and from parents in particular, and is under little pressure to take account of their norms and expectations for his role'.[15]

The theme of accountability in this chapter has been used as a general focus in summarizing the context of the Record Keeping project. The records kept by primary school teachers are but one aspect of professional accounting. Research will no doubt be carried out into other aspects of accountability, for example to parents through school reports.[16] The reports from the DES Assessment of Performance Unit will provide generalized survey data and information about pupils' performance for anyone who wishes to know.

It would be naive to expect that the Record Keeping project can provide any 'final' solution to the technical problems associated with school records, and immodest to suggest that any project could do so for the political problems. In any case, similar problems require different solutions in different situations, and primary schools in England and Wales today display a rich variety in aims (explicit and implicit), methods, organization and, of course, size.

The rest of this report describes and analyses efforts made by teachers to record the progress of children and the circumstances in which this takes place. It discusses the political and technical problems of so doing, informed by the opinions of teachers who have worked with the team. Its purpose is the improvement of record keeping practice in primary schools. It therefore contains a certain (minimal) amount of theoretical information and discussion where this was found helpful by the co-operating teachers, a great deal of information about the current 'state of the art', and many examples of primary school records chosen to illustrate what teachers found useful.

REFERENCES

1  M. Woodhall and V. Ward, *Economic Aspects of Education*, Slough:  NFER Publishing Co., 1972.
2  C. Jencks, *Inequality*, Allen Lane, 1973 (Penguin, 1975).
3  Editorial comment, *Daily Mail*, 6 June 1978, on a feasibility study of voucher systems.
4  J. Bolton and G. Richardson, 'Facing up to shaping a framework for operations', *Education* 147, 11 June 1976, p.514.
5  *Education in Schools: a Consultative Document* (Cmnd 6869), HMSO, July 1977, paragraph 3.1.
6  N. Wright, *Progress in Education*, Croom Helm, 1977, p.193.
7  *Education in Schools: a Consultative Document* (see note 5),

paragraph 1.3.

8  Central Advisory Council for Education (England), *Children and their Primary Schools* [Plowden Report], 2 vols, HMSO, 1967.

9  J. Freeman, *Team Teaching in Britain*, Ward Lock, 1969.

10  E.g. S.N. Bennett, 'Plowden's progress - informal one in six', *Times Educational Supplement*, 18 October 1974.

11  L. Hodges, 'We need a system whereby what is happening in schools in Leicester bears some sort of relationship to what is happening in Grimsby', *Times Educational Supplement*, 8 April 1977.

12  R. Cyster, P.S. Clift, and S. Battle, *Parental Involvement in Primary Schools*, Slough:  NFER Publishing Co., 1980, p.70.

13  DES/Welsh Office, *A New Partnership for our Schools* [Taylor Report], HMSO, 1977, paragraph 5.28.

14  *Education in Schools:  a Consultative Document* (see note 5), paragraph 10.3.

15  D. McIntyre, 'The teacher - roles and responsibilities', *Primary Education Review* (NUT) 3, spring 1977, p.8.

16  A project entitled 'School Reports to Parents' has been est-ablished at the National Foundation for Educational Research (1978-81).

# 2   The method of research

The knowledge that primary teachers have traditionally
been expected to keep records as part of their professional commitment, and that all schools today keep
some form of school records, had continual impact on
the work of the project.   Unlike many other Schools
Council projects, which have been concerned with
curriculum innovation either in terms of restructuring
curriculum areas or in suggesting innovative teaching
methods, the principal concern of the Record Keeping
project has been to help teachers record existing
classroom practice.   Essentially the team interpreted
their brief as:

(1)   identifying, as far as possible, good practice
      in record keeping;
(2)   discussing this with teachers;
(3)   evaluating records on the basis of these dis-
      cussions and developing ideas in collaboration
      with project teacher groups.

As an end result of these activities, primary teachers
who have read this report should be able to evaluate
their own record systems and improve on them if found
lacking.
    Throughout the duration of the project, whether the
team were visiting schools, attending consultative
committee meetings or meeting with groups of teachers,
the constant message they received was that the discussion and ideas should be kept at a practical level.
Thus, most emphasis in the project has been placed on
the year-long collaboration with the six teacher
groups.   Aware of the comment from Lawrence Stenhouse
that 'educational ideas expressed in books are not
easily taken into possession by teachers',[1] the team
spent much time 'on the road', running workshops and
giving talks, not only to disseminate ideas but to
find out how other practising teachers responded to
them.
    The rest of this chapter briefly reviews the work
of the project.   The overall programme was divided

into three main phases:

(1)  research:  visits to schools, working parties
     and educationists working in similar or rela-
     ted fields;
(2)  collaborative work with six teacher groups to
     discuss ideas, develop and try out new
     systems of record keeping;
(3)  data analysis, report writing and dissemina-
     tion.

Ten main project activities were defined, contained
within the three stages mentioned above.  These activities emerged sequentially, though subsequently
they might occasionally have occurred at the same
time.

*I  Preliminary contacts*
Initially the project contacted local education
authorities (LEAs) seeking permission to correspond
with and visit schools in their area which had something of interest on record keeping to pass on to the
team.  When permission was granted, each LEA was
asked to recommend approximately six such schools in
its area.  The headteachers of these schools were
then contacted, introduced to the project and asked
to send brief descriptions of their schools in terms
of size, type and curriculum organization.

Over 200 replies were received and these schools
provided the sample for the research phase of the
project.  Thus the research data were quite deliberately not derived from a random sample of schools
but came from those with teachers who had shown a positive interest in record keeping.  The reason for
selecting a sample in this way was that the information which the team needed, i.e. well thought out recording examples, was more likely to be found in
schools where record keeping was acknowledged to be
important.  Furthermore, the team felt that there
would be no purpose in visiting schools where little
or no record keeping was going on.  Since the project
depended on the goodwill of teachers in allowing the
researchers to visit their schools, a sample of
'interested' teachers would be potentially more fruitful than any other.

*II  School visits*
It was decided to collect data on the wide variety of
record systems currently in operation in schools
throughout England and Wales, and examine their relevance to the particular context in which they were

being used.  Visits to schools were thus planned so
that the team would see a wide range of differing
school organizations and environments.

The general aim when visiting these schools was to
discover the views of teachers on:

(1)   the purpose of record keeping;
(2)   how the day-to-day recording of pupil activity
      should be summarized and communicated to
      others either within schools or between
      schools, i.e. liaison between the producers
      and the recipients of the record;
(3)   the preferred method and frequency of recor-
      ding;
(4)   the content of records - what is/should be
      written on them;
(5)   confidentiality - who has/should have access
      to school records;
(6)   assessment techniques:  the place of standar-
      dized tests, grading, ranking and other forms
      of assessment on the school record.

Between October 1976 and March 1977, 97 schools
throughout England and Wales were visited and, in
addition to the data from the interviews, the team
took away examples of every record (where available)
currently in use at the schools.  The researchers were
unable to visit all the schools which had been contacted initially, due to constraints on project time and
because travelling to the north of England, the south
coast, north Wales, etc. proved to be exceedingly ex-
pensive.  However, as it was considered important that
knowledge of as many school recording systems as
possible should be gathered, those that had not been
visited were asked to provide descriptions and samples
of records by post;  95 schools responded to this request.

In addition, the research team made contact with
other research workers and educationists in order to
obtain a wider view of recording and assessment.

III   *Teacher group activities*
Six teacher groups were set up, composed of members
serving in a variety of primary schools characterized
by different kinds of school organization, e.g. integrated day, vertical grouping, class-based teaching,
team teaching.  Because it was recognized that teacher
experience is strongly related to LEA policy and local
influences, the groups were given a wide geographical
distribution and were located in Slough, Reading,
Birmingham, Cardiff, Haverfordwest and Whitby.  In

addition, there was an associate group that wished to discuss project issues but was not included in the main project teacher group activity;  this met regularly at Newbury.

After discussion within the teacher groups and at project consultative committee meetings it was decided that the main concerns of the teacher groups would be:

(1)   to consider the principles and objectives of record keeping and hence what records are needed throughout the primary age range;

(2)   collectively to discuss and evaluate a variety of systems for assessing and recording

    (*a*)   pupils' day-to-day learning experiences (what is attempted),

    (*b*)   pupils' responses to learning experiences (what is achieved);

(3)   collectively to generate, try out and modify new systems of primary school records across the curriculum.

Figure 1 indicates the scope and sequence of teacher group activities and the interaction between project teacher groups and the team.

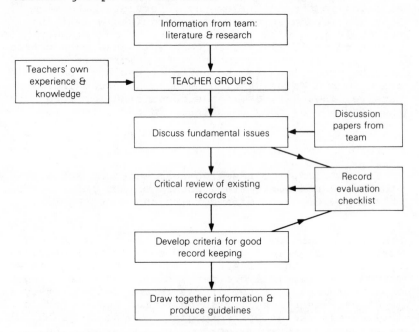

Fig.1   Teacher group activities

Whilst all six groups discussed the general principles of record keeping, four also focused on more
specific issues.  Two groups were particularly interested in the recording and assessment of pupils'
social/personal and aesthetic development;  one group
looked closely at record design and ease of communication between schools;  another group reviewed the
area of confidentiality and record keeping.

*IV  Papers by the research team*
In response to comments from teachers in the research
phase of the project and from teacher group discussion, a number of papers were written by members
of the team.  Some were purely informational, and reported on initial research findings, e.g. papers on
confidentiality.  Others were reviews of the literature on a certain area produced at the request of
project teachers, e.g. 'frameworks' for aesthetic
development.  Yet others were stimulus papers to be
used as the basis for discussion, e.g. on 'The need
for aims and objectives'.  As these papers proved
valuable in helping to illuminate the area of school
record keeping, some have been included in appendix F.
It is hoped that they may be of use at in-service and
other courses connected with record keeping.
    In addition, two issues of a project newsletter
were distributed to all those who had been involved
in the project and to a large number of inquirers.
Two thousand copies of the first newsletter were sent
out at the end of the project's first year and the
same quantity of the second at the end of the project.
These newsletters gave informal interim accounts of
the work of the team.

*V  Analysis of information obtained in the
    research phase*
The analysis of the data gathered earlier in the project took the form of two studies:  (1) on curricular
content of records, and (2) on teachers' views about
record keeping.

    (1)   An analysis was made of curricular emphases
          as depicted in the records accumulated by the
          team.  The records were carefully reviewed
          and classified according to the range of pupil
          skills and experience indicated.  Table 1
          shows the range of curriculum categories re-
          presented on records and the proportion of
          schools in the sample which recorded each
          category (chapter 4 gives a more detailed
          breakdown).

Table 1  Proportion of sample schools including curriculum
categories in records ($n$ = 192)

| Skill/curriculum category | % of schools |
|---|---|
| Reading development | 96 |
| List of mathematical topics covered | 81 |
| Social/personal development | 55 |
| Writing development | 35 |
| Oral language development | 34 |
| Physical development | 31 |
| Concept attainment in mathematics | 29 |
| Scientific skills and experience | 17 |
| Aesthetic development - craft skills | 14 |
| Study skills | 3 |

(2)   A study was made of teachers' statements in
interviews concerning their general feeling
about records.  The sample teachers' attitudes
varied somewhat.  Most felt that there was
some value in keeping school records (the
reader should remember that these teachers
were specifically selected for their interest
in school records), but a few stated that all
records were a waste of time and teacher time
would be more profitably spent in teaching,
marking or preparing work.
   The interview statements were classified
into three sets:
(a)   attitudes of teachers towards records;
(b)   comments on the purpose of keeping school
      records;
(c)   views on the confidentiality issue, i.e.
      whether or not parents should have access
      to school records.

*VI   Record evaluation*
The evaluation of existing systems of school records
was one of the team's major tasks.  The original proposal specified that the project should 'evaluate each
[recording] system against facility of use, comprehen--
siveness and detail of information recorded, ease of
summation'.  A number of possible approaches to the
evaluation of school records were available to the
team.  One was to give selected records to project
teachers who would try them out in school and then
report back.  This was much the most preferred
approach, since evaluation by project teachers would
be made on practical as well as theoretical grounds.
However, as there was not sufficient project time for

teachers effectively to evaluate the number of records
accumulated in this way, two other methods of evaluation were adopted:

(1)    using a record evaluation checklist;
(2)    seeking and aggregating teacher opinions on
       particular kinds of record in a more informal
       way.

   *(1)    Record evaluation checklist:*  The team drew up
a list of topics which had arisen repeatedly in the
teacher groups when discussing 'good practice' in record keeping.  The first draft of the checklist was
used by teachers to appraise a variety of school records.  The teachers were asked to evaluate the records using the criteria indicated in the provisional
checklist and also to offer criticism and amendments
to the checklist itself.  Hence the development of the
checklist had a twofold purpose:

(*a*)    to inform the team which kinds of  school
        records teachers prefer;
(*b*)    when fully developed, to provide the basis
        for drawing up a set of criteria by which
        teachers themselves could formulate and evalu-
        ate their own school records.

After going through a number of drafts, a final and
rather more lengthy checklist evolved, incorporating
many suggestions from project teachers and also rather
more sophisticated aspects of record and questionnaire
design.  (It appears in full on pp.54-7.)
   *(2)    Informal evaluation:*  So as to keep the evaluation of records as open as possible, in addition to
the development of the evaluation checklist, teachers
at project workshops and teacher group meetings were
asked to discuss and write down comments on the whole
range of selected records.  Immediate visual impact
and ease of comprehension were important criteria.
                              *
   Using these two approaches to evaluation, eighty
records exemplifying current record keeping practice
in terms of curricular area, primary age range and
record design were chosen for appraisal.  The data
gathered from the checklist and from the informal
evaluation assisted the team in identifying both criteria and actual records which are seen as useful and
relevant to primary school teachers.

*VII    LEA record study*
A study was made of all the LEA official record cards

obtained by the project.  This was by no means a full set, as some LEAs were unable to send in their record cards since they were being revised and others because no current card existed.  This study focused on the items of information recorded rather than the format. As well as the more obvious categories of information, e.g. pupil's name, home address and date of birth, other data requested included comments on social background, medical information, information on academic and social development and test results.

The LEA official record was a frequent cause of complaint by teachers to the team members.  Hence it was decided that another checklist, based on the LEA record analysis, should be composed and distributed amongst teachers involved with the project.  The motive for this exercise was again twofold:

(1)  to identify which items were seen by teachers as most useful in pupil transfer;

(2)  to identify differences (if any existed) in attitudes towards transfer records between primary teachers.

*VIII  Open plan study*

The project undertook this study not as part of the original project proposal, but as a result of an incident in the research phase of the project.  During an early excursion to Wales a school was visited which had been described in the correspondence as principally geared to team teaching.  However, on arrival it was found that the teachers had returned to class-based teaching since, as they were quick to explain, they could not deal with the record keeping and monitoring aspect of team teaching.  They had abandoned their chosen way of teaching because they could not cope with the record keeping.

This led the researchers to ponder on the reasons for such difficulties and to suggest that school records may have a different and perhaps more complex function in open plan schools (or in schools in which team teaching is the dominant form of organization). The researchers already had access to the names and addresses of all the open plan schools in England and Wales via another Schools Council project, Open Plan Schools:  an Inquiry.[2]  Five questions connected with record keeping were included in the questionnaire sent out by the Open Plan Schools project and, in addition, headteachers were asked to indicate whether they wished to provide information to the Record Keeping project.

Of six hundred schools initially contacted, well

over half replied.  Their replies were analysed in
terms of type of school (e.g. primary, middle);  type
of records kept (e.g. phonics, science, transfer);
organizational factors specifically related to open
plan schools (e.g. predominant teaching style);  and
problems or special factors connected with record
keeping in open plan schools.  (For a detailed analysis, please see chapter 9.)

## IX   *Case study*

In the attempt to produce helpful information of a
practical nature for teachers, the team decided to
focus on a particular school which was in the process
of re-formulating its own record system.  Using various methods of gathering data including informal
visits, taped interviews, written statements of method
(from the teachers) and the production of diagrams and
slides to show the relationship between school records
and classroom activities, the team hoped that a picture would emerge of the whole *process* of developing
and introducing a new system of record keeping.

The particular school chosen for the study was a
large inner-city, ethnically mixed, recently combined
Junior Mixed and Infants school in an old, though well
kept building;  it was selected because it had problems similar to other such schools yet had formulated
a record keeping system to meet its specific requirements.  This study was thus an attempt to give the
research significance by placing it firmly in the context of school practice.

## X   *Dissemination*

Throughout the lifetime of the project, the team participated in in-service courses and workshops on record keeping and the work of the project.  In fact,
such was the demand for the services of the team, that
a halt had to be called to this aspect of project work
early in 1978, since it was encroaching on time set
aside for other activities.

The deliberate geographical dispersal of school
visits, workshops and teacher groups ensured, to some
extent, the dissemination of the work of the project.
However, this was constrained by lack of time.  At one
time it was envisaged that several dissemination conferences would be held in the final stages of the project.  However, the team accepted the suggestion that
dissemination conferences were best organized at the
time of report publication when materials would be
readily available for discussion, and not before, when
no such material yet existed.

REFERENCES

1   L. Stenhouse, *An Introduction to Curriculum Research and Development*, Heinemann Educational Books, 1975, p.142.
2   The final report of this project has been published as *Open Plan Schools: Teaching, Curriculum, Design*, by S.N. Bennett *et al.* (Slough:  NFER Publishing Co., 1980).

# 3 The functions and purposes of school records: teachers' views

In the literature produced on school records over the past decade or so, there have been few attempts to define their principal components. Writers have focused on the function or the purpose of records and then categorized school records in these terms.[1,2] This strategy was adopted to some extent by the project team - not, however, without some review of alternative approaches.

In the interviews at the earlier stages of the project it was found that teachers looked at record keeping from two points of view: first, their perception of the *purpose* of keeping school records and, secondly, what these records were expected to *do*. Thus, teachers in the main research sample were asked what they personally saw as the purpose of keeping school records. The responses gave a number of generally agreed typical reasons for school record keeping and also some unexpected ones.

*Typical reasons* given by the teachers for keeping records were:

(1)  to chart pupil progress and achievement;
(2)  to communicate information to other teachers;
(3)  to ensure continuity of education throughout the school;
(4)  to ensure continuity of education on transfer to other schools;
(5)  to guide a replacement or supply teacher;
(6)  for diagnostic purposes - to spot problems, identify under-achievement and pupils needing extra help;
(7)  to provide teachers with information on the success (or failure) of teaching methods and materials;
(8)  as a statement of 'what has happened' - to inform interested parties (parents, educational psychologists, headteacher);
(9)  to give headteachers a general picture of achievement within the school.

Some of the *less expected* replies to the question concerning the purpose of school records included:

(10)  to be used as a defence against accusations of falling standards;

(11)  as an insurance policy - the record is an account of what has gone before which may be needed in the face of hostile attacks;

(12)  for the head to gain control over the class-room curriculum;

(13)  to keep balance in areas of study;

(14)  to reassure teachers as to what progress has been made;

(15)  in a large school, to keep 'tabs' on each pupil.

The great variety of reasons for keeping records has been criticized as counter-productive to good teaching practice. 'One of the strongest impressions gained ... is that records are expected to fulfil too many purposes simultaneously and that, as yet, in-sufficient consideration has been given to methods of using the information collected.'[3] A great deal of evidence was found to support Walker's statement in that, whereas many teachers recognized a need to pro-duce careful and detailed records, these were often unread by those for whom they were written. This was particularly apparent at one of the schools visited, where the infant head complained bitterly that, though she and her staff had worked hard to produce a useful set of records, it had recently come to her knowledge that these records were totally disregarded by the staff of the neighbouring junior school. When this point was raised at the junior school, its teachers explained that the infant records were useless since the sort of information written therein, e.g. child studies written in long-hand and vague checklists, were not specific or objective enough.

Obviously, for the communication of information on school records to be useful, there must be some agree-ment between teachers on criteria and content. Part of the project's brief has been interpreted as being to initiate discussion leading ultimately, it is hoped, to a record keeping consensus.

The frameworks chosen by the team for the analysis of record keeping in primary schools were not entirely based on the stated purposes for keeping school re-cords (see above), which were often complex and some-what idiosyncratic. It was decided to adopt two approaches:

(1)  analysis of records in relation to curriculum
     content;
(2)  analysis of records in relation to record
     function or stated purpose.

Alternative frameworks, such as those based on age of
pupil or school type (nursery, infant, junior) were
considered, but rejected on the grounds that the two
chosen methods appeared closest to the thinking of
teachers.  When asked to describe the record systems
operating in their schools, teachers invariably either
listed records in terms of function (e.g. teacher's
day-to-day notes for curriculum planning, transfer
records) or referred to curriculum content categories
(e.g. reading, mathematics, topic work).

*Curriculum content*
It was decided not to adhere strictly to classroom
practice and adopt the 'three Rs' plus topic work
curriculum model so often found in the primary school.
Instead, records were analysed according to the areas
adopted by the APU.  The reason behind this decision
was that, whereas general classroom practice is principally concerned with curriculum content, and is sub-
ject- or knowledge-based, the APU model places emphasis on the acquisition of skills and concepts rather
than specific areas of knowledge.[4]
   An early APU model contains six areas of pupil
development.[5]

(1)  *Language:* Communication.  To include oral
     communication in a variety of forms to suit
     different occasions as well as listening,
     reading and writing in their various forms.
(2)  *Mathematical:* Communication.  Expression of
     ideas of relationship and quantity through
     symbols or pictorial forms such as number,
     graphs, models and diagrams, etc.
(3)  *Scientific:* Methods of dealing with phenomena
     and data.  These include observation;  the se-
     lection, evaluation and use of evidence;  the
     testing of hypotheses;  the use of experiment.
     This area is concerned with techniques and
     approaches to subjects in history, geography,
     chemistry, physics and biology.
(4)  *Personal and social:* The development of the
     pupil in personal and social relationships.
     The increase in self-awareness and sensitivity
     to other people as well as his moral attitude
     towards his environment.
(5)  *Aesthetic:* The pupil's appreciation of form,

colour, texture, sound.  His affective
response to his environment and respect for
quality.  'The capacity to harness imagination
and feeling in creative work'.

(6)  *Physical:*  The body and muscular development
of the pupil.  The ability to control and use
the body efficiently and expressively including the use and handling of tools and appa-
ratus.

Adopting this curriculum model caused the team some
problems, since many teachers were not entirely clear
how the APU model of the curriculum related to their
own classroom practice and record keeping.  Also, although many teachers were extremely interested in
category (5), aesthetic development, it was generally
felt that the area provided little meaning in the record keeping context.  In addition, teachers attached
little importance to the recording of scientific development and some argument occurred as to whether it
was possible to place history in the scientific mode
of thought.

*Function of records*
The main survey found that there were currently seven
different functions of record keeping in primary
schools:

(1)  *day-to-day* record of the teacher - kept for
planning and organization of classroom work,
e.g. notes on attainment in reading and mathematics, topic work covered and so on;

(2)  *summary* record for the transfer of information
within school (either teacher to teacher or
teacher to head):
(*a*)  half-termly,
(*b*)  termly,
(*c*)  half-yearly,
(*d*)  at the end of each year;

(3)  *transition* record for the transfer of information from school to school at the end of each
educational stage:
(*a*)  from nursery to infant or first school,
(*b*)  from infant or first school to junior
or middle school,
(*c*)  from junior or middle to secondary
school;

(4)  *transfer* record sent from school to school
when a pupil changes schools for reasons other
than transition;

(5)  *diagnostic* record

(*a*)    either used at the instigation of the
class teacher to identify educational
weakness,

(*b*)    or used at the instigation of the LEA to
identify children at risk, e.g. in
Croydon, Birmingham;

(6)    records, reports and referrals to and from
the supporting *welfare* agencies, i.e. the
school medical, psychology, welfare and social
services;

(7)    reports to *parents*.

(Further information on the analysis of how school
records were compiled is given in chapter 5.)

Finally, it may be interesting to mention here what
teachers suggested a school record should *not* be:

(1)    a waste of teacher time;

(2)    too jargonistic or too lengthy;

(3)    used to check up on the work of the teacher;

(4)    a substitute for, or an addition to, gossip in
the staff room, designed to transmit to a new
teacher the opinions, impressions and preju-
dices of his/her predecessor;

(5)    used as a bureaucratic device to increase the
school's control over the lives of its pupils.

### REFERENCES

1  A.S. Walker, *Pupils' School Records*, Slough:  NFER Publishing
Co., 1955.

2  P. Rance, *Record Keeping in the Progressive Primary School*,
Ward Lock Educational, 1971.

3  Walker (see note 1), p.33.

4  B.W. Kay, 'Monitoring pupils' performance' (in section entitled 'Educational standards today'), *Trends in Education*
1975/2, 11-18.

5  Adapted from Kay (see note 4), p.15.

# 4 Internal records: analysis

*Introduction*
The general state of primary school record keeping in
England and Wales is one of immense variety in content, design and layout. Many of the records collected were idiosyncratic to the schools which originated
them, or even to the teachers, reflecting particular
curricular assumptions, schemes of work, equipment in
use. Such idiosyncratic records, whilst useful in
their context, are unlikely to be very meaningful to
teachers elsewhere and are thus of little or no value
as they stand when children change schools. Children
*do* change schools; all of them between stages (e.g.
primary to secondary), and a substantial number at
other times (see chapter 1), and teachers are then
faced with the task of summarizing information in a
way which is meaningful to their 'receiving'
colleagues. The topic of transfer records is dealt
with fully in chapter 6, but it may be commented here
that much unnecessary labour might be avoided if those
who design record keeping systems always paid attention to the explicit and unambiguous expression of
what has been attempted and achieved (see chapter 7)
at the time when the systems are devised.

This chapter examines the kinds of school record
that primary teachers keep. It is in two sections:

(1) an overview of the subjects and skills which
teachers record as relating to pupil progress;
(2) a detailed analysis of the items used on
records.

Appendix A contains further sources of information
which may be found useful in compiling records.
Actual examples of records are reserved for chapter 5.

### OVERVIEW

For the reasons discussed in chapter 3, record items
have been classified according to the following categories:

24

    (i)    reading development;
    (ii)   oral language development;
  (iii)   written language development;
   (iv)   mathematics:
          (1)   topics list,
          (2)   concepts list;
    (v)    social and personal development;
   (vi)   scientific development;
  (vii)   study skills development;
 (viii)   physical development;
   (ix)   aesthetic development.

The main survey indicated that teachers keep several different kinds of record for use within school:

(1)  A *summary record*, filled in at the end of each term or year.  Such records are used:
    (*a*)   to pass on information to the next class teacher;
    (*b*)   to keep the headteacher informed of pupils' progress, particularly in larger schools;
    (*c*)   to act as a report to parents or as a basis for writing reports to parents.

(2)  *Class records* are kept more fully by teachers who see their teaching role in terms of organizing a whole class of children.  Ticks, marks or grades are the basic methods of indicating assessments of pupils' progress.  These records are kept in mark books or class lists.

(3)  *Individual pupil records* are principally kept by teachers who see pupils as individual learners.  A record sheet is kept for each pupil and generally contains considerable detail about that pupil's strengths and weaknesses, and has information added frequently (i.e. daily or weekly).

(4)  *Pupils' own records:*  Children in some schools are encouraged to keep their own records of work done.  The form that these take ranges from charts kept in the back of pupils' own exercise books and individual assignment sheets to wall charts used by the whole class.

(5)  *Samples of pupils' work:*  Teachers in some schools keep samples of work throughout a pupil's school career as a measure of progress.  Methods of selecting the work vary from a sample taken at random throughout the year to the setting of prescribed exercises on a regular basis perhaps once or twice a term.  In some cases the children themselves were

responsible for the selection.

The following analysis is based on the project's survey of records used in nearly two hundred primary schools as described in chapter 2.  A detailed examination was made of all the individual pupil records collected.

I   READING AND PRE-READING RECORDS

From the project's study of primary school records, it appears that, in so far as quantity and frequency of recording are measures of importance, language and reading development in particular are considered the most important aspects of the primary curriculum. The records collected by the team also gave insights into the knowledge teachers have of the reading process and its development.  These records indicate that in many schools the reading process begins as soon as a pupil is faced with the first book on a graded reading scheme and ends when all the books in the scheme have been successfully completed.  At the latter stage the pupil is frequently classified as an 'independent' reader.

In other schools, the records used reflect a more elaborate view of the reading process, extending from the acquisition of pre-reading skills through to the higher reading skills.  Some of the more detailed records indicate that many teachers are concerned with identifying pupils with reading difficulties and, with the aid of the diagnostic record, are attempting to treat these problems in a systematic and analytic way.

In many schools the project found evidence that teachers are recording the development of pre-reading skills.  Some assess 'reading readiness' when the pupils are admitted to the reception class.

*(1)  Pre-reading and reading readiness*
Pre-reading records varied considerably in length and content.  Many records contained checklist items about physical aspects of perception (e.g. How well can the pupil see and hear?   How well is the pupil physically co-ordinated?).  The quality of a pupil's spoken language was frequently noted as a factor in readiness to read.  A pupil's attitude and curiosity about books was included on some records, but by no means all, and was considered a significant factor at the pre-reading stage by the compilers of these records.  The following range of items (not all mutually exclusive) has been extracted from examples studied by the project.

*Auditory skills*
Listening:  good/poor.

*Attitudes*
Enjoys listening to stories:  always/usually/
  seldom.

*Memory*
Able to repeat a given:  sound/word/phrase.
Repeats from memory:  'one', 'two', 'three' (etc.)
  words/a number of non-consecutive digits/a sen-
  tence/a short story.

*Physical aspects of hearing*
(see also section VIII below)
Does he/she respond to a question or directions?
Is he/she apparently able to hear what is said in
  class?
Does he/she respond:
  to a low voice at six metres?
  to a whisper at half a metre?
Is his/her audiometer test normal?
Does he/she:
  hear within normal limits?
  listen to commands and carry them out effici-
    ently?
  follow simple instructions:  easily/with help/
    with difficulty?

*Auditory discrimination*
Can he/she detect differences and similarities in
  sound images [*sic*]?
Does he/she:
  listen rather than interrupt?
  listen to all of a story with evident enjoyment
    so that (s)he can retell all or part of it?

*Visual perception*
Do the child's eyes seem comfortable [*sic*]?
Are the results of clinical tests or an oculist's
  examination favourable?

*Matching*
Able to:
  match picture with picture;
  match picture + word with picture + word;
  match word with picture + word;
  match word with picture;
  match word with word;
  reconstruct a number of pegs in a pattern;
  reconstruct jigsaw;
  reconstruct mixed jigsaws;
  copy a shape.

*Discrimination*
Able to:  sort/find a shape/find the 'odd man out'/
    identify 'same' and 'different'.

*Spatial discrimination*
Able to differentiate between shapes.

*Discrimination of size*
Able to:  match by size/grade 'bigger than' and
    'smaller than'.

*Sequencing* (using equipment like logic blocks)
Able to add the next two or three items in a
    series:  by colour only/by shape only/by colour
    and shape.
Able to continue a pattern previously drawn.

*Motor skills*
Right/left-handed.
Can trace:  shapes/letters/drawings.
Can copy:  shapes/letters/drawings.
Can copy from a distance:  shapes/letters/drawings.
Does he/she make hands work together:  in cutting/
    in using tools?

*Eye-hand co-ordination*
Can he/she:
    throw, catch or bounce a ball?
    use constructional toys?
    use building blocks?
    use crayons for colouring in drawings?
    draw a recognizable picture of a human figure?
    draw a reasonably straight line about six inches
        in length?

*Spoken language*
Is speech well articulated?
Does he/she:
    speak clearly (noting volume and articulation)?
    pronounce words:  correctly (allowing for local
        accents)/with slight error/in a babyish manner?
    speak more correctly after being helped over a
        difficulty by teacher?
    speak in sentences?
    speak fluently?
    have any speech defect (e.g. stutter, lisp, etc.)?
    substitute one sound for another (e.g. $f$ for $v$,
        $v$ for $th$)?
    use non-verbal gestures/movements in preference
        to spoken language?
Is English his/her native language?

Records of pupils' attitudes and personal social
development have been seen covering most aspects of

the curriculum.  But the items listed below are taken
specifically from pre-reading records:

*Interest*
Shows an interest in words and books.
Shows a desire to read.
Needs encouragement to read.

*Social*
Does he/she:
  co-operate:  with teacher/with other adults/with
    other children?
  work well in groups?
  work well on his/her own?
  take a share of responsibility?
  share materials?
  wait his/her turn to play in games?

*Self-reliance*
Does he/she:
  work things through with teacher's help?
  need constant guidance from teacher?
  ask other people for help?
  find other constructive activities to do after
    completing a set task, without being reminded?
  take care of materials and clothing?

*Attitudes and emotional development*
Does he/she:
  see a task through to completion?
  accept changes in school routine calmly?
  appear to be happy and well adjusted to school
    work?
  avoid work when not being supervised?
  accept a certain amount of failure without with-
    drawing, crying or sulking?
  accept a certain amount of opposition?
  try hard to ignore distraction?
  behave impulsively?
  behave reflectively?
Is he/she:
  easily distracted?
  restless?

A further category, found only in a minority of
records, focuses attention on a pupil's conceptual
development.

*Conceptual skills*
Can he/she:
  classify objects:  according to one attribute
    only/according to two attributes/according to

three or more attributes?
repeat or reconstruct a sequence of objects (e.g.
beads)?
recall a series of digits/letters/words/objects
(e.g. 'Kim's game')?

It can be seen from this analysis that there are
several ways of asking similar questions about a
pupil's state of development.  There are many items
which do not follow a particularly clear developmental
order.  In some areas of development, a definite sequence may not be appropriate since children follow
different paths towards maturity.

*(2)   Reading records*
Once a child has begun to read, records of progress
fall into four main categories.

(a)   (i) Phonic checklists
Numerous examples of this type of record were seen by
the researchers, mostly in infant schools.  Some
teachers devised their own lists, based either on
their teaching experience or on the sequence in which
sounds were introduced in the reading scheme in use.
Other teachers preferred to use one of the published
lists (see appendix A) or an adaptation of such a
list.  Other teachers said they used this kind of record only for pupils who were finding difficulty with
the decoding process and that keeping such detailed
records was unnecessary for most pupils.
   (ii) Sight checklists
In some schools, similar checklists were seen which
contained lists of 'sight vocabulary' based either on
the reading scheme in use or compiled from one of the
published lists (again, see appendix A).

(b)   Reading stage records
Records of two types were found in this category:

   (i)   lists of books and/or pages read by pupils;
   (ii)  lists of books classified in order of read-
         ability.

The latter type of record was more frequently encountered where several parallel reading schemes were in
use.  Teachers used this method of record keeping as
a means of planning work for pupils, particularly
those requiring extra reading practice at some stage
of development.  The grading of reading schemes was
based either on a teacher's experience and assessment
of the books in reading schemes or on a published list

of books and their readability levels (see appendix
A).

(c)   Records of reading test scores
Two main ways of recording results were in evidence.

(i)    Numerical reading ages or reading quotients
       were listed, frequently without dates of
       testing.  These took the form of rank ordered
       class lists of results (at one testing
       session) and also results gained by indivi-
       dual pupils over a period of time.

(ii)   Reading scores were presented graphically.
       An individual pupil's set of scores over a
       period of time was plotted as a linear graph.
       Histograms, or block graphs, were also in
       evidence in some schools.  The project sample
       teachers found that presentation of reading
       scores for one or several classes as a block
       graph gave a useful visual impression of the
       distribution of reading ability in a partic-
       ular grouping of children.  Information de-
       rived from these records was found valuable
       in allocating resources to pupils who needed
       them.  Over a period of time it would be
       possible to compare distributions (see
       examples in chapter 5).

Comment
From the evidence seen, reading progress is largely
measured by using tests of the word recognition variety (e.g. Schonell, Burt;  see p.181).  The limitations of such tests[1] should be recognized if teachers
are to make an accurate diagnosis of a pupil's reading
difficulties.

(d)   Diagnostic and monitoring records
Several LEAs have instituted schemes for 'screening'
all children at certain ages in order to identify any
with actual or potential learning problems.  These
screening programmes include a variety of assessments:

(i)     readiness in language development;
(ii)    readiness in physical and sensory develop-
        ment;
(iii)   readiness in emotional and social develop-
        ment;
(iv)    associated social and environmental informa-
        tion considered to be significant in the
        diagnosis of children 'at risk'.[2]

The construction of these records requires the involvement of teachers and psychologists who have a thorough knowledge of the learning processes required for reading.  Comments from teachers about the difficulties in using such records suggest a need for further in-service training, and also for a one to one pupil teacher ratio.

## II   ORAL LANGUAGE DEVELOPMENT RECORDS

Records of reading development, particularly those concerned with the pre-reading stage, included statements about pupils' oral language development.

A child's development interacts in three aspects of language:  oral, reading and written.  However, facility in each of these will be qualitatively different at any given time.  In the earlier stages of primary education a child's oral ability exceeds his reading ability, which in turn generally exceeds his written language ability.  For this reason, records of oral language were more commonly found in infant schools than at later stages of education.  The construction of the records collected varied a great deal.  Many of them appeared in the form of checklists;  assessment of the items was either on a yes/no basis, or on a rating scale (e.g. A-E or 1-5).  The following examples (A to F) indicate the kinds of item included in such records.

> (A)   Talks freely to other individual friends.
>        Talks freely to others in his/her group.
>        Talks freely to all children.
>        Talks to teacher when questioned.
>        Talks to teacher freely.
>        Talks to adults in school.
>        Talks quite freely to everyone.
>        Speaks clearly but quietly.
>        Speaks clearly and confidently.
>        Enjoys reading or talking in front of other
>            individuals.

> (B)   Uses short phrases only.
>        Uses sentences in normal conversation.
>        Talks about pictures, names objects.
>        Recounts an experience.
>        Relates main theme of a story.
>        Asks appropriate questions.
>        Describes a picture in some detail and says
>            what is happening.
>        Knows the words of common nursery rhymes and
>            songs.

Tells a simple story with a picture stimulus.
Can project what might happen from an action
  picture.
Describes personal experience of events with
  correct use of past tense.
Can express differences in terms of shape,
  size and texture.
Can link similar objects and events.
Describes coherently and in sequence how a
  model was made.

(C)   Chatters with friends.
      Talks with teacher.
      Answers - mainly in monosyllables.
      Can and will recite.
      Comprehends oral sentences, questions and
        instructions.
      Answers in a rambling fashion.
      Can give coherent explanation or account of
        an event.
      Can speak in front of class (e.g. with pre-
        pared report).
      Can take part confidently in class drama.
      Answers readily and fluently in sentences.
      Will converse freely in novel situations with
        unfamiliar adults.
      Can take part in class discussion or debate.
      Has the language and confidence for all
        normal situations encountered at his/her
        age.

(D)   Uses:  only simple statements and sentences/
        complex sentences.
      Can use past tense.
      Understands past tense.
      Limited/wide vocabulary.
      Can use prepositions correctly.
      Articulation poor/clear.
      Confuses word order in sentences/word order
        usually correct.

(E)   *Vocabulary*
      Meagre/rich;  accurate/incorrect;  words mis-
      pronounced.

      *Sentence structure*
      Incomplete/simple/complex sentences.
      Says little/is very voluble.

      *Imagination*
      Creative/bizarre.

      *Organization*
      Events recounted in proper sequence, well

organized/disjointed/repetitive.

(F)   (*With children of non-English origin*)
Understands but does not speak English.
Speaks English in disjointed words.
Speaks in phrases or sentences.
Uses idiomatic English.
Questions and discusses.
Speaks English:  clearly/fluently/confidently.

Two main aspects of oral language are contained within the above examples:

(1)   level of social interaction and degree of spontaneity;
(2)   quality of thought expressed in oral language.

Example A is entirely of the former category.
Examples B and D are entirely of the latter category.
Examples C and E contain elements of both categories.

III   RECORDS OF WRITTEN LANGUAGE DEVELOPMENT

The methods of recording development in written language skills varied from longhand comments to checklist ratings.
At the infant and lower junior school age range, records of the checklist kind were frequently found. The following examples (A to C) will give some idea of their general form.

(A)   *Handwriting development*
(1)   Holds pencil satisfactorily.
(2)   Can trace over simple shapes or pictures.
(3)   Can trace over complex shapes or pictures.
(4)   Can trace over writing patterns.
(5)   Can trace over letters directly (or with tracing paper).
(6)   Can write underneath teacher's writing.
(7)   Can write, copying from a workcard.
(8)   Can write, copying from a blackboard.
(9)   Can write from dictation:  (*a*) words; (*b*) short sentences;  (*c*) complex sentences (material appropriate to pupil's reading age).

| (B) | *Writing record* | Date and comment |
|---|---|---|
| | (1) Scribble - no attempt at representation. | |
| | (2) First attempts at representation. | |
| | (3) Good picture representation. | |
| | (4) Fair attempt at writing pattern. | |
| | (5) Good attempt at writing pattern. | |
| | (6) Good individual letters. | |
| | (7) Good copy of single words. | |
| | (8) Good copy of sentences. | |
| | (9) Writes own name without help. | |
| | (10) Pretend writing by child. | |
| | (11) Desire to write own sentences. | |
| | (12) Writes own phrases. | |
| | (13) Writes simple sentence about a picture. | |
| | (14) Writes many sentences using word book. | |
| | (15) Good style when writing an account with some spelling errors. | |
| | (16) Good imaginative writing with some spelling errors. | |
| | (17) Fluent writing with fewer errors. | |

(C)  *Written expression*
    (1)  Attempts at free expression using odd words.
    (2)  Can compare sentences.
    (3)  Can write about own experiences.
    (4)  Can write story.
    (5)  Can write freely using dictionary.
    (6)  Writes imaginatively.
    (7)  Has good command of language.
    (8)  Enjoys writing.

Checklists records are based on the observations teachers have made, over the years, of the way children's written language develops.  Teachers seemed to find this to be a satisfactory pragmatic approach to recording progress in the absence of an overall, clearly defined, theory of written language development.

At the upper junior/middle school age range, records of written language development relied on the individual teacher being able to identify important or significant aspects of progress, since a blank space was frequently provided for comments.  Often the only guidance given to the teacher completing the record was in the following form.

Please comment on:

*Handwriting:*  legibility, fluency, style, left-handedness.
*Use of language:*  spelling, comprehension, punctuation, grammar.
*Creative writing:*  stories, poems, diaries, descriptive writing.

No further information was given about what was to be recorded nor details as to how the assessments were to be made.  The quality of what is recorded thus depends entirely upon the individual teacher's expertise.

Despite the absence of an overall theory about how children's written language develops, there exist reports of research which focus on particular aspects of development such as 'visual perception', 'spelling', 'analysis of typical errors' and 'grammar'.  From the material that is currently available it may be possible to construct frameworks of development as a basis for more systematic, practicable record keeping.

*Spelling*
No systematic records of spelling were seen by the team though occasionally 'spelling ages' or grades were included under language or writing records. Qualitative assessment of spelling was not covered. According to the 1977 Green Paper, it is suggested that '... in primary schools, improved fluency in writing has been achieved at the expense of accuracy in spelling and punctuation'.[3]  This seems to be supported by the present study.

IV   MATHEMATICS RECORDS

Of the various kinds of record examined by the team,

those of mathematics progress were the second most
prevalent.  Despite the frequency and quantity of
mathematics records, many teachers admitted difficulty
in producing satisfactory forms which could be easily
understood by teachers from other schools.

Mathematical abilities seem to be more readily
ordered hierarchically than most other areas of development.  The problems in compiling mathematics records arise when deciding which aspects of progress
need to be recorded, rather than in the sequencing of
subject-matter.  Also, many teachers expressed the
view that their mathematics records, despite regular
revision, were somehow inadequate.

Checklists of one form or another were a common
form of recording progress.  Teachers had varying
views regarding the reliability of assessments of progress as shown on these checklists, particularly when
interpretated by teachers in other schools.  Because
of this problem of interpretation, some teachers
suggested that such records comprised nothing more
than a list of a pupil's mathematical experiences and
not the level of competence attained.

It has not been an easy task to categorize and
analyse the variety of mathematics records collected,
except in fairly general terms.  Three main types
predominate:

(1)   lists of mathematical topics experienced by
      the pupil - based on a textbook scheme or
      schemes;
(2)   checklists of mathematics concepts and skills;
(3)   list of topics (similar to item (1) above),
      based on guidelines produced by a local
      authority.

*(1)   Topic lists*
Most of the records analysed here originated in junior
and middle schools.  They were based on lists of
mathematics *topics* devised by analysing the textbook
scheme(s) in use.  This kind of record has been found
comparatively simple to produce but, where several
schemes were in use, a good deal of preliminary cross-
referencing was required.

Mathematics at the junior and middle school level
is more complex than at the infant level, in that
pupils are required to use a number of concepts and
skills in combination.  The use of topic lists, as
opposed to checklists, was preferred by teachers in
primary and middle schools because of their relative
simplicity.  Checklists containing lists of the wide
range of concepts and skills taught to 8-13 year-old

pupils were considered too lengthy to be of practical
use.

Though many ways of designing records based on book
schemes were seen, the principal form of construction
was in the form of a 'matrix', where the subject/topic
areas were listed down one side of the record and the
pages or stages of development were listed along the
top.  Such lists can be derived simply from the contents page of the textbook.

With records of this type for individual pupils,
the project sample teachers expressed their doubts as
to how valuable such a record would be to other
teachers, particularly those in other schools.  It was
felt, as with checklists, that the main value was the
information given about a pupil's mathematical experiences.  Where the same mathematics scheme was in use
in another school, pupils were (obviously) more easily
placed at an appropriate point in the scheme as a result of having this kind of information on record.

*(2)  Concept checklists*
The checklist records of concepts learned and skills
acquired were seen mainly in infant and first schools.
The sample teachers felt they were a useful check when
used as a curriculum guide or syllabus, thereby ensuring that pupils were receiving a broad and balanced
'diet' of mathematical experiences.  Two main criticisms of checklist records emerged:

(*a*)  they tended to be lengthy and unwieldy, especially where one list was required for each
pupil (some of the checklists seen had over
100 items);

(*b*)  the marks or ticks against particular items
did not appear to indicate, with any degree
of accuracy, pupils' competence in applying
the concepts and skills indicated.

Methods of filling in this kind of record varied.
Frequently a single tick indicated that a pupil 'can
do' the item.  Other lists were checked off on a *yes/
no* basis.  One further method attempted to increase
the precision of the assessments, and was being filled
in as follows:

√  Has been introduced to this concept or skill.
×  Has had practice in using this concept or skill.
*  Has a sound understanding of this concept or
skill.

The project team saw several variations of this

method.  Unfortunately, teachers use three-point
scales similar to the one illustrated with different
criteria.  Where other teachers have to interpret such
records, it is therefore vital that a key to facilitate interpretation is included.

*(3)  LEA development guidelines*
Many LEAs have set up working parties of teachers and
advisers to devise a common policy in the field of
mathematics teaching in their area.  The outcome of
some of these working parties has been the production
of mathematics curriculum guidelines.  Several of
these have been published and many teachers have used
such guidelines as a basis for devising their own records.  The following guidelines were collected by the
project team.

(i)   Title:  *Redditch Mathematics Flow Diagrams:*
      (*a*) 5-9 years;  (*b*) 9-13 years
      Publisher:  Redditch Teachers' Centre*

(ii)  Title:  *Guidelines in School Mathematics:*
      (*a*) *Guidelines wallchart*;  (*b*) *Notes on*
      *Guidelines*
      Author/s:  Staff of Mathematics Department,
      Manchester College of Education
      Publisher:  Hart-Davis Educational (1971)

(iii) Title:  *SMP 7-13* (primary level mathematics
      course):  supporting texts for each unit
      Author/s:  School Mathematics Project
      Publisher:  Cambridge University Press
      (1977—)

(iv)  Title:  *Bulmershe Mathematics Programme*
      (for 4-9 years):  supporting texts
      Author/s:  Staff of Bulmershe College of
      Education and associates (incorporating
      learning aids by Dr Z.P. Dienes)
      Publishers:  ESA Creative Learning, Harlow
      (main output);  individual supporting
      texts from other publishers (detailed in
      ESA catalogue)

(v)   Title:  *Checking Up*, I-III
      Author/s:  Nuffield Mathematics Project
      Publisher:  W & R Chambers/John Murray
      (1970-3)

* This teachers' centre in Hereford & Worcester LEA is no longer
  open.

(vi)   Title: *Guidelines in Mathematics for
       Teachers:  5-12/13 years*
       Publisher:  West Sussex LEA[4]

(vii)  Title: *Progression in Primary Mathematics*
       Publisher:  Educational Development Centre,
       Birmingham[5]

(viii) Title: *Mathematics Guidelines*
       Author/s:  British Families Education
       Services (part of Service Children's
       Education Authority[6])
       Publisher:  Service Children's Education
       Authority

(ix)   Title: *Mathematics Manual, 5-13 years*
       Publisher:  Croydon LEA[7]

(x)    Title: *ILEA Curriculum Guidelines:
       Primary School Mathematics Checkpoints*
       Publisher:  Inner London Education Authority
       (1978)[8]

(xi)   Title: *Content Guidelines in Mathematics
       5-13 years*
       Publisher:  Wiltshire LEA (1977)[9]

*Comment*

The major problem faced by teachers is that of communicating assessments of pupils' mathematical abilities
in a way which is readily understood by teachers in
other schools.  Assessment data on the records collected were of two kinds.

(*a*)  *Quantitative:*  Usually in terms of numerical
       marks, percentages, ratings or grades.  These
       were given as a brief summary of a pupil's
       mathematical attainment.  Often information
       such as this merely gives a teacher some rough
       indication of how a pupil stands in relation
       to other pupils in his/her age group but does
       not indicate what the pupil has learned.

(*b*)  *Qualitative:*  Information of this kind is
       difficult to present in an abbreviated form
       (by number or letter codes) unless accompanied
       by lengthy notes on how the abbreviations
       should be interpreted.  E.g. after some in-
       formation is given about the task set or skill
       to be learnt, the following 'qualitative'
       ratings may be given:

*Acquired*
1.  Skill well developed, has good proficiency.
2.  Skill developed satisfactorily, profici-
    ency could be improved.
3.  Basic skill developed, low proficiency,
    needs additional work.

*Not acquired*
4.  Basic skill not acquired.

The reporting of pupils' mathematical development
in qualitative terms may be further enhanced by describing reasoning ability.  Piagetian tests (which
have been replicated by Beard and Lovell)[10] have been
used to demonstrate that a child's thinking has a
logical consistency which is different from that of an
adult.  The Nuffield Mathematics *Checking Up* books
(see (v) on p.39) are designed to show how pupils'
mathematical development has progressed and at what
stage they happen to be.  The conceptual understanding
of pupils can be reported on a scale of Piagetian
stages such as that described in the *Manual* to the
first of the CSMS mathematics tests (*Number Operations*).[11]

Presentation of abbreviated information of mathematics test results can be carried out on an item
(question) analysis basis and in the form of a grid
(see example from *Basic Mathematics Test B* in appendix
A, p.252).  When a grid is completed for each pupil, a
survey of items incorrectly answered can supply diagnostic information about pupils' weaknesses.  Aspects
of mathematics which require further teaching are thus
highlighted and work can be planned for individual
pupils or groups.

Analysis of errors made or habits used by pupils in
their mathematics tasks can provide information for
other teachers which is possibly of more use than
numerical grades or ratings.  A list of this kind, of
American origin, is included in appendix A.

Reporting development in this kind of detail involves teachers observing pupils' work habits and analysing written work carefully.  Under present conditions it may only be possible to concentrate detailed
analysis on a few pupils.  However, the project sample
teachers felt that the greater problem with this kind
of information was not so much the bulk of information
but its short-term validity;  information about a
child's level of competence soon becomes superseded by
new information as the child goes on learning.  The
more detailed the information, the sooner it becomes
outdated.

One of the most frequent comments from the sample
teachers at both primary and secondary level about
this kind of information was that teachers can find
out for themselves, within an hour or two, most of
what they need to know about a pupil and, furthermore,
children need to go over work they have done before in
order to consolidate their learning.  Different
teachers required different amounts of detail about
new pupils' mathematical ability and attainment.  To
an extent, these variations in quantity of information
required were dependent on how far they were prepared
to adjust new work in mathematics to individual pupils'
past experiences.

It is therefore recommended that any attempt at
expressing the quality of a pupil's work and learning
should include information on the topic content or
stage reached, in addition to some indication of how
the pupil performed on the tasks set.

### V   RECORDS OF SOCIAL AND PERSONAL DEVELOPMENT

The records of pupils' social/personal development
seen by the project team were of two kinds:

(1)   unstructured comments about pupils' adjustment
to school and their relationships with adults
and peers, variously called 'pen-portraits',
'pupil profiles' or other similar titles;
(2)   structured records or reports in the form of:
(a)   rating scales,
(b)   attitude scales,
(c)   gradings linked to a set of criteria,
(d)   a list of personality traits on which the
teacher is asked to make comments.

Equivocal comments have been received from the
sample teachers about the usefulness of personal/
social development records.  Some teachers have indicated their value, saying that it is interesting to
compare one's own impressions of a child with those of
other teachers.  On the other hand, some teachers have
dismissed such records because of the subjective and
possibly prejudicial nature of the comments contained
in them.

### (i)   Unstructured comments
The pen-portrait relies on a teacher's ability to
structure what he or she has to say about a pupil.
The terms and categories of information used by individual teachers are dependent on their perceptual
constructs, that is, on the way they see the world and

the different meanings they attach to words.[12]    This
is borne out somewhat by the frequency with which
teachers made comments like '... they [the records of
personal/social development] say more about the
teacher than the pupil'.

*(2)   Structured records*
Many schools visited were using various rating scales,
attitude scales and other methods of structuring
teachers' subjective impressions of pupils.   When
asked about their preference for this kind of record,
teachers felt that a list of behavioural traits on a
record helped them in focusing attention on children
and in their observations.

The majority of records seen were 'home-made';
that is, they were produced by individual teachers for
their own use without any evidence of being standardized and validated.   Thus, they lacked the sophisti-
cation of professionally produced scales used by psychologists.   As an exception to the predominance of
teacher-made scales, a few schools used the Rutter
Child Scale B (see p.136), an instrument for identifying children who have possible neurotic or anti-
social tendencies.   The Rutter scale is of course an
assessment procedure and not primarily intended as a
format for record keeping.

The idiosyncratic nature of records of pupils'
personal development is probably best illustrated by a
few examples.   For instance, 'dependability' on one
record can appear as 'reliability' on another;   definitions in dictionaries show that the two terms are
closely related but individual interpretations may
vary.   The following examples from two separate records reveal something of the perceptions of the
teachers who compiled them.

    (A)   *Reliability*
        rating 1   unable to lie, volunteers informa-
                  tion
             2   truthful and honest
             3   will lie to escape punishment
             4   lies, cheats as a matter of course
             5   lies to incriminate others
             6   compulsive thief
             7   light-fingered

    (B)   *Dependability*
        rating 1   uses own initiative
             2   completes jobs without supervision
             3   needs continual teacher guidance
             4   leaves jobs incomplete

      5   generally adopts accepted behaviour
           regardless of immediate teacher/
           adult presence

Variants of these two examples include the following.

  (C)  The child is reliable:
      1  always
      2  usually
      3  sometimes
      4  seldom
      5  never

  (D)  *Reliability*
      rating 1  extremely reliable
            2  reliable
            3  normally reliable
            4  unreliable

The weakness of example (C) is common to all rating scales using absolute criteria such as 'always' and 'never'.  It is very difficult to rate any person on the extreme ends of the scale with any amount of certainty.  The five-point scale is thus immediately reduced to three.  The problems with scales similar to example (D) is the notion of 'normality' as related to pupils' reliability.  What is normal for a five-year-old may not be so for a ten-year-old.  This is a particular problem when assessing 'maturity', as in the following example:

   *Temperament*
   rating 1  very stable (mature)
          2  average
          3  easily upset (immature)
          4  unstable

The recording of personal/social information about pupils raises a whole range of questions as to the ethics of the exercise, and the legal implications in relation to confidentiality (see chapter 8).  Few teachers were able to say precisely why they kept such information except in the most general terms, e.g. 'so that a teacher has a better understanding of the child'.  Other teachers felt that keeping such information was important in the case of a minority of children who were at physical and/or psychological 'risk'.

From opinions expressed by members of one of the project teacher groups, the use of records of social/personal development appears '... to imply the use of

objective methods to collect subjective data ...   This
seems to be an inadequate way of treating this information'.   Another teacher in the same group said:
'Most of the records appear to aim at a general profile of the child without any in-depth examination of
any of the problems they may reveal'.   If records of
this kind are kept, it is important for teachers to
accept that such problems may arise from school environment, neighbourhood environment, clash of child's
personality with teachers, peers and parents.[13]

### VI   RECORDS OF SCIENTIFIC SKILLS DEVELOPMENT

Records kept in this area of the curriculum were seen
in just less than one in five of the survey schools,
and may be categorized as follows:

(1)   areas of study to be followed – in the form
      of flow diagrams,
(2)   lists of topics studied;
(3)   lists of equipment used;
(4)   lists of scientific skills used or acquired.

Of these, flow diagrams of topics were the most common
type.   It was sometimes difficult to see whether they
were intended for planning a course of study or to be
used purely as a record afterwards.   The flow diagrams
revealed some remarkable ramifications from the main
theme.
      Lists of scientific skills were rarely seen.   Some
of the skills which were included are similar to what
may also be called 'study skills' (see section VII
below).   (See the definition of scientific skills as
applied by the APU, p.21.)
      Only one or two schools included lists of equipment
used in connexion with work in science, for example:

*Section five*
1$a$   Setting up circuits on the circuit board.
1$b$   What happens when thin wires are joined to a
       battery?
1$c$   Magnets and electricity.
1$d$   Making and using a current balance.
1$e$   Using ammeters.
1$f$   Measuring electricity in different parts of a
       circuit.
1$g$   Different ways of changing the flow of elec-
       tricity in a circuit.
1$h$   Investigating the resistance of wire of various
       sizes and kinds.
1$i$   Testing fuses.

1*j*  Further circuit investigations.
1*k*  A simple computer.

2*a*  Do all substances let electricity flow through them?
2*b*  Does using a larger driving force make electricity flow through gases?
2*c*  Making batteries.
2*d*  Measuring the driving force of batteries.
2*e*  Do all batteries give the same voltage?

3*a*  Trying to find out about electricity.

In general, teachers do not feel the necessity to record pupils' progress in this area of the curriculum. This is borne out in the survey of transfer records (chapter 6) in which teachers rated information about pupils' abilities in science at a low priority.

One of the project teacher groups studied the area of science in some detail, basing their work on a study of the Science 5-13 project (sponsored by Schools Council, the Nuffield Foundation and the Scottish Education Department). As teacher group time was limited, the stage of producing records was not reached at the conclusion of the Record Keeping project. Progress had been halted by concern with how pupils were to be assessed in the area of science.

## VII   STUDY SKILLS DEVELOPMENT RECORDS

Records showing pupils' development in the use of study skills were found in very few schools. The sort of items used might well be seen as an extension of a reading record:

(1)  can find books in the library;
(2)  can use contents page;
(3)  can use a book index;
(4)  can comprehend main ideas;
(5)  can comprehend details.

From the survey of categories of information on transfer records, teachers appear to accord a very low level of importance to recording the development of study skills, and yet many teachers appear to assume that their pupils can use them, particularly in 'project' work.

## VIII   RECORDS OF PHYSICAL DEVELOPMENT

Physical development records seen in the survey may be divided into two main categories:

(1)   medical factors;
(2)   physical co-ordination.

In the schools which kept records of physical development, there was a wide range in the amount of detail
included.

*(1)  Medical factors*
Records containing medical factors appear to overlap
with records kept by the School Health Service.  This
is further complicated by the practices adopted by
medical authorities in different areas whereby pupils'
medical records are kept within the school in some
areas and in a central office in others.
      The medical factors recorded by teachers in the
survey were mainly concerned with pupils' hearing and
sight, e.g.

(*a*)   Does vision appear normal?
       Is hearing normal?

(*b*)   *Eyes*
       Do the child's eyes seem comfortable?
       Are the results of clinical tests or an
          oculist's examination favourable?

       *Ears*
       Does the child respond to a question or direc-
          tions, and is he/she apparently able to hear
          what is said in class?
       Does he/she respond to a low voice at six
          metres and a whisper test at half a metre?
       Is the child's audiometer test normal?

The wording used in the second example was seen on
several records.  Barbe's *Checklist for Reading Readiness* (1968)[14] includes criteria identical to the items
above.
      Apart from these items, three further sections
appear under the title of 'physical readiness':

(*c*)   *Speech*
       Does he/she speak clearly and well?
       Does he/she respond to correction readily?
       Does he/she show freedom from 'baby talk'?

(*d*)   *Hand-eye co-ordination*
       Does he/she make his/her hands work together
       well in cutting, using tools, or bouncing a
       ball?

(*e*)   *General health*
       Does he/she give an impression of good health?

Does he/she seem well nourished?
Does the school physical examination reveal
   good health?

Other medical factors which appeared to be worthy
of note on internal school records include:

(a)   allergies;
(b)   vaccinations (particularly date when last
      anti-tetanus injection was given);
(c)   activities which should be avoided because of
      medical factors (such as heart weakness).

*(2)   Physical co-ordination*
Records concerned with physical co-ordination included
both gross and fine motor skills, i.e. large bodily
movements involved in physical education (PE) and
games;  finely controlled movements used in handwriting.  One of the records collected was set out
thus.

*Crawling*

*Balance*
Walk along line alone.
Walk along plank alone.

*Jumping*
Off the ground.
Off a raised surface.
Over a raised object.

*Running*

*Hopping*

*Climbing*
Over a fence.
On tables.
   [etc.]

*Throwing*
Quality of aim.

*Kicking*
Quality of aim.

*Catching*
Size of object which can be managed.
                   [etc.]

| Activity | Date |
| --- | --- |
| Balancing along a beam | |
| Forward roll | |
| Backward roll | |
| Climbs rope | |
| Climbs ladder | |
| Travels over ladder bridge | |
| [etc.] | |

   Discussion in one of the project teacher groups
highlighted the problems of assessment in this area of
a child's development.  Group members also questioned
the need to record this kind of information.  A physical development record devised by this group (p.120)
includes a list of activities seen as indicating the
quality of a child's co-ordination.  They also
asserted that, for many children within the normal
range of abilities, a record of physical activity
development was largely unnecessary.  For the minority
of children who have a learning difficulty deriving
from physical deficiencies, a record was felt to be an
important way of building up a more detailed profile
of the child and giving some indication of where additional help was required.

IX   RECORDS OF AESTHETIC DEVELOPMENT

Records collected by the project and classified under
this heading reflected several aspects of aesthetic
development and indicated the way teachers attempted
to assess pupils' development in what was seen to be
a difficult area.
   Aspects of development seen on records included
attitudes, appreciation, skills and interests.  The
APU defines the area of aesthetic development in the
following words:

   '... the pupil's appreciation of form, colour, texture,
   sound;  his affective response to his environment, his
   respect for quality, his capacity to harness imagination
   and feeling in creative work'.[15]

The following examples illustrate how teachers are
thinking about the area of aesthetics.

   *Creative work and special interests*
   Shows initiative
   Enjoys working alone
   Enjoys group work

Seeks adult help
Special interest
Bricks
Sand
Wendy house
Clay
Painting
Craft
Muscular control:   good/poor
Has difficulty

*Music*
Finds enjoyment
Ability to listen
Recognition of rhythm
Reproduction of rhythm
Music ability
Special instrument:   violin/recorder/cello/other

*Art*
Crayons to outline
Uses colour well/uses only a few colours
Uses scissors well
Uses paintbrush well
Creative with clay/creative junk modelling/shows
   general creativity
Can draw well/can draw people/can draw houses

General assessment:   very poor/poor/fair/good/
excellent

Comments:
   (space allowed for comments)

### PUPILS' OWN RECORDS

No detailed analysis was made of the ways children
were encouraged to make, and keep, their own records.
Suffice it to say that, in many of the schools visited,
pupils kept a record of the work they had done or the
activities in which they had participated.  The
methods of recording varied from notes kept at the
back of an exercise book to wall charts for a whole
class.  Assignment sheets were also seen completed by
pupils as well as their teachers.  Examples of pupils'
own recording are given in Joan Dean's (1972) book on
this topic.[16]
   The value and reliability of pupils' self-accoun-
ting rests in the attitudes encouraged by teachers and
developed by pupils.  If the 'name of the game' is a
race to colour in as many squares as possible in a
week (each square representing a unit of work), what

pupils learn from their experiences may not be what
teachers expect.

*Samples of pupils' work*
Samples of work collected at regular intervals - termly, for instance - as a record of pupils' development
were frequently encountered by the project team.
Teachers favoured this way of recording progress, considering that, amongst the methods of keeping school
records, it was unique in having a meaning for the
children, their parents and their future teachers.

Against this method was its inevitably bulky and
selective nature:  flat pupil-products only are practicable!  Some teachers also felt that colleagues who
favoured this method of school recording to the exclu-
sion of other methods were in fact side-stepping the
difficult task of assessment.  The selection amongst
children's work was also questioned:  should it be of
the child's best (as judged by the teacher) or should
it also include his worst in order to give an idea of
his range?  Only a few of the schools in the sample
made a practice of sending records of this kind on to
another school at the point of transfer or transition
(see chapter 6).  Indeed, how far can a few pages of
mathematics work indicate mathematical competence or
a few pieces of written work indicate language
ability?  Without being too pernickety about detail,
samples of work of this kind can at best complement,
not supplement records of the more usual kind.

### SUMMARY

It can be seen from the examples that an immense variety of methods of recording pupils' progress exists in
primary schools.  Records of pupils' reading and mathematical development were by far the most common whereas those concerned with science and art were seen in-
frequently.

The records appear to reflect the teacher's understanding of how development occurs in relation to
different aspects of the primary curriculum.  Where
teachers are aware of a structural and systematic
framework (or theory) of development, this is reflected in the compiling of records.  These tended to be
considered much more favourably by other teachers and
any criticism of them focused on the amount of detail
included.

REFERENCES

1   See, for instance, D. Vincent and M. Cresswell, *Reading Tests in the Classroom*, Slough:  NFER Publishing Co., 1976.

2   See K. Wedell and E.C. Raybould (eds), *The Early Diagnosis of Educationally 'at risk' Children (Educational Review* Occasional Publication 6), University of Birmingham School of Education, 1965.  A screening procedure for school entrants has also been developed by the Schools Council Compensatory Education project;  this kit, the *Swansea Evaluation Profile*, by R. Evans *et al.* (Slough:  NFER Publishing Co., 1978), is at present still experimental and available only to researchers.

3   *Education in Schools:  a Consultative Document* (Cmnd 6869), HMSO, July 1977, paragraph 3.2.

4   County Hall, West Street, Chichester, W. Sussex, PO19 1RF.

5   Educational Development Centre (teachers' centre), Garrison Lane, Birmingham, B9 4BS.

6   Service Children's Education Authority, Empress State Building, Fulham, London SW6 1TR.

7   Croydon LEA, Taberner House, Park Lane, Croydon, CR9 1TP.

8   Inner London Education Authority, County Hall, London SE1 7PB.

9   Wiltshire LEA, County Hall, Trowbridge, Wiltshire, BA14 8JB.

10   See K.R. Fogelman, *Piagetian Tests for the Primary School*, Slough:  NFER Publishing Co., 1970.

11   Concepts in Secondary Mathematics and Science Programme, *CSMS Test N1:  Number Operations* (by M. Brown), Slough: NFER Publishing Co., 1978.

12   C.E. Osgood, G.J. Suci, P.H. Tannenbaum, *The Measurement of Meaning*, Urbana, Ill.:  University of Illinois Press, 1957, new ed. 1968;  G.A. Kelly, *The Psychology of Personal Constructs*, vol.1, New York:  Norton, 1955.

13   R.S. Illingworth, *The Child at School*, Oxford:  Blackwell, 1974.

14   W. Barbe, *Checklist for Reading Readiness*, Frontenac, USA: County Special Education Dept, 1968;  included in *Individual Pupil Monitoring System:  Reading*, Houghton Mifflin, 1974.

15   B.W. Kay, 'Monitoring pupils' performance' (in section entitled 'Educational standards today'), *Trends in Education* 1975/2, 15.

16   J. Dean, *Recording Children's Progress*, Macmillan Education, 1972.  Also included in Anglo-American Primary Education Project, *British Primary Schools Today*, vol.3, Macmillan Education, 1972.

# 5 Internal records: evaluation and synthesis

Central in importance to this project was the evaluation of the rich variety of records collected in the research phase (see chapter 2). By this means a broadly acceptable, practical as distinct from theoretical, understanding of what constitutes a good school record was achieved. It was therefore the major task undertaken by all the project teacher groups.

The project team were faced with the monumental task of evaluating literally hundreds of different examples of school records, all considered to be valuable by their originators. In order to make this task feasible, the records were first sorted into the general areas of function described in chapter 4, and a selection then made of those which best exemplified each type. This resulted in the retention of eighty in all, and these were reproduced in sufficient quantity for distribution to the members of the teacher groups in such a way that approximately 25 teachers had copies of each record.

The method of evaluation initially favoured would have been to distribute these records amongst the teachers to use, as far as they were able, over the period of at least one school term, and then report back to the team on the various merits and demerits of each. A consensus of strengths and weaknesses could thus be achieved, and remedial action where appropriate, taken prior to another round of trials.

Given more time than the project had, this slow but sure method would have produced eighty sets of records refined, in so far as they were inherently capable of detail refinement, to be generally suitable to some extent for most teachers, but wholly suitable for none. Early piloting of this strategy clearly pointed to this conclusion, which logic suggests anyway: only when schools teach a common curriculum by a laid-down pedagogy will 'off-the-peg' records of this kind be totally applicable. In spite of public airing of such notions, implicit in some of the quotations in chapter 1, the dominant trend in British primary school [58

53

Example 5.1  Record evaluation checklist (4pp)

Name .............................................................

Address ..........................................................

Age range of your school ........................................

### A. This section is concerned with DESIGN only

|  |  | (Tick) | | Comment |
|--|--|--|--|--|
|  |  | Yes | No |  |
| 1. | Is the title of the record clear? | ☐ | ☐ | ........................ |
| 2. | Is the name of the pupil easily located on the form? | ☐ | ☐ | ........................ |
| 3. | Are there instructions for the use of the record? | ☐ | ☐ | ........................ |
| 4. | Are coding or abbreviations used? | ☐ | ☐ | ........................ |
| 5. | Is the layout easy to follow? | ☐ | ☐ | ........................ |
| 6. | Is the wording unambiguous throughout the record? | ☐ | ☐ | ........................ |
| 7. | Is the printing on the record easy to read throughout? | ☐ | ☐ | ........................ |
| 8. | Could the information on the record be extracted readily? | ☐ | ☐ | ........................ |
| 9. | Is there adequate space for entries? | ☐ | ☐ | ........................ |

By each entry or section:

| 10. | Is there space for a date? | ☐ | ☐ | ........................ |
|--|--|--|--|--|
| 11. | Is there space for comments? | ☐ | ☐ | ........................ |
| 12. | Is there space for a signature? | ☐ | ☐ | ........................ |
| 13. | Is the record of a manageable size? (a) in shape? | ☐ | ☐ | ........................ |
|  | (b) to read? | ☐ | ☐ | ........................ |
|  | (c) to fill in? | ☐ | ☐ | ........................ |
| 14. | Could the record be simplified without serious loss of information? | ☐ | ☐ | ........................ |

(1)

B. This section is concerned with CONTENT only

1. What do you see as the purpose of this record?

Yes  No<br>☐  ☐

2. Is this the kind of information that you need?

Comments on what you would omit

Comments on what you would include

Yes  No<br>☐  ☐<br>☐  ☐

3. (a) Do the content-categories follow a sequence?

   (b) If NO, could this be sequenced effectively?

   Comments

Yes  No<br>☐  ☐

   (c) If YES (to 3a), is it appropriate?

   Comments

Yes  No<br>☐  ☐

4. Does the record give indications for future teaching?

   Comments

Yes  No<br>☐  ☐

5. (a) Is this a record of work experience/attempted?

   Comments

Yes  No<br>☐  ☐

   (b) Is this a record of pupil achievement/attainment?

   Comments

(2)

6. What factors (if any) are considered in assessing the level of pupil attainment?

   (i) <u>Relative ratings</u> (if used)

      E.g. ratings such as 'below average' or 5 point scale (A-E)

      Indicate (by a tick) which reference group you think is being used:

<br>

                                                    <u>Type of test</u> (if used)

      (a) national group    ☐  ...........................................

      (b) LEA area          ☐  ...........................................

      (c) district/
           catchment area   ☐  ...........................................

      (d) school group     ☐  ...........................................'

      (e) year group       ☐  ...........................................

      (f) class group      ☐  ...........................................

      (g) other            ☐  ...........................................

      (h) not clearly
           indicated        ☐  ...........................................

  (ii) <u>Criteria</u>

      Is there an indication on the record of how assessments are being made, e.g. some form of guidelines or instruction?

<br><br>

7. Have you any other comments to make about the contents of this record?

<br><br><br>

## C. Overall

1. Do you think this is a good record?

Yes ☐
No ☐
Doubtful ☐

Comments

2. Would you use it in your class?

Yes ☐
No ☐
Doubtful ☐

Comments

3. In what way do you think it could be improved?

practice remains firmly outside such an educational
strait-jacket. The very existence of such records
could in fact be damaging, in that their apparently
impeccable credentials might encourage inexperienced
teachers to teach in such a way as to 'fit' the record, a case of 'the tail wagging the dog' with a
vengeance.

It was decided that the proper purpose of this
evaluation exercise was the formation of general principles for recording, by the critical appraisal of
these specific, real-life examples. The teacher
groups were therefore asked to assist in formulating
a record evaluation checklist, as described on p.15.

The final form of the checklist (example 5.1, pp.
54-57) represents the consensus view of the teachers
who took part in the project as to what a good primary
school record should be. It was circulated with the
accompanying comment: 'This form, produced by the
project team as an attempt to evaluate the efficiency
of records, is *provisional* and open to *amendment*.'

The rest of this chapter consists of a selection,
from amongst the eighty evaluated records, of those
most favoured by the teachers who studied them. They
are presented as examples only of records in use, included to amplify and illustrate the general principles embodied in the checklist and not because they
are necessarily suitable for general use as they stand.
Accompanying each are teachers' comments, selected to
express the dominant views about them, and a short
summary evaluation by the project team. In general,
layout has been slightly modified in order to fit
within the present page size (the extent in pages,
given in the example titles, relates to pages occupied
within this book); and references to the child have
been standardized in the 'he/she' form.

SELECTED EXAMPLES OF RECORDS

*School admission form/pre-school profile*
(example 5.2, pp.60-63)

Teachers' comments
(*a*)   'This record contains much of the information an
        infant headteacher requires.'
(*b*)   'It contains useful information but is rather
        lengthy and may be off-putting to some parents
        perhaps!'
(*c*)   'Good, if parents can read it and be confident
        to complete the answers (50% of mothers in my
        school would find it difficult and embarrassing).'
(*d*)   'Clearly presented record.'
(*e*)   'Format is such that it is not easy to find in-
        formation quickly.  Could be presented in a more
        condensed form.'

Project's evaluation
This record does have the disadvantage of being
rather too long but has the advantage of allowing
plenty of space for making longer comments where
necessary.  One cannot have both space and a condensed format without reducing the number of items of
information.

Example 5.2  School admission form/pre-school profile, based on interview
            with parent:  Isle of Wight LEA (4pp)


Name ................................  Date of birth ................

Address ...................................................................

..........................................................................

Previous school(s) or
playgroup(s) (please give dates) ..........................................

..........................................................................

..........................................................................

Position
in family .................................................................

Family
doctor ....................................................................

..........................................................................

Name, address and telephone number of
person to be contacted in cases of emergency ..............................

..........................................................................

..........................................................................

Letters/notes
to be sent to .............................................................

..........................................................................

Parent/guardian
having actual custody .....................................................

..........................................................................

Is there any help or information you require from the school
about such things as meals, milk, uniform and transport?

..........................................................................

..........................................................................

..........................................................................

Has he/she had any serious accident or illness or spent
any length of time in hospital or away from the family?

Inoculations

Is he/she receiving any form of medication or
subject to any restriction on physical activities?

Are you aware of anything that worries or disturbs
him/her with which you feel the school should be acquainted?

Any further relevant information

PRE-SCHOOL PROFILE                    (To be completed in respect of a child
                                      before admission to the primary school)

## Self-care

Can he/she dress and undress
him/herself - including footwear?


Is he/she able to go to
the toilet without help

### and

can he/she ask correctly?



Is he/she able to feed him/herself
using a knife and fork
and a spoon and fork?

## Physical development

Does he/she enjoy
physical activities?


Is he/she left- or
right-handed?


Can he/she recognize
and name basic colours?



## Social development

Does he/she prefer to play
alone or with other children?


Does he/she talk readily to
adults/other children?  (Any speech
difficulty may be noted here.)


Any other information, e.g.
timid


(3)

School meals/milk

Is there any food he/she
should not eat?


Do you wish him/her to have milk?



Headteacher's notes

(Notes for guidance of parents showing what they can do to help their
child/children before starting their first term at school may be given
to parents at the head's discretion.)

Date of                                    Parent
interview ......................           interviewed ......................

Signature of headteacher ................................................

(4)

*Pre-reading guide* (example 5.3, pp.66-69)

Supplementary information
This record has been based on work carried out by
A. E. Tansley (see footnote, p.67).  It focuses on the
early identification, or screening, of children who
may be educationally 'at risk', i.e. who are most
likely to have some form of learning problem.  The record has been amended slightly to avoid some of the
awkward wording in the original and references to
specific workcard activities meaningful only to the
originating school.

Teachers' comments
(*a*)   'This asks for a lot of information:  I think it
        would be useful, but would a teacher with a large
        class use it carefully enough?'
(*b*)   'A clear and precise record.'
(*c*)   'A useful record for diagnosing children with
        learning difficulties but would not need to be
        used for all children.'
(*d*)   'There is not enough room to make extra comments.'
(*e*)   'Some items would demand more than a tick if
        meaningful information is to be given.'

Project's evaluation
The 'tick and date' entries are somewhat inadequate as
a record since some items require observations to be
carried out on several occasions, noting both
successes and failures.  As this checklist is basically an assessment schedule, notes about a pupil's
performance should be kept on a separate sheet of
paper, giving some indication of the quality of performance on the items being tested.

*Language record* (example 5.4, pp.70-75)

Teachers' comments
(a)  'I consider this to be a comprehensive list of
     items for a language record for use by the
     teacher in class.  The purpose of the record
     would be to acquaint the teacher with the nature
     of the tasks completed and skills successfully
     used.'
(b)  'May be highly desirable, but could take more
     time to complete than to actually do the work
     with the child.'
(c)  'More space should be allocated to accommodate
     comments where necessary (e.g. speech diffi-
     culty).'
(d)  'No dates or indication to suggest whether the
     record is a summary or continuous record - over
     a year or over a four-year period.'

Project's evaluation
This is as comprehensive a checklist of language
development as was found used in schools.  Fortunately
it is somewhat shorter than similar checklists of
reading and language development emanating from
America.[1]
     As with other checklists, items which are broad in
scope are often presented somewhat ambiguously, e.g.
'can reason in language'.  A checklist consisting of
a small number of very specific items can also be
criticized, for omitting important aspects of development.

Example 5.3  Pre-reading guide (4pp)*

Pupil's name ........................

Date of birth ........../........../..........

| | Tick | Date observed |
|---|---|---|
| | | |

EMOTIONAL/SOCIAL DEVELOPMENT AND ATTITUDES

Does he/she play well with other children?

Does h/she share belongings with others?

Is behaviour stable (not easily upset)?

Does he/she concentrate on what he/she is doing?

Can he/she tolerate changes in routine without stress?

Is he/she interested in books and printed material?

Has he/she a desire to read?

SKILLS

Visual discrimination

Can he/she detect differences and similarities
in shape, size and colour?

Matching:  picture to picture

picture + word to picture + word

word only to picture + word

word only to picture only

word only to word only

pairs

shapes

(1)

| | Tick | Date observed |
|---|---|---|

## Aural discrimination

Can he/she detect differences and similarities between given sounds?

## Language development

Does he/she use good sentences in his/her normal conversation?

Does he/she know common nursery rhymes?

Is he/she interested in listening to stories?

Can he/she relate the main ideas of a story in sequence?

Can he/she talk about a given picture?

Can he/she describe in detail what is happening, or likely to happen, in the picture?

Can he/she talk about what he/she has seen or done?

Is he/she interested in reading signs and advertisements?

## CONVENTIONS

When using a book does he/she:

(a) follow the front to back sequence of pages?

(b) follow the top to bottom sequence of lines?

(c) follow the left to right sequence of words?

(d) understand the difference between letters and words?

(e) understand the different forms of each letter, including capitals and lower case?

---

\* Adapted from A. E. Tansley, Reading and Remedial Reading (Routledge, 1967, new ed. 1972)

(2)

Tick    Date observed

## PHYSICAL AND SENSORY DEVELOPMENT

Is his/her eyesight normal?

Can he/she hear within normal limits?

Does he/she carry out spoken instructions efficiently?

Is he/she active and in good health?

Are his/her physical actions well co-ordinated?

Has he/she a good sense of rhythm?

Does he/she use pencils, crayons and paintbrushes with reasonable efficiency?

Can he/she draw a recognizable picture of a human figure and a house?

Can he/she draw a reasonably straight line about 6 inches in length without the aid of a ruler?

Can he/she do simple jigsaws?

Is his/her speech clearly articulated?

Can he/she draw the following forms as well as the majority of his/her peers?

(3)

69

RESULTS OF TESTS

| | Name of test | Date tested | Comments |
|---|---|---|---|
| Intelligence tests | | | |
| Reading tests | | | |
| Other tests | | | |

(4)

Example 5.4  Language record (6pp)

Name ............................     Date of birth .................

SPEECH

Articulates clearly ☐

Has speech difficulty (specify) ☐

Can understand teacher's language structure ☐

Can talk about first-hand experience:   (a) to teacher ☐
                                         (b) to group ☐
                                         (c) to class ☐

Can deliver a simple message ☐

Can carry on a simple conversation ☐

Can relate a story ☐

Takes part in class discussion ☐

Can talk about probability and possibility ☐

Can express emotion and feeling ☐

Can reason in language ☐

Can explain or teach something ☐

Can give directions ☐

Answers telephone and takes messages correctly ☐

Interviews and asks questions to find out ☐

Uses past tense ☐

Uses future tense ☐

Uses prepositions correctly ☐

LISTENING

Listens to teacher in a group ☐

Is distractible ☐

Listens to (and watches) radio (television) ☐

Listens to stories and comments on content ☐

Can recall stories ☐

Listens to and responds correctly to instructions and explanations ☐

Concentrates on a given task ☐

(1)

HANDWRITING/MANUAL DEXTERITY/HAND-EYE CO-ORDINATION

Hand used (L or R)  ☐

Can copy simple shapes  ☐

Can complete simple jigsaws  ☐

Can reproduce familiar shapes as asked  ☐

Can thread large beads  ☐

Holds pencil correctly  ☐

Traces over teacher's writing (date)  ☐

Copies teacher's writing (date)  ☐

Can use a word book  ☐

Can copy from book or workcard  ☐

Can form letters correctly  ☐

Can join letters  ☐

Can space out and present work:  (a) without lines  ☐
                                 (b) with lines  ☐

PRE-READING SKILLS

Spends time in book corner with books  ☐

Understands concept of reading  ☐

Recognizes the word as a unit of speech  ☐

Visual discrimination

Can match picture to picture  ☐

Can match shape to shape  ☐

Can match initial letter to word  ☐

Can match word to word  ☐

Can pick 'odd man out' in series of pictures  ☐

Can pick 'odd man out' in series of words  ☐

Can pick 'odd man out' in series of letters  ☐

Can match letter and letter  ☐

Auditory discrimination

Can identify a sound in a word  ☐

Can play 'I spy' with sounds  ☐

Can pick phonic 'odd man out' in spoken list  ☐

Recognizes familiar everyday sounds  ☐

(2)

CONVENTIONS OF WRITTEN LANGUAGE

Usually gets letters in right order ☐

Usually writes in sentences ☐

Usually writes in paragraphs ☐

Uses capitals correctly ☐

Uses punctuation (see p.5 below for notes on marking boxes):

| . | ☐ |
|---|---|
| , | ☐ |
| " " | ☐ |
| ! | ☐ |
| ' | ☐ |
| ? | ☐ |

Understands the meaning of the following words:

    word ☐
    letter ☐
    capital letter ☐
    small letter ☐
    fullstop ☐
    sentence ☐
    magic 'e' ☐
    paragraph ☐

Uses past tense correctly ☐

Uses future tense correctly ☐

Uses present tense correctly ☐

USE OF WRITING

Writes own 'news' ☐

Writes stories and other imaginative work ☐

Writes rhymes ☐

Writes poetry ☐

Writes to a given title or outline ☐

Distinguishes fact from fiction and writes one or the other
   intentionally ☐

Reports factual information and first-hand experience ☐

Writes letters in their correct form ☐

Makes notes: (a) from books ☐
           (b) from TV or radio ☐
           (c) from interviews or discussion ☐

Puts together notes to make coherent whole ☐

Writes appropriately for a given purpose ☐

(3)

USING BOOKS AND WRITING

Knows alphabetical order ☐

Uses alphabetical order ☐

Uses indexes ☐

Finds books needed for information ☐

Compares different accounts in different books ☐

Works from written instructions ☐

Can use a workcard ☐

ADVANCED SKILLS

Can read fluently with good expression ☐

Can skim ☐

Shows enjoyment in reading ☐

READING (use in conjunction with appended checklist, pp.5-6 below)

Knows 100 key words on checklist ☐

Knows sounds as list ☐

Blends sounds to build/read new words ☐

Blends sounds as list indicates ☐

(4)

READING

NOTES on completing the boxes:

◻ first experience   ⊠ practice satisfactory   ▨ understanding

BOOKS                                    SOUNDS

| | | | | |
|---|---|---|---|---|
| a | ☐ | 3 letter words | ☐ |
| b | ☐ | 4 letter words | ☐ |
| c | ☐ | ch | ☐ |
| d | ☐ | ing | ☐ |
| e | ☐ | oo | ☐ |
| f | ☐ | ee | ☐ |
| g | ☐ | ea | ☐ |
| h | ☐ | ai | ☐ |
| i | ☐ | ay | ☐ |
| j | ☐ | oa | ☐ |
| k | ☐ | ar | ☐ |
| l | ☐ | or | ☐ |
| m | ☐ | er | ☐ |
| n | ☐ | ir | ☐ |
| o | ☐ | ur | ☐ |
| p | ☐ | ow | ☐ |
| qu | ☐ | ou | ☐ |
| r | ☐ | y | ☐ |
| s | ☐ | ies | ☐ |
| sh | ☐ | aw | ☐ |
| t | ☐ | au | ☐ |
| th | ☐ | all | ☐ |
| u | ☐ | silent | |
| v | ☐ | (magic) e | ☐ |
| w | ☐ | silent k | |
| x | ☐ | "   gh | ☐ |
| y | ☐ | "   b | ☐ |
| z | ☐ | "   w | ☐ |

(5)

BOOKS

| | | | | | | |
|---|---|---|---|---|---|---|
| and | it | walk | man | going | read | horse |
| here | says | by | car | of | not | house |
| is | have | play | good | off | but | puts |
| the | he | up | an | about | will | do |
| dog | look | at | apple | talk | there | thank |
| likes | wants | doing | give | run | fire | him |
| I | no | on | red | make | little | sea |
| a | you | boat | boys | children | two | all |
| shop | some | see | was | work | which | cat |
| toy | for | get | girls | game | draw | milk |
| in | this | me | bus | after | then | what |
| has | can | cake | school | she | big | why |
| ball | jump | please | tea | be | my | who |
| tree | into | with | bed | away | her | |
| they | we | one | said | or | our | |
| are | to | help | them | flowers | us | |
| water | go | Mummy | now | out | things | |
| fun | yes | Daddy | where | let | keep | |
| come | home | that | so | his | farm | |

(A sheet is included on the end of this record.  On it please note
any problem - consistent errors, refusals and, if possible, the
reason for a change in reading scheme.  Please date each entry.)

(6)

*Child's book record* (example 5.5, p.77)

Teachers' comments
(a)   'Good to focus children's attention on personal
      achievement - a danger of "quantity" rather than
      "quality" - children should be made aware of the
      possibilities of what having a book means.'
(b)   'There should be a column where the teacher in-
      dicates that he has discussed the book with the
      child, not just signed in the "finished" column.'
(c)   'More suitable for older children - more space
      should be allowed for their own comments.'
(d)   'Simple and easy record of what a child has read.
      Could enable a teacher to suggest further reading
      or alternatives.'

Project evaluation
Older primary children can be reasonably expected to
keep this kind of record themselves thus reducing the
'clerical' demands on teachers and allowing more time
for the qualitative assessment of reading.  The record
affords opportunity for pupils to evaluate what they
have been reading, though perhaps, to avoid the repe-
titive use of phrases 'I like it' or 'I didn't like
it', some children will need guidance on how to fill
it in.  Recording by pupils needs to be encouraged in
a controlled manner lest the 'name of the game' becomes a race to 'read' (or list) as many books as
possible, to beat one's friends.

Example 5.5  Book record to be filled in by child

Name _____          Year _____

| Date chosen | Date finished | Title and author | No. of pages | Comments – like or dislike |
|---|---|---|---|---|
|  |  |  |  |  |
|  |  |  |  |  |
|  |  |  |  |  |
|  |  |  |  |  |
|  |  |  |  |  |
|  |  |  |  |  |
|  |  |  |  |  |
|  |  |  |  |  |

*Reading record:   comparative list*
(example 5.6, pp.80-81)

Supplementary information
Several versions of records of this type were seen,
each reflecting the schemes used in a particular
school.  This record was based on the analysis of
reading schemes carried out by Moon (see footnote,
p.80), who links reading development to thirteen
stages,* including the following.

*stages 1-4:*  pre-reading stage - introductory readers,
  pictures and sight vocabulary;
*stage 6* (approximate reading age 6-6½ years):  Children should have an adequate sight vocabulary and
  need extension work in phonics;
*stage 10:*  by this stage children will have mastered
  'decoding';
*stages 11-13* (approximate reading age 8½-9½ years):
  at these stages children will have mastered the
  mechanics of reading and will be able to extend
  their comprehension and higher reading skills.

Teachers' comments
(*a*)   'This record is a straightforward information
       sheet for teachers.  It is useful where several
       reading schemes are used in a school or even as
       a transfer record.'
(*b*)   'I would need some indication of the meaning of
       "stages" but assume that the books are itemized
       at the same level.'
(*c*)   'More information on level of competence for
       successful completion of books at each stage is
       needed.'
(*d*)   'Would be most helpful to teachers in enabling
       children to be "slotted in" at an appropriate
       level.'
(*e*)   'It would be better to use reading age levels
       rather than "stages".'

Project evaluation
This is basically a record of pupils' reading experiences.  However, it is of limited use since any

---

*  The twelfth edition of Moon's book (1980) categorizes
   reading matter for the stages as follows:
   *Stage 0*   Pure picture books - the first reader
   *Stages 1, 2, 3*   Introductory readers - caption books
   *Stages 4-10*   Developmental readers
   *Stages 11, 12, 13*   Bridging readers - bridging from
      shorter to longer books and out to general fiction, etc.

assessment of reading capability can only be inferred
from knowledge of the books and the skills required
to read them.


*Reading age distribution form* (example 5.7, pp.82-83)

Supplementary information
The purpose of this record is to present graphically
the distribution of reading ages in a class or year
group as half-yearly blocks (yearly from age eight).
Children's names are entered in the appropriate column
according to reading test results.  When the entry is
completed, a coloured line needs to be entered down
the column indicating the average *chronological* age of
the group in order that the reading age distribution
can be seen in relation to actual ages.

Teachers' comments
(*a*)   'Possibly useful, although addition of average
        age might add substantially to the record's
        interpretation.'
(*b*)   'Would give the headteacher an idea of the range
        of reading ability in each class.'
(*c*)   'There is no indication of the type of test used
        to assess the reading ability.'
(*d*)   'There is no indication for future teaching.'
(*e*)   'There needs to be some instruction for the use
        of this record.'

Project evaluation
This is an interesting method of presenting data about
a whole class or year group.  If the age range in a
class is more than six months (that is, more than one
column in width) the data may be better presented in
standardized scores or *z* scores (see appendix D) in
order to give a better picture.  The usefulness of
the record may be no more than administrative in that
a headteacher can view such records over the whole
school prior to making decisions about allocating resources and identifying pupils who may need extra
provision (both gifted and slow learners).

Example 5.6   Reading record:   comparative list (2pp)*

| STAGE | SCHEMES | | | |
| | Sparks | One, Two, Three & Away | Breakthrough | Griffin Pirates |
| --- | --- | --- | --- | --- |
| 2 | Stage 1 | Intro bk A | | |
| 3 | Stage 2 | Intro bks B, C, D | | Pre-readers |
| 4 | Stage 3 | | Yellow bks | Bks 1, 2 |
| 5 | Stage 4 | Platform level 1 | Red, Green bks | Bk 3 |
| 6 RA:[+] 6y to 6.5y | Stage 5 | Bks 1, 1A, 2, 2A | Blue bks ABC, About the House | Bks 4, 5 |
| 7 | Stage 6 | Platform level 2 bks 3 to 4A | - | Bks 6, 7 |
| 8 | - | Bks 5, 6, 7 | | Bks 8, 9 |
| 9 | | - | | Bks 10, 11 |
| 10 | | | | Bks 12 to 16 |
| 11 RA:[+] 8.5y | | | | Bks 17 to 20 |

*   Compiled from lists in C. Moon, Individualised Reading, Centre for the Teaching of Reading, University of Reading (updated twice yearly).
[+]   RA: reading age.

(1)

| SCHEMES (cont) | | | |
| Through the Rainbow | Time for Reading | Macdonald Starters | Ladybird |
| --- | --- | --- | --- |
| Red | | | Bks 1, 2 |
| Orange | | | Bk 3 |
| Yellow, Green | Story bks 1 to 4 | | Bk 4 |
| Blue | Story bks 5 to 8 | Activities | Bk 5 |
| Indigo | Story bks 9 to 12 | Places, Maths | Bk 6 |
| Violet | - | A Long Time Ago, People, Legends | Bk 7 |
| Gold, Silver 1 to 4 | | Science | Bk 8 |
| - | | - | Bk 9 |
| | | | Bk 10 |

(2)

Example 5.7   Reading age distribution form (2pp)

Class ...................................    Date ...................

Teacher ..................................

| Non-reading -5:0 | Pink 5:0-5:5 | Brown 5:6-5:11 | Mauve 6:0-6:5 | Black 6:6-6:11 | Orange 7:0-7:5 |
|---|---|---|---|---|---|
|  |  |  |  |  |  |

(1)

| Yellow | Red | Green | Blue | Free reader |
|---|---|---|---|---|
| 7:6-7:11 | 8:0-8:11 | 9:0-9:11 | 10:0-10:11 | 11:0+ |
|  |  |  |  |  |

(2)

*Reading age graph* (example 5.8, p.85)

Teachers' comments
(a)   'Confusing on first impression - notes for use
      would be helpful.'
(b)   'A clear and simple visual expression of a
      child's progress as demonstrated by reading age
      tests.'
(c)   'Perhaps more comment space would be required
      where some explanation was needed when rates of
      progress fluctuate.'
(d)   'Simple and clear, but how much testing would
      this involve?'

Project evaluation
The original record received by the project was somewhat confusing to the teachers to whom it was shown
as the 'above average' results were shown *below* the
average line.   The example here has been made clearer
in that the axes of the graph have been reversed,
showing 'above average' results visually above the
average line.   Also certain extra 'notes' which made
the original graph look cluttered have been omitted.
On the original, dates of testing and name of test
used were left out, but have been added here.
    This kind of presentation allows for easy extrac-
tion of information;   however, reading age results
give very little information about the quality of a
child's reading ability, except by implication, and
then only in broad terms.

Example 5.8   Reading age graph

Name _____

Date of birth _____

Test dates _____

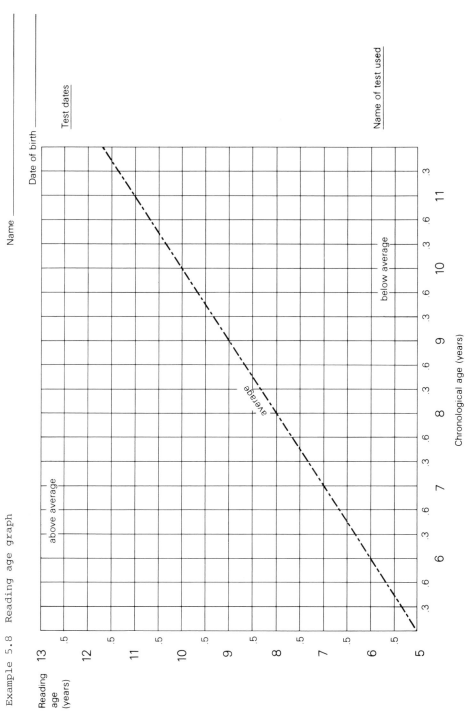

Name of test used _____

Chronological age (years)

*Phonic skills record card*

Supplementary information
This record was one from a series linked to a handbook of tests, *Get Reading Right* by S. Jackson;[2]
unfortunately it was not possible to include a facsi-
mile of the actual card.   This is divided into sections corresponding to tests 3-11 in the series, and
occupies both sides of an A4 sheet.   Each section
contains a tabular checklist of items being tested,
which range from letter names and sounds (lower and
upper case presentation) and short words, through
consonant and vowel blends and silent letters, to
word endings and multisyllabic words.   In each case
space is allowed for 'Notes for future lessons' and
the date at which the test was correctly read.

Teachers' comments
(a)   'Very handy for use with children with difficul-
      ties, as a diagnostic record.'
(b)   'Useful as a record of individual progress in
      phonic development, but perhaps too detailed for
      use with every child.'
(c)   'Can be used at any school age level where some
      reading weakness is apparent.'
(d)   'Tests not indicated by full titles.   There is
      sufficient room only for checking off each
      phonic item.   There is no room for indicating
      the time taken or the order in which sounds were
      mastered.'

Project evaluation
The accompanying book needs to be used as explanatory
instructions do not appear on the record.   Teachers
working in the project groups generally liked this
record and considered it to be a good example of
clear layout and purposeful items.

*Junior mathematics record for Fletcher scheme,*[3]
*level II, books 1-4* (example 5.9, pp.88-90)

Teachers' comments
(*a*)    'This record is based on a weak assumption that
        slavishly following the Fletcher scheme will be
        sufficient as the sole scheme of work in mathe-
        matics.'
(*b*)    'The sequential content of the record gives
        scope for assessment on a three-point scale.'
(*c*)    'Little room for diagnostic comments to be made.'
(*d*)    'There is no key and [it] would need quite
        intensive study by a receiving teacher in order
        to interpret the record.'
(*e*)    'The record is well designed.'

Project evaluation
Records based on mathematics schemes are currently
being used in many schools. This particular record
is restricted to internal use within only one school,
since the assumptions behind 'PA cards completed'
would only be understood by the teachers who had a
hand in compiling the record. Though one may guess
that 'FA' could represent 'further activity', there
is little indication of the scope and depth of work
contained on the cards. The columns headed 'Fully
understood', 'Fair', 'Not comprehended' imply norms
set by teachers for their own classes. Without more
detailed information on scaling, this kind of assessment is of little use for transferring information
between schools.
    This, then, is a record of pupils' past experien-
ces in mathematics rather than one accurately indicating mathematical competence. Teachers evaluating
this record considered its design and layout (originally on two A4 pages) favourably, though suggestions
were made that perhaps more space could be allowed
for teachers' comments.

Example 5.9   Junior Fletcher mathematics record (3pp)

| Name | | Level I, book 7 completed on | | Remarks | | |
|---|---|---|---|---|---|---|
| PA cards com- pleted | Book and section | Date com- pleted | FA cards com- pleted | REMARKS Fully under- stood | Fair | Not compre- hended |
| | **Level II, book 1** | | | | | |
| ..... | 1. Tallying and addition | | | | | |
| ..... | 2. Difference and 'take away' | | | | | |
| ..... | 3. Enrichment and number facts | | | | | |
| ..... | 4. Addresses and regions | | | | | |
| ..... | 5. Measurement - length and mass | | | | | |
| ..... | 6. Multiplication | | | | | |
| ..... | 7. Measurement - time | | | | | |
| ..... | 8. Sharing | | | | | |
| ..... | 9. Symmetry | | | | | |
| | 10. Addition - tens and units | | | | | |
| | **Level II, book 2** | | | | | |
| ..... | 1. Addition and differ- ences | | | | | |
| ..... | 2. Measurement - various | | | | | |
| ..... | 3. Multiplication | | | | | |

| PA cards completed | Book and section | Date completed | FA cards completed | REMARKS Fully understood | Fair | Not comprehended |
|---|---|---|---|---|---|---|
| | **Level II, book 2** | | | | | |
| | 4. Angles and direction | | | | | |
| | 5. Addresses and regions | | | | | |
| | 6. Sharing | | | | | |
| | 7. Shapes | | | | | |
| | 8. Enrichment | | | | | |
| | **Level II, book 3** | | | | | |
| | 1. Statistics | | | | | |
| | 2. Addition - hundreds, tens, units | | | | | |
| | 3. Statistics | | | | | |
| | 4. Measurement - area | | | | | |
| | 5. Difference - hundreds, tens, units | | | | | |
| | 6. Measurement - mass | | | | | |
| | 7. Multiplication | | | | | |
| | 8. Angles | | | | | |
| | 9. Number patterns | | | | | |
| | 10. Enrichment | | | | | |

| PA cards com- pleted | Book and section | Date com- pleted | FA cards com- pleted | REMARKS Fully under- stood | Fair | Not compre- hended |
|---|---|---|---|---|---|---|
| | Level II, book 4 | | | | | |
| | 1. Money | | | | | |
| | 2. Measurement - length | | | | | |
| | 3. Multiplication | | | | | |
| | 4. Angles | | | | | |
| | 5. Division | | | | | |
| | 6. Introducing probability | | | | | |
| | 7. Fractions | | | | | |
| | 8. Algebraic relations | | | | | |
| | 9. Shapes - the circle | | | | | |
| | 10. Introducing decimals | | | | | |
| | 11. Enrichment | | | | | |

(3)

*Mathematics assessment card*
(example 5.10, pp.92-95)

Supplementary information
Abbreviated headings to the right-hand boxes denote
year groups in the infants (I) and juniors (J);  SU =
standard unit.  The original layout is a single sheet
with two columns of items.

Teachers' comments
(*a*)  'A useful record to move through a school with
       a child showing work experienced - no space pro-
       vided for concept mastery (perhaps this is not
       such a bad recording technique since it is very
       difficult to estimate if a concept has been
       mastered).'
(*b*)  'Clear layout and forms a good record, providing
       that it is not supposed that topics must, or
       ought, to be taught in that order.'
(*c*)  'A reasonable record;  I presume that the more
       obscure headings in the list would have been
       more fully explained to the teacher.'
(*d*)  'The position in the scheme would denote work
       done but further tests would be needed to iden-
       tify what work has been assimilated.'

Project evaluation
The overall design of this record was liked by the
majority of teachers taking part in the project,
though the content of the record was viewed less
favourably.  The weakness in content lies not so much
in the list of mathematical topics but in the stated
purpose of the record.  The title implies that
'assessment' of levels of attainment is the main purpose.  However, there is no indication on the record
of how the assessments should be made or how they
should be recorded.
    As a cumulative record of mathematical experiences
pupils have had each year, it gives a comprehensive
summary of work done in the primary years.  Providing
the limitations are recognized, this record can be
used with a variety of published mathematics schemes.

Example 5.10   Mathematics assessment card (4pp)

Name ............................   Date of birth .......................

| | | I1 | I2 | I3 | J1 | J2 | J3 | J4 |
|---|---|---|---|---|---|---|---|---|
| **N U M B E R** | Sorting, threading - grouping - colour and size | | | | | | | |
| | Finger rhymes - recognition of symbols | | | | | | | |
| | One-to-one correspondence | | | | | | | |
| | Recognition        1-5 | | | | | | | |
| | Setting            1-5 | | | | | | | |
| | Recognition        5-10 | | | | | | | |
| | Setting            5-10 | | | | | | | |
| | Number line        1-10 | | | | | | | |
| | Number bonds       1-10 | | | | | | | |
| | Addition of 3 numbers | | | | | | | |
| | Number bonds to 20 | | | | | | | |
| | + Addition (vertical and horizontal) | | | | | | | |
| | — Subtraction | | | | | | | |
| | x Multiplication | | | | | | | |
| | ÷ Division | | | | | | | |
| | Counting on and back in ones, twos, threes, etc. | | | | | | | |
| | Number square to 100 | | | | | | | |
| | x Tables | | | | | | | |
| | Place value        TU, HTU, THTU | | | | | | | |
| | Number patterns and groups | | | | | | | |

(1)

| | | I1 | I2 | I3 | J1 | J2 | J3 | J4 |
|---|---|---|---|---|---|---|---|---|
| **N U M B E R** | Fractions - vulgar | | | | | | | |
| | Fractions - decimal | | | | | | | |
| | Averages | | | | | | | |
| | | | | | | | | |
| **M O N E Y** | Shopping to 10p | | | | | | | |
| | Shopping to 20p | | | | | | | |
| | Shopping and recording | | | | | | | |
| | Change - counting up | | | | | | | |
| | +   and   − | | | | | | | |
| | x   and   ÷ | | | | | | | |
| **T I M E** | Time          o'clock | | | | | | | |
| | ½ hour        ¼ hour | | | | | | | |
| | to and past | | | | | | | |
| | hours       minutes | | | | | | | |
| | am       pm | | | | | | | |
| | +  and  −  intervals | | | | | | | |
| | Calendar and intervals | | | | | | | |
| | 24 hour clock | | | | | | | |
| | Speed, distance and time | | | | | | | |
| | Problems      +  −  x  ÷ | | | | | | | |

| | | I1 | I2 | I3 | J1 | J2 | J3 | J4 |
|---|---|---|---|---|---|---|---|---|
| | Sets | | | | | | | |
| | | | | | | | | |
| LENGTH | Sorting - strips - longest, shortest | | | | | | | |
| | Measure and record - own units - span, shoe, etc. | | | | | | | |
| | Standard units | | | | | | | |
| | Conservation | | | | | | | |
| | Computation      + and − | | | | | | | |
| | do.        x  and ÷ | | | | | | | |
| | Longer measures - km, miles | | | | | | | |
| WEIGHT | Simple balance - heavier, lighter | | | | | | | |
| | Balancing non-standard units - shells, etc. | | | | | | | |
| | Weighing set amounts      100g, etc. | | | | | | | |
| | Making own weights | | | | | | | |
| | Systematic recording and computation      + and − | | | | | | | |
| | do.        x  and ÷ | | | | | | | |
| CAPACITY & VOLUME | Experimental play | | | | | | | |
| | Standard measures - comparisons | | | | | | | |
| | Computation    + and − | | | | | | | |
| | do.      x  and ÷ | | | | | | | |
| | Cubes | | | | | | | |
| | The cubic centimetre | | | | | | | |
| | Estimation and measurement | | | | | | | |

(3)

| | | I1 | I2 | I3 | J1 | J2 | J3 | J4 |
|---|---|---|---|---|---|---|---|---|
| **S H A P E** | Vocabulary and recognition of shapes | | | | | | | |
| | Angles | | | | | | | |
| | Direction and bearings | | | | | | | |
| | Symmetry | | | | | | | |
| | Parallels | | | | | | | |
| | Perimeter | | | | | | | |
| | Solid shapes | | | | | | | |
| | Flat shapes - properties and relations | | | | | | | |
| | Circle - area, pattern, diameter | | | | | | | |
| **A R E A** | Conservation - area and volume | | | | | | | |
| | Non-SU tiles - stamps | | | | | | | |
| | Standard units - practical | | | | | | | |
| | Area = L x B | | | | | | | |
| | Area of triangle | | | | | | | |
| | Area - irregular figures | | | | | | | |
| | Graphs - picto, block | | | | | | | |
| | do.    line and pie | | | | | | | |
| | Statistics | | | | | | | |
| | Scale - proportion - maps | | | | | | | |
| | Problem solving | | | | | | | |
| | | | | | | | | |
| | | | | | | | | |

*Number checklist and mathematical vocabulary list*
(examples 5.11a and b, pp.98-103)

Teachers' comments
(*a*)   'This record is quite sound in content and easy
        to use.'
(*b*)   'It is not very "progressive" in thinking but
        covers what most infant teachers would expect.'
(*c*)   '... not sure whether the record covers the work
        tackled or pupils' attainment.'
(*d*)   'It would be impossible to test a class of chil-
        dren on all the items, especially the mathema-
        tics language.'
(*e*)   'A good guide for teachers but not for use as
        individual pupils' records - could be improved
        with more detailed guide to assessment of items.'
(*f*)   'A need for more space to make comments.'
(*g*)   'Could be improved by deciding on the main beha-
        vioural objectives.'

Project evaluation
Many of the items on this checklist are abbreviated
to the point of ambiguity and leave out the essential
words which indicate the kind of mental activity a
pupil is expected to demonstrate.  In common with
many other mathematics checklists, the main weakness
is the assessment of attainment.  The marking off of
items by a tick and date apparently indicates that
this is a record of mathematical experiences rather
than mathematical attainment.  The mathematical vocabulary list may be useful, though one would perhaps
question the need to make a termly mark for each of
the three infant school years.
    Checklists such as this have been used as means of
assessing language at structured teacher-pupil interviews.  The teacher, in a one-to-one situation and
with the use of the checklist, is able to observe and
assess a pupil's understanding of mathematical terms,
concepts and operations.

*Lower and upper junior mathematics records*
(examples 5.12a and b, pp.104-111)

Supplementary information
The abbreviation MAB in item 2 of the lower junior
record stands for Multibase Arithmetic Blocks (mathematics materials designed by Z.P. Dienes, publisher:
Educational Supply Association).

Teachers' comments
(a)  'Appears to be fairly comprehensive record and
     helpful in the classroom.'
(b)  'This is possibly the best way to monitor a
     child's progress in maths and should be a part
     of a continuous process throughout the child's
     time in school.'
(c)  'A well-planned record which could be easily
     used and information easily extracted.'
(d)  'The inclusion of a double check in the upper
     junior section is to be commended.'
(e)  'There is no indication of how assessments were
     made.'

Project evaluation
This record is similar to the previous checklist in
content but more space is available where necessary
to check and comment on each item.  Similar criticism
with regard to assessment applies here as to the
primary record in example 5.11a (there is room for
the inclusion of qualitative statements about pupils'
understanding in the comments column).
    The lower and upper junior sections may be kept
separately to reduce the physical bulk of the record
when in use.

*Flow diagram* (example 5.13, p.112)

Teachers' comments
(a)  'This is the kind of record used in preparing
     lines of thought in a project.'
(b)  'There is no indication given of the skills to
     be used or learned, or levels of work and
     achievement.'

Project evaluation
This kind of record is a popular means of presenting
project planning in diagrammatic form.  In addition,
wall-mounted versions of flow diagrams enable pupils
to see the way that their work might be developed and
make it possible for them to extend the area of study
themselves.
    Records in this form can only give an indication
of what pupils have experienced and should not be
considered in any way as assessments of levels of
attainment competence.

Example 5.11a  Number checklist (3pp)

Date of birth ........................

Name .........................

| | ✓ | Date |
|---|---|---|
| 1. Sorting/classifying - 1 cond. | | |
| 2. Sorting/classifying - 2 conds | | |
| 3. Sorting/classifying - more than 2 conds | | |
| 4. Finding pairs - pictures | | |
| 5.       "    " - symbols | | |
| 6.       "    " - patterns | | |
| 7. Finding differences - pictures | | |
| 8.     "      " - patterns | | |
| 9.     "      reversals | | |
|                    - pictures | | |
| 10.    "     reversals | | |
|                    - patterns | | |
| 11. Pattern completion - pictures | | |
| 12.    "           " - symbols | | |
| 13.    "           " - random patterns | | |
| 14. Ordering - orally | | |
| 15a.   "   - practically | | |
| 15b. Sets | | |

| | ✓ | Date |
|---|---|---|
| 16. Set language | | |
| 17. Introduction of signs - > ∨ | | |
| 18.     "        "    " - ↑ | | |
| 19.     "        "    " - ↔ | | |
| 20. Finding relationships | | |
| 21. Matchings | | |
| 22. One-to-one correspondence | | |
| 23. Many-to-one correspondence | | |
| 24. Recognition of numerals 0-9 | | |
| 25. Placing of 0-9 in ordered sequ. | | |
| 26. Cardinal aspect of nos 0-9 | | |
| 27. Mappings | | |
| 28. Graphs | | |
| 29. Pict. representation - diff./sum | | |
| 30. Ordinal aspect of nos 0-9 | | |
| 31. Writing of numerals 0-9 | | |

(1)

| | | Date |
|---|---|---|
| 32. | Recognition of and writing of names - zero (or nought) | |
| | one | |
| | two | |
| | three | |
| | four | |
| | five | |
| | six | |
| | seven | |
| | eight | |
| | nine | |
| | ten | |
| 33. | Number patterns in 2s ⎤ start from 0 | |
| 34. | " " 3s ⎬ | |
| 35. | " " 5s ⎦ | |
| 36. | " " 2s ⎤ start from any no. | |
| 37. | " " 3s ⎬ | |
| 38. | " " 5s ⎦ | |
| 39. | Conservation of nos - 9 | |
| 40. | Partitioning of nos - 9 | |
| 41. | Recognition of numerals 10-19 | |
| 42. | Placing of nos 10-19 in sequ. | |

| | | Date |
|---|---|---|
| 43. | Cardinal aspect of nos - 19 | |
| 44. | Ordinal " " - 19 | |
| 45. | Writing of numerals 10-19 | |
| 46. | Recognition and writing of names - ten | |
| | eleven | |
| | twelve | |
| | thirteen | |
| | fourteen | |
| | fifteen | |
| | sixteen | |
| | seventeen | |
| | eighteen | |
| | nineteen | |
| 47. | Conservation of nos - 19 | |
| 48. | Recognition of 20, 30, 40, 50 | |
| 49. | " 60, 70, 80, 90, 100 | |
| 50. | " nos - 100 | |
| 51. | Counting on and back from any no. - in 1s | |
| 52. | " - in 2s | |

(2)

| No. | | ✓ | Date |
|---|---|---|---|
| 53. | Counting on and back from any no. - in 5s | | |
| 54. | "                  - in 10s | | |
| 55. | Use of signs - > ∨ | | |
| 56. | "    "    "  → | | |
| 57. | "    "    "  ←→ | | |
| 58. | "    "    "  + | | |
| 59. | "    "    "  − | | |
| 60. | "    "    "  = | | |
| 61. | Use of number line | | |
| 62. | "    "  100 squares | | |
| 63. | Counting in groups - 2s | | |
| 64. | "        "      "  - 3s | | |
| 65. | "        "      "  - 5s | | |
| 66. | Understanding of tens and ones | | |
| 67. | "              " place value | | |
| 68. | Multiplication as repeated addition - 2s | | |
| | 3s | | |
| | 5s | | |
| | 10s | | |
| 69. | Language for multiplication | | |
| 70. | Division as sharing | | |
| 71. | "        " repeated subtraction | | |

(3)

Example 5.11b  Understanding of mathematical language (3pp)

Name ...........................

Date of birth ...............

| | RECEPTION CLASS | | | FIVES CLASS | | | SIXES CLASS | | |
|---|---|---|---|---|---|---|---|---|---|
| | Term 1 | Term 2 | Term 3 | Autumn | Spring | Summer | Autumn | Spring | Summer |
| big | | | | | | | | | |
| bigger | | | | | | | | | |
| bigger than | | | | | | | | | |
| biggest | | | | | | | | | |
| too big | | | | | | | | | |
| as big as | | | | | | | | | |
| small | | | | | | | | | |
| smaller | | | | | | | | | |
| smaller than | | | | | | | | | |
| smallest | | | | | | | | | |
| too small | | | | | | | | | |
| as small as | | | | | | | | | |
| tall | | | | | | | | | |
| taller | | | | | | | | | |
| as tall as | | | | | | | | | |
| short | | | | | | | | | |
| shorter | | | | | | | | | |
| shortest | | | | | | | | | |

(1)

| | RECEPTION CLASS | | | FIVES CLASS | | | SIXES CLASS | | |
|---|---|---|---|---|---|---|---|---|---|
| | Term 1 | Term 2 | Term 3 | Autumn | Spring | Summer | Autumn | Spring | Summer |
| large | | | | | | | | | |
| largest | | | | | | | | | |
| heavy | | | | | | | | | |
| heavier than | | | | | | | | | |
| too heavy | | | | | | | | | |
| light | | | | | | | | | |
| lighter than | | | | | | | | | |
| lightest | | | | | | | | | |
| first | | | | | | | | | |
| last | | | | | | | | | |
| next | | | | | | | | | |
| before | | | | | | | | | |
| after | | | | | | | | | |
| the same as | | | | | | | | | |
| more than | | | | | | | | | |
| less than | | | | | | | | | |
| fewer than | | | | | | | | | |
| too many | | | | | | | | | |
| too few | | | | | | | | | |
| how many? | | | | | | | | | |
| how much? | | | | | | | | | |

(2)

| | RECEPTION CLASS | | | FIVES CLASS | | | SIXES CLASS | | |
|---|---|---|---|---|---|---|---|---|---|
| | Term 1 | Term 2 | Term 3 | Autumn | Spring | Summer | Autumn | Spring | Summer |
| enough | | | | | | | | | |
| little | | | | | | | | | |
| fast | | | | | | | | | |
| slow | | | | | | | | | |
| late | | | | | | | | | |
| early | | | | | | | | | |
| on | | | | | | | | | |
| off | | | | | | | | | |
| full | | | | | | | | | |
| empty | | | | | | | | | |
| float | | | | | | | | | |
| sink | | | | | | | | | |
| pour | | | | | | | | | |
| thin | | | | | | | | | |
| thick | | | | | | | | | |
| wide | | | | | | | | | |
| narrow | | | | | | | | | |

(3)

Example 5.12a  Lower junior mathematics record (4pp)

Name ...................................

Date of birth ...............

| Mathematical concept and experience | Intro. | Checked | Comments |
|---|---|---|---|
| NUMBER | | | |
| 1. Recognition of numbers and recording in words and figures ............ 100 ............ 1000 | | | |
| 2. Revision of infant number using cards  1 + 1 − 1 *  2 + 2 − 2 *  3 + 3 − 3 *  4'4"  5'5"5"' | | | |
| MAB Changing practice | | | |
| " Cards 1-6 | | | |
| 3. Addition of number | | | |
| Tens and units  no carrying horiz. vert. | | | |
| "    "    "  with    "    " | | | |
| Addition language | | | |
| 4. Subtraction of number | | | |
| Tens and units  no changing horiz. vert. | | | |
| "    "    "  with    "    " | | | |
| Subtraction language | | | |
| 5. Division and multiplication of number | | | |
| Table squares 1-10 | | | |
| Activities - games | | | |
| Interrelationship of $\div$, x | | | |
| Division and multiplication language | | | |

(1)

| Mathematical concept and experience | Intro. | Checked | Comments |
|---|---|---|---|
| **NUMBER** | | | |
| 6. Multiplication and division facts (4 ways) | | | |
|   E.g.   $2 \times 6 = 12$ <br>        $6 \times 2 = 12$ <br>        $12 \div 2 = 6$ <br>        $12 \div 6 = 2$ | | | |
| 7. Odd and even numbers | | | |
| 8. Signs $= \neq$ | | | |
| 9. Extension of addition through to thousands, hundreds, tens and units with problems | | | |
| 10. Extension of subtraction as above | | | |
| 11. Extension of multiplication and division as above | | | |
| 12. Square numbers | | | |
| **MONEY** | | | |
| 13. Handling and changing | | | |
| 14. Addition of money | | | |
| 15. Subtraction of money | | | |
| 16. Multiplication of money | | | |
| 17. Division of money | | | |

(2)

| Mathematical concept and experience | Intro. | Checked | Comments |
|---|---|---|---|
| The whole and its parts | | | |
| 18. Practical work in fractional parts, $\frac{1}{4}$, $\frac{1}{2}$ & $\frac{3}{4}$ and of whole nos and fractions. Introduction of tenths | | | |
| Introduction to decimalisation | | | |
| 19. The meaning of the decimal point | | | |
| 20. Addition of decimals (1 place) | | | |
| 21. " " (2 places) | | | |
| 22. Subtraction of decimals (1 place) | | | |
| 23. " " (2 places) | | | |
| 24. Simple multiplication (2 places) | | | |
| 25. " division " " | | | |
| LENGTH | | | |
| 26. Revision of limb measurements | | | |
| 27. Practical work (with recording) in metres and cm | | | |
| 28. Mental facts - mm, cm & m | | | |
| WEIGHT | | | |
| 29. Revision of infant work | | | |
| 30. Extension of practical work in grammes and kg | | | |
| 31. Mental facts - gm and kg | | | |
| CAPACITY | | | |
| 32. Revision of infant work | | | |

(3)

| Mathematical concept and experience | Intro. | Checked | Comments |
|---|---|---|---|
| CAPACITY (cont) | | | |
| 33. Extension of practical work in ¼, ½ and 1 litre | | | |
| 34. Mental facts - ml and litre | | | |
| TIME | | | |
| 35. Revision of infant work | | | |
| 36. Extension of practical work | | | |
| 37. Introduction of 24 hr clock | | | |
| 38. Mental facts - sec, min, hr & days | | | |
| 39. The calendar, months of the year, leap year | | | |
| 40. Simple timetables | | | |
| 41. Graphs | | | |
| 42. Recognition of basic shapes - circle / square / rectangle / triangle / rhombus / ellipse / polygons | | | |
| 43. Tesselations - practical work | | | |
| 44. Right angles - " " | | | |
| 45. Perimeter, circumference - " " | | | |
| 46. Area - " " | | | |
| EXTRA MATHEMATICAL EXPERIENCES (list) | | | |
| [½ page allowed for list] | | | |

(4)

108

Example 5.12b  Upper junior mathematics record (4pp)

Name of child ...................................

Date of birth ...................................

| Mathematical concept and experience | Intro. | Checked | Checked | Comments |
|---|---|---|---|---|
| NUMBER | | | | |
| 1. Recognition of numbers and recording in words and figures ........... 1,000 ........... 1,000,000 | | | | |
| Order of size - extent to incl. fractions and decimals Simple arithmetic series | | | | |
| 2. Revision and extension of 4 rules Mathematical language, e.g. product, etc. Addition Subtraction Multiplication - simple extending using 2 or 3 figs Division - simple extending to use 2 figs | | | | |
| 3. Place value (revision) | | | | |
| 4 Use of other bases (Dienes) in 4 rules  2  3  5 | | | | |
| 5. Mental practice in addition and subtraction - 100 | | | | |

(1)

| Mathematical concept and experience | Intro. | Checked | Checked | Comments |
|---|---|---|---|---|
| **NUMBER** | | | | |
| 6. Multiplication and division facts (stress relationships) e.g. $3 \times 8 = 24$ $8 \times 3 = 24$ $24 \div 3 = 8$ $24 \div 8 = 3$ | | | | |
| 7. Odd and even numbers | | | | |
| 8. Prime numbers (use A.E.M.) incl. positive and negative nos and zero | | | | |
| 9. Square numbers (use A.E.M.) | | | | |
| 10. The whole and its parts | | | | |
| Practical work in fractional parts $\frac{1}{4}, \frac{1}{2}, \frac{3}{4}, \frac{1}{5}, \frac{1}{10}$ , etc. | | | | |
| Addition | | | | |
| Subtraction | | | | |
| Multiplication | | | | |
| Division | | | | |
| 11. DECIMALISATION | | | | |
| Meaning of the decimal point | | | | |
| Addition to 3 places | | | | |
| Subtraction to 3 places | | | | |
| Simple multiplication to 2 places | | | | |
| Long multiplication extended to 3 places | | | | |
| Simple division to 2 places | | | | |
| Long division by 2 figures (e.g. 26) | | | | |

(2)

| Mathematical concept and experience | Intro. | Checked | Checked | Comments |
|---|---|---|---|---|
| 12. PERCENTAGES (correlate with 10 and 11) | | | | |
| 13. MONEY | | | | |
|     Handling and changing | | | | |
|     Addition | | | | |
|     Subtraction | | | | |
|     Multiplication | | | | |
|     Division | | | | |
| 14. LENGTH (metric) | | | | |
|     Extension of practical work in mm, m and km | | | | |
|     Mental facts - mm, cm, m and km | | | | |
|     Correlate with 4 rules in decimals | | | | |
| 15. WEIGHT (metric) | | | | |
|     Extension of practical work in grammes and kg | | | | |
|     Mental facts - gm, kg and metric tonne | | | | |
| 16. CAPACITY AND VOLUME (metric) | | | | |
|     Extension of practical work in ml and litres | | | | |
|     Mental facts - ml and litres | | | | |
|     Correlate with 4 rules in decimals | | | | |
| 17. TIME, DISTANCE AND SPEED | | | | |
|     Extension of practical work | | | | |
|     Mental facts (using abacus) - sec, min, hr, days | | | | |

(3)

| Mathematical concept and experience | Intro. | Checked | Checked | Comments |
|---|---|---|---|---|
| 17. TIME, DISTANCE AND SPEED (cont)<br>Calendar months and years (incl. leap year)<br>24 hr clock, timetables<br>Journeys (speed and distance)<br>Universal time - rotation of earth - time change | | | | |
| 18. GRAPHS<br>Histograms, st. line conversion<br>Correlation with previous experience | | | | |
| 19. AVERAGES | | | | |
| 20. SHAPE<br>Various shapes, perimeters<br>Area - square, rectangle and triangle<br>Volume - cubes and cuboids<br>Angles in shapes - right angle<br>acute angle<br>obtuse angle | | | | |
| 21. RATIO | | | | |
| 22. SIMPLE ALGEBRAIC EQUATIONS<br>(Use balance at outset) | | | | |
| 23. SETS | | | | |
| EXTRA EXPERIENCE<br>[½ page allowed for list] | | | | |

(4)

112

Example 5.13  Flow diagram:  the lunch in my pocket

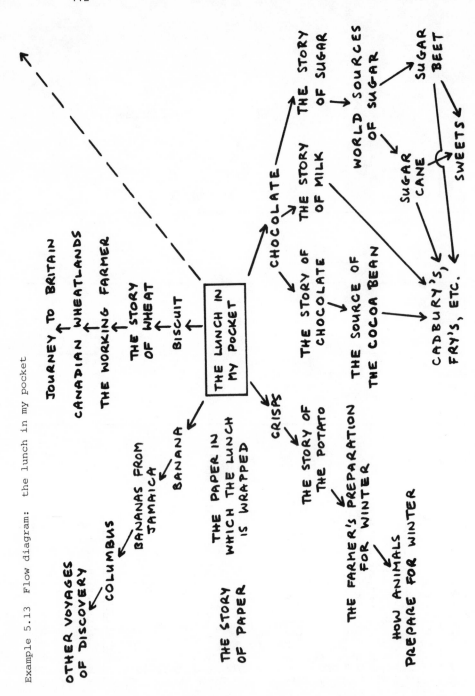

*Record of aesthetic skills and abilities*
(example 5.14, p.114)

Supplementary information
Abbreviated headings to the right-hand columns denote year groups in the infants (I) and juniors (J).

Teachers' comments
(*a*)  'This is more a list of art and craft skills and the use of the word "aesthetic" is inappropriate.'
(*b*)  'A relatively useful list of skills for a class teacher to have, but not sure that a written record of competence is necessary for every child.'
(*c*)  'If used for every child I would require more space for comments.'

Project evaluation
Some of the project groups studied the area of aesthetic development in the hope of finding some suitable frameworks as a basis for assessing pupils (see appendix E, Frameworks for Aesthetic Development). When considering record keeping, teachers tended to emphasize the development of the physical co-ordination aspects of art and craft rather than the aesthetic aspects.

Without an easily understood framework of aesthetic development (a research topic in itself), the assessment and recording of this area will remain neglected.

*Record of development in science*
(example 5.15, p.118)

Supplementary information
This record comes from the Schools Council Progress in Learning Science project[4] (director: Wynne Harlen) and seeks to help teachers identify, through observation, stages of development in individual pupils with a view to 'matching' them to appropriate learning activities. There are two versions of the record, suitable respectively for earlier and later development; the example shown is that for *later* development. In each case the record is supported by a checklist incorporating criteria for assessing levels of development in each of the areas listed. For example, for *independence* (in thinking) and for *observing*, the criteria for three points on the dimension of (later) development are shown in Fig. 2.

Example 5.14   Aesthetic skills and abilities

|  | I/2 | I/3 | J/1 | J/2 | J/3 | J/4 |
|---|---|---|---|---|---|---|
| 1. Uses scissors correctly |  |  |  |  |  |  |
| 2. Uses ruler for drawing straight lines |  |  |  |  |  |  |
| 3. Uses ruler for drawing lines and measuring |  |  |  |  |  |  |
| 4. Uses compasses, without measuring |  |  |  |  |  |  |
| 5. Uses protractor correctly, and set squares for drawing shapes |  |  |  |  |  |  |
| 6. Uses protractor and set squares for measuring angles |  |  |  |  |  |  |
| 7. Uses dividers |  |  |  |  |  |  |
| 8. Uses wax crayons for drawing |  |  |  |  |  |  |
| 9. Uses coloured pencils for colouring pictures |  |  |  |  |  |  |
| 10. Able to shade areas of pictures with coloured pencils, carefully |  |  |  |  |  |  |
| 11. Able to draw and shade pictures with felt pens |  |  |  |  |  |  |
| 12. Uses large paintbrush correctly |  |  |  |  |  |  |
| 13. Uses smaller brushes |  |  |  |  |  |  |
| 14. Uses ready-mixed paint |  |  |  |  |  |  |
| 15. Uses powder colour |  |  |  |  |  |  |
| 16. Able to mix own colours from individual powder colours |  |  |  |  |  |  |
| 17. Models in plasticine |  |  |  |  |  |  |
| 18. Models in clay |  |  |  |  |  |  |
| 19. Uses woodwork tools carefully and creatively |  |  |  |  |  |  |
| 20. Uses balsa knives carefully and creatively |  |  |  |  |  |  |
| 21. Sews with needle and thread |  |  |  |  |  |  |
| 22. Sews with machine |  |  |  |  |  |  |
| 23. Able to work and use tape-recorder/ cassette competently |  |  |  |  |  |  |

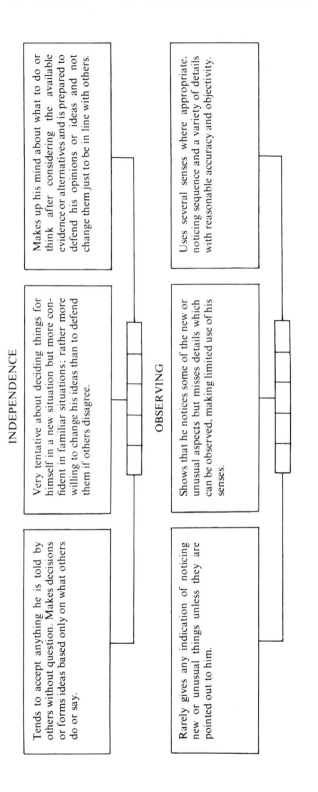

INDEPENDENCE

Tends to accept anything he is told by others without question. Makes decisions or forms ideas based only on what others do or say.

Very tentative about deciding things for himself in a new situation but more confident in familiar situations; rather more willing to change his ideas than to defend them if others disagree.

Makes up his mind about what to do or think after considering the available evidence or alternatives and is prepared to defend his opinions or ideas and not change them just to be in line with others.

OBSERVING

Rarely gives any indication of noticing new or unusual things unless they are pointed out to him.

Shows that he notices some of the new or unusual aspects but misses details which can be observed, making limited use of his senses.

Uses several senses where appropriate, noticing sequence and a variety of details with reasonable accuracy and objectivity.

Fig. 2 Criteria for levels of development. Reproduced from *Raising Questions* (see reference 4), checklist for later development, p.241.

Teachers' comments
(a)   'This is an interesting record which incorpo-
      rates the most important concepts and skills
      necessary for scientific development.  I don't
      know how I could fit this record with the
      science lessons carried out at my school.'
(b)   'There is no space for comments.  I do not think
      that a tick in the appropriate box is sufficient.'

Project evaluation
This record is the outcome of a structuring of
teachers' observations of their pupils' behaviour
during day-to-day activities.  Observations have to
be made in a variety of situations and over a period
of time in order to gather information about the 24
different skills, abilities and attitudes which indicate a broad interpretation of 'science'.  Science is
seen as a way of approaching and investigating problems which is relevant to a wide variety of activities.
    Reference must be made to the detailed criteria if
the objections to 'ticking boxes' are to be overcome.
It is preferable to read parts of *Raising Questions*[4]
if the context and intended uses of this record are
to be understood.  Its use can result in individual
child-profiles such as Fig. 3.


*Physical development record*
(example 5.16, pp.120-126)

Supplementary information
This differs from records presented so far in that it
was actually produced by a group of teachers con-
currently with the project.  No extant records of
this kind were collected from schools.

Project evaluation
Initially this record may appear complex but familiarity with the notes should help the user to make
efficient use of time and energy in completing the
record.
    Special attention should be paid to note 7 and the
relevant section 7 on the record.  This feature provides at a glance the numbers of section to which one
must refer for important information about a child.
This method of 'advance warning' can save teachers
from going through many pages of information of
little importance.  The responsibility for deciding
when information becomes important enough to be
marked at section 7 rests with the teacher completing
the record.  The decision to draw certain sections to

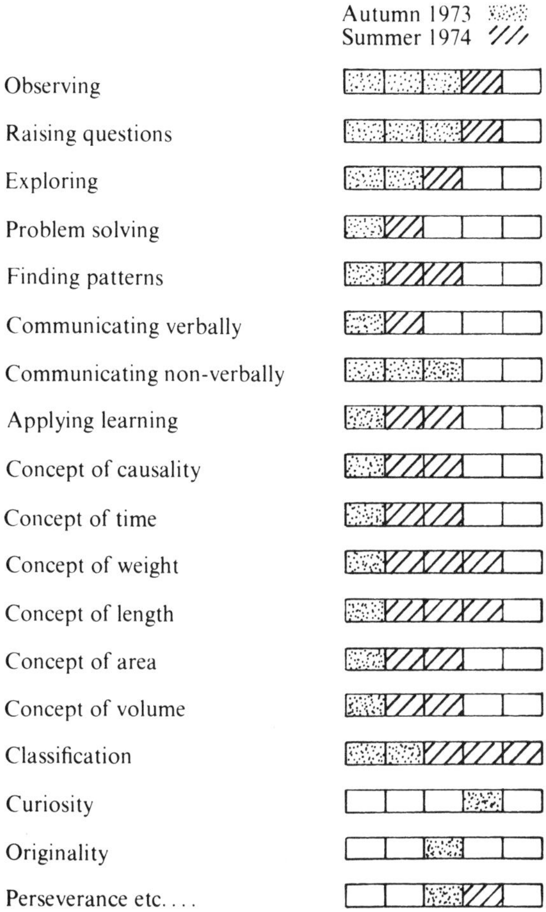

Autumn 1973

Summer 1974 ////

Observing

Raising questions

Exploring

Problem solving

Finding patterns

Communicating verbally

Communicating non-verbally

Applying learning

Concept of causality

Concept of time

Concept of weight

Concept of length

Concept of area

Concept of volume

Classification

Curiosity

Originality

Perseverance etc....

Fig. 3   Profile of a six-year-old (abridged) based on record
for *earlier* development. Reproduced from *Raising
Questions* (see reference 4), p.55.

another teacher's attention by this method must, in
the last resort, be an arbitrary one.  The overriding
consideration when making such a decision should be:
'Does the physical problem noted in this section
affect the child's adjustment to, or coping with,
activities in school?'  Where the answer to this
question is *yes*, the appropriate box at section 7
should be ticked.  Where the answer is *no*, the box
should be left blank.  Where doubt exists, a second
opinion should be sought or, in the final event, the

Example 5.15   Record of development in science*

Child's name ........................   <u>Second record</u>
Date of birth .......................   Filled in by ........................
                                        Date of completion ..................
                                        Additional comments


<u>First record</u>                     <u>Third record</u>
Filled in by ........................   Filled in by ........................
Date of completion ..................   Date of completion ..................
Additional comments                     Additional comments


Curiosity
Originality
Willingness to co-operate
Perseverance
Open-mindedness
Self-criticism
Responsibility
Independence
Observing
Proposing enquiries
Experimenting/investigating
Communicating verbally
Communicating non-verbally
Finding patterns in observations
Critical reasoning
Applying learning
Cause and effect
Measurement
Volume
Force
Energy
Change
Interdependence of living things
Adaptation of living things

* Reproduced from *Raising Questions* (see reference 4),
  checklist for later development, p.258.

'fail-safe' decision of *yes* (tick) should be made.
In any case, the receiving teacher may wish to read
the record in detail at a time when he or she suspects
a child has a difficulty.

A prime objective of this record (Aims and objectives, 6) is to reduce the amount of information a
teacher needs to read about a child at the point of
transfer, particularly at transition (e.g. change-
over from primary to secondary) where many such records have to be read.

*Personal development record*
(example 5.17, pp.127-129)

Teachers' comments
(*a*)   'Easy to complete as the five-point scale simpli-
        fies the task of finding the right comment.'
(*b*)   'Could form the basis of a report to parents on
        a child's behaviour in school.  The category
        "general intelligence" may however be classed as
        "sensitive".'
(*c*)   'The content of the record is useful.'
(*d*)   'I like the multi-choice format but could do
        with space for an alternative if it arose.'
(*e*)   'The record lacks instructions as to how the
        squares are to be filled in and the frequency of
        entries.'
(*f*)   'There is an unanswered question as to what
        criteria the ratings are based on - and I hope
        that the era in record keeping of ticking pre-
        emptive statements is both discredited and
        dying.'
(*g*)   'There is no provision for the child whose atti-
        tudes in some subjects are better than in others.'

Project evaluation
This form of recording was being used by several LEAs
on their transfer cards;  it contains a mixture of
types of assessment, some of which are based on a
notion of norms for a particular trait, while others
provide a range of qualitative statements to describe
various aspects of the trait.

The problems of assessing children on the basis of
what is average are greatly increased when records
are used between different schools, since the level
of expectations of average behaviour varies from
school to school and even from teacher to teacher.

For those teachers wishing to extend and standar-
dize their observations (see section on rating scales,
p.176) this record may provide a starting point.

Example 5.16   Physical development record* (7pp)

AIMS AND OBJECTIVES

(1) To provide a full record of all aspects of a child's physical development.

(2) To make the recording simple.

(3) To separate facts and subjective comments.

(4) To help the teacher in planning a curriculum.

(5) To allow for the co-ordination of school, home and support facilities.

(6) To ensure that a child who develops normally does not involve the teacher in extensive record keeping, but that when a child does have problems all the facts may be noted.

(7) To ensure that all facts are dated and initialled.

---

\*   © Copyright October 1977 J. L. Houghton

(1)

NOTES ON USE OF PHYSICAL DEVELOPMENT RECORD

Nos 1-5 Should be filled in on arrival at the school.

No. 6 Should be filled in on arrival at school and added to if need be.
B = boy, G = girl, e.g. Ⓑ/G/B. The record is for the eldest of three
(ringed), and new additions to the family can easily be added to the
existing children.

No. 7 A quick checklist of areas of special note. E.g. if a hearing loss is
noted then section 15 will be ticked. If an illness of over 3 weeks
is noted then section 11 will be ticked. A teacher receiving the
record will then know straight away which sections to look at first.

No. 8 E.g. asthma, hay fever, hole in heart, epilepsy, etc.

No. 9 On entry into the school at either 5 years or later a parent/guardian
should be asked for this information. Pre-school hospitalization may
be relevant.

No. 10 The height and weight should be recorded at the same time each year
(i.e. beginning or end) and the months added (i.e. 5-3).

No. 12 Short- or long-sighted.

No. 13 E.g. squint, lazy eye, etc. If rectified please note date informed.

No. 14 Pass or Fail. If Fail registered then tick checklist on sheet 1
(section 7), and refer to medical record.

No. 15 Insert words Pass or Fail. If Fail registered tick checklist on
sheet 1 (section 7), and refer to medical record.

No. 17 Comments must be factual, respecting confidentiality of support
agencies.

Notes on PDR (sheet 3)

No. 18 The skills should not be specifically taught for the completion of
this record. The examples given are an indication of a stage in
motor development. This section should be seen as an indication of
the development of motor control.

PDR sheet 4 would be filled in each year by the class teacher. A new sheet
each year. This section of the PDR is therefore subjective and should
be read as such. The comments made should be along the lines of those
entered on a report for parents and include technical ability as well
as creativity. Each sheet should then be attached to the back of
the PDR.

General notes

(1) Date noted = date school notified. If very different from date detected
by outside agency, etc. make reference to this in the comments
section.

(2) Section 7 The relevant number must be ticked if a section is filled in,
or, in the case of sections 14 and 15, if a Fail is recorded. Failure
to tick the box may result in a teacher or head failing to look at or
notice a certain section.

(3) It is the responsibility of the head teacher and class teacher to ensure
that the record is maintained as an accurate statement.

(4) Init. = initials  . . . . . . . . . . . . . . . . . . . . . . . . . . . . . . . . . . . . .

(2)

(1) School ......................... (2) Name ...........................

(3) MALE/FEMALE ....................

(4) Date of birth

| | | |
|---|---|---|
| | | |

(5) Date of entry

| | | |
|---|---|---|

(6) Position in family
(Enter eldest child first)

| | | | | | | |
|---|---|---|---|---|---|---|
| | | | | | | |

(7) Please make special note of the following sections where ticked:

| 8 | | 9 | | 11 | | 12 | | 13 | | 14 | | 15 | | 16 | | 17 | |
|---|---|---|---|---|---|---|---|---|---|---|---|---|---|---|---|---|---|

(8) Known allergies or problems

| Complaint | Date noted | Comments | Init. |
|---|---|---|---|
| | | | |
| | | | |
| | | | |
| | | | |

(9) Hospitalization

| Date in | Date out | Time off school | Reason | Comments | Init. |
|---|---|---|---|---|---|
| | | | | | |
| | | | | | |
| | | | | | |

(3)

(10) Height record

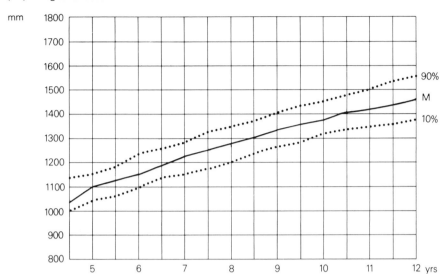

Weight record

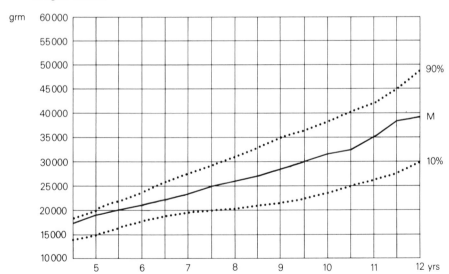

KEY  ..... 90% (percentile)
     ——— Mean
     ..... 10% (percentile)

(4)

PDR sheet 2

(11) Illness requiring absence from school of over 3 weeks

| From | To | Reason | Comments | Init. |
|------|-----|--------|----------|-------|
|      |     |        |          |       |
|      |     |        |          |       |
|      |     |        |          |       |

(12) Should glasses be worn? ..... If YES then why? ........................

(13) Visionary defects or problems other than short and long sight

| Date noted | Problem | Init. | Rectified | Init. |
|------------|---------|-------|-----------|-------|
|            |         |       |           |       |
|            |         |       |           |       |
|            |         |       |           |       |

(14) Routine eyesight tests

| Age | Eyes tested? Yes No | Pass | Fail | Comments | Init. |
|-----|---------------------|------|------|----------|-------|
| 5-6 | | | | | |
| 6-7 | | | | | |
| 7-8 | | | | | |
| 8-9 | | | | | |
| 9-10 | | | | | |
| 10-11 | | | | | |
| 11-12 | | | | | |

(15) Hearing tests

| Age | Ears tested? Yes No | Pass | Fail | Comments | Init. |
|-----|---------------------|------|------|----------|-------|
| 5-6 | | | | | |
| 6-7 | | | | | |
| 7-8 | | | | | |
| 8-9 | | | | | |
| 9-10 | | | | | |
| 10-11 | | | | | |
| 11-12 | | | | | |

(5)

PDR sheet 3

(16) Is a hearing aid worn? ................. Date first worn ..............
Date noted ..............

(17) Support agencies, e.g. Education Welfare Office (EWO), Child Guidance (CG)

| Agency dates | Comments | Init. |
|---|---|---|
|  |  |  |
|  |  |  |
|  |  |  |
|  |  |  |
|  |  |  |
|  |  |  |

(18) Specific motor skills not yet achieved (see note)

| Skill | Date | Notes | Init. |
|---|---|---|---|
| Uses scissors |  |  |  |
| Draws straight line with ruler |  |  |  |
| Can cut with scissors accurately |  |  |  |
| Draws straight lines without ruler |  |  |  |
| Can draw round a 10p piece |  |  |  |
| Holds pencil properly |  |  |  |
| Ties own shoelaces |  |  |  |
| Grasps small objects |  |  |  |
| Catches ball (2 hands) |  |  |  |
| Catches ball (dom. hand) |  |  |  |
| Catches ball (rec. hand) |  |  |  |
| Balances on upturned bench |  |  |  |
| Completes simple jigsaw (25 piece) |  |  |  |
| Can jump off box |  |  |  |
| Hops on both feet |  |  |  |

(19) Handedness     Right dominant [ ]
                    Left dominant  [ ]

(6)

<u>PDR sheet 4</u> (1 per year)

Name .......................................... Date ......................

(1) <u>Gym</u>   (a) <u>Floor work</u>


       (b) <u>Apparatus</u>


(2) <u>Outdoor games</u>


(3) <u>Drama</u>


(4) <u>Movement</u>


(5) <u>Art</u>


(6) <u>Craft</u>


(7) <u>Health/sex education</u>


(8) <u>Clubs (membership of)</u>


Signed ...................................

(7)

Example 5.17 Personal development record (3pp)

Form teacher's initials

Form

|  |  |  |  |  |  |  |  |
|---|---|---|---|---|---|---|---|

I  GENERAL INTELLIGENCE

1. Has considerable ability
2. Above average ability
3. Average
4. Somewhat below average
5. Lacking ability

II  INDUSTRY

1. Very industrious, does more than required
2. Works very well and completes task
3. Works reasonably well; average output
4. Makes some effort occasionally
5. Does as little work as possible

III  CONCENTRATION

1. Attentive and accurate
2. Sustained for considerable period
3. Average, but easily distracted
4. Concentrates spasmodically
5. Inattentive; unable to concentrate

(1)

IV PERSEVERANCE

1. Tenacious, determined to succeed

2. Usually perseveres until successful

3. Works steadily, often sees task through

4. Works fairly steadily, often leaves task unfinished

5. Gives up easily; no attempt at completion

V CONDUCT/CO-OPERATION

1. Controlled, obedient, willing and helpful

2. Controlled, obedient, sometimes willing and helpful

3. Occasional lapses in behaviour, co-operation spasmodic

4. Neg. attitude to authority, rather unwilling; co-operative if convenient

5. Hostile, impertinent, non-co-operative

VI RELATIONSHIPS WITH PEER GROUP

1. Very sociable, popular; some natural leadership

2. Friendly; mixes well

3. Tolerated by most people - one or two friends

4. Reserved; shy - ignored by most people

5. Does not mix; sometimes hostile

(2)

VII GROUP WORK

1. Works very well with others; an
   initiator and major contributor

2. Co-operates with others well

3. Only a moderate contribution made

4. Joins in reluctantly; uninterested

5. Cannot work with others; isolates self

VIII SELF-CONFIDENCE

1. Assured and confident

2. Has some poise and confidence

3. Average in confidence and assurance

4. Requires constant encouragement

5. Nervous; self-effacing; timid; lacking

IX ADDITIONAL CHARACTERISTICS

1. Well-dressed and well-groomed

2. Shows initiative

3. Courteous

4. Trustworthy

5. Resents correction

(3)

*Record of personal characteristics*
(example 5.18, pp.131-133)

Teachers' comments
(*a*)   'A clear and precise record form, easy to follow,
        good content.'
(*b*)   'The categories imply a fair spread of knowledge
        about each child.'
(*c*)   'Intervals for recording (once per term) are
        reasonably spaced.'
(*d*)   'A more acceptable and useful checklist.'
(*e*)   'Dangerous area of content for assessment - too
        many subjective values required.'
(*f*)   'Assumes predetermined standard of child's
        ability and alignment with peers.'
(*g*)   'No explanation or key for using the record,
        therefore the record is somewhat valueless
        especially for transfer.'

Project evaluation
Variations on this record were frequently used in
many schools that we visited (derived possibly from a
similar record example in the book by Rance)[5].

  Conclusions about the previous personal development record (example 5.17) also apply here.  The
ratings for some categories are reduced to three
points thereby limiting 'precision'.  Since assessment of these characteristics tends to be imprecise,
such a reduction may not be a bad thing, but for many
children it may not even be worthwhile keeping any
record of these traits, since they will just be
marked average.

  Notes about particular traits may only be required if a child is outstanding at either end of the
scale.  If this record is kept only for these children, the clerical chore of completing such records
may be reduced by between 60% and 80% and, in the
time saved, teachers may be able to devote themselves
to analysing the causes of problems more systematically for the 20-30% of children for whom such records are felt to be necessary.

Example 5.18  Record of personal characteristics (3pp)

| | J1 | J2 | J3 | J4 |
|---|---|---|---|---|
| **CAPACITY FOR WORK** | | | | |
| Always works to capacity | | | | |
| Average | | | | |
| Underfunctioning | | | | |
| **PERSISTENCE** | | | | |
| Very persevering | | | | |
| Average | | | | |
| Gives up easily | | | | |
| Hardly ever tries | | | | |
| **SPEED OF LEARNING** | | | | |
| Quick | | | | |
| Average | | | | |
| Very slow | | | | |
| **POWERS OF RETENTION** | | | | |
| Good | | | | |
| Average | | | | |
| Poor | | | | |

(1)

|  | J1 | J2 | J3 | J4 |
|---|---|---|---|---|
| **TEMPERAMENT** |  |  |  |  |
| Easily upset |  |  |  |  |
| Average |  |  |  |  |
| Very stable (mature) |  |  |  |  |
| Defiant - never upset |  |  |  |  |
| **NEATNESS OF WORK** |  |  |  |  |
| Painstaking - meticulous |  |  |  |  |
| Usually good |  |  |  |  |
| Average |  |  |  |  |
| Untidy |  |  |  |  |
| Couldn't care less |  |  |  |  |
| **BEHAVIOUR IN CLASS** |  |  |  |  |
| Very attentive - never needs correction |  |  |  |  |
| Usually good |  |  |  |  |
| Often inattentive |  |  |  |  |
| Frequently disruptive |  |  |  |  |
| **SOCIABILITY WITH CHILDREN** |  |  |  |  |
| A good mixer |  |  |  |  |
| Average |  |  |  |  |
| Has only a few friends |  |  |  |  |
| Solitary |  |  |  |  |

(2)

133

| | J1 | J2 | J3 | J4 |
|---|---|---|---|---|
| ATTITUDE TO ADULTS | | | | |
| Seeks attention | | | | |
| Friendly | | | | |
| Reserved | | | | |
| TEST RESULTS | | | | |

(3)

*Child's behaviour questionnaire*
(example 5.19, pp.136-137)

Supplementary information
This questionnaire by M. Rutter (see footnote, p.137) was designed to be filled in by teachers and suitable for use with children of ages 7-13 years.
   Items marked in the column 'Doesn't apply' score 0.
   Items marked in the column 'Applies somewhat' score 1.
   Items marked in the column 'Certainly applies' score 2.
   Children with a total score of nine or more are designated as showing some disorder.
   A 'neurotic' subscore is obtained by summing the scores for items 7, 10, 17 and 23.
   An 'anti-social' subscore is obtained by summing the scores of items 4, 5, 15, 19, 20 and 26.

Teachers' comments
(a)   'Simple to read and easy to fill in.'
(b)   'Useful for certain children.  I would not like
      to complete one for each member of the class.'
(c)   'A very negative record - only makes use of
      information on bad behaviour.'

Project evaluation
The ease of completion and scoring will enable teachers to fill in the scale for a whole class for survey purposes.  The scale can be used to discriminate between different types of behavioural or emotional disorder, as well as discriminating between children who show disorder and those who do not.
   Although this record has been regarded by some teachers as a very useful measure of the pupil's behaviour in the school, its undoubted limitations need to be emphasized.  First, it is a simple and crude measure and for clinical purposes it needs to be supplemented by other information from the teacher. Secondly, as scored in the way described, it cannot be used to pick out children with monosymptomatic - very specific - disorders.  Thirdly, it is less efficient in differentiating children with certain less common disorders of a circumscribed kind such as anorexia nervosa, conversion hysteria and some obsessional disorders.
   Lastly, the value of any scale for completion by teachers depends on the skill of the teacher as an observer, and on the opportunities for the teacher to observe the child in varied situations.

*Literacy record card (early version[6])*
(example 5.20, pp.138-139)

Teachers' comments
(*a*)  'A useful record, as it is fairly brief and yet comprehensive.'
(*b*)  'I think many of the items are very important but I am not sure how to operate the four-point scale - oral practice, written practice, instruction level, independent level.'
(*c*)  'What do some of the statements mean, i.e. expresses and recognizes tentativeness, reflects on own feelings?'

Project evaluation
This record has resulted from a series of working parties, the main aim of which has been to devise a new LEA record card. It has been designed to be minimal yet comprehensive. The literacy section of this record reflects recommendations made in the Bullock Report (1975).[7] A major fault of many records is that though a three-point scale is included for assessment purposes and may have a key, teachers are left to their own devices as to how they interpret 'average', 'above average', 'below average', etc.
     In this case the criteria for assessment implied by the key need to be made explicit before accurate interpretation and use of the record can be made.  No mention is made on the record of how a teacher should evaluate 'instruction level'.  The levels of competence at the 'instruction level' and 'independent level' may be set arbitrarily by individual teachers.
     However, the Bullock Report, in chapter 17 on 'Screening, diagnosis and recording', gives some guidance:

'At the *independent* level, the child is able to read aloud in a natural and easy manner, without help from the teacher and with 99 per cent accuracy in word recognition.  If the child makes more than one error in a hundred running words or has less than a 90 per cent comprehension of the passage he is not reading at this level.  The teacher can then determine whether he is at the *instructional* level with this particular material.  This involves 95 per cent word recognition, the child making no more than five errors in a hundred running words, and he should be able to give a satisfactory answer to 75 per cent of the questions asked by the teacher.  At this standard of performance the child can be expected to reach independent level on that material in response to appropriate teaching.  Below it he can be said to be operating at the *frustration* level, and the

Example 5.19  Child Scale B* (2pp)

TO BE COMPLETED BY TEACHERS

Below are a series of descriptions of behaviour often shown by children. After each statement are three columns: 'Doesn't apply', 'Applies somewhat', and 'Certainly applies'. If the child definitely shows the behaviour described by the statement place a cross in the box under 'Certainly applies'. If the child shows the behaviour described by the statement but to a lesser degree or less often place a cross in the box under 'Applies somewhat'. If, as far as you are aware, the child does not show the behaviour place a cross in the box under 'Doesn't apply'.

Please put ONE cross against EACH statement.  Thank you.

| Statement | Doesn't apply | Applies somewhat | Certainly applies |
|---|---|---|---|
| 1. Very restless. Often running about or jumping up and down. Hardly ever still | ☐ | ☐ | ☐ |
| 2. Truants from school | ☐ | ☐ | ☐ |
| 3. Squirmy, fidgety child | ☐ | ☐ | ☐ |
| 4. Often destroys own or others' belongings | ☐ | ☐ | ☐ |
| 5. Frequently fights with other children | ☐ | ☐ | ☐ |
| 6. Not much liked by other children | ☐ | ☐ | ☐ |
| 7. Often worried, worries about many things | ☐ | ☐ | ☐ |
| 8. Tends to do things on his own - rather solitary | ☐ | ☐ | ☐ |
| 9. Irritable. Is quick to 'fly off the handle' | ☐ | ☐ | ☐ |
| 10. Often appears miserable, unhappy, tearful or distressed | ☐ | ☐ | ☐ |
| 11. Has twitches, mannerisms or tics of the face or body | ☐ | ☐ | ☐ |
| 12. Frequently sucks thumb or finger | ☐ | ☐ | ☐ |
| 13. Frequently bites nails or fingers | ☐ | ☐ | ☐ |
| 14. Tends to be absent from school for trivial reasons | ☐ | ☐ | ☐ |

15. Is often disobedient ☐ ☐ ☐ ☐ ☐ ☐

16. Has poor concentration or short attention span ☐ ☐ ☐ ☐ ☐ ☐

17. Tends to be fearful or afraid of new things or new situations ☐ ☐ ☐

18. Fussy or over particular child ☐ ☐ ☐

19. Often tells lies ☐ ☐ ☐

20. Has stolen things on one or more occasions ☐ ☐ ☐

21. Has wet or soiled self at school this year ☐ ☐ ☐

22. Often complains of pains or aches ☐ ☐ ☐

23. Has had tears on arrival at school or has refused to come into the building this year ☐ ☐ ☐

24. Has a stutter or stammer ☐ ☐ ☐

25. Has other speech difficulty ☐ ☐ ☐

26. Bullies other children ☐ ☐ ☐

Are there any other problems of behaviour?

..............................................................................................

..............................................................................................

Signature: Mr/Mrs/Miss ...............

How well do you know this child?   Very well ☐   Moderately well ☐   Not very well ☐

THANK YOU VERY MUCH FOR YOUR HELP

---

* Reproduced from M. Rutter, 'A child's behaviour questionnaire for completion by teachers', J. Child Psychol. Psychiat. 8 (1967), 11. A revised and improved version, Child Scale B(2), is not yet published (copies from Professor Rutter, Institute of Psychiatry, De Crespigny Park, London SE5 8AF).

Example 5.20  Literacy record card (early version): Avon LEA (2pp)

FULL NAME OF PUPIL:

SCHOOL:

KEY
| | |
|---|---|
| O | oral practice |
| ∅ | written practice |
| ⊠ | instruction level |
| ■ | independent level |

USE OF LANGUAGE

- Reports on present experience ☐
- Reports on recalled experience ☐ ☐ ☐
- Projects to anticipate ☐ ☐ ☐
- Projects to predict ☐ ☐ ☐
- Perceives causal dependent relationships ☐ ☐
- Gives explanation (how) (why) ☐ ☐
- Expresses and recognizes tentativeness ☐ ☐ ☐
- Deals with imaginary problems ☐ ☐ ☐
- Creates imaginary experiences ☐ ☐ ☐
- Reflects on own feelings ☐ ☐
- Collaborates ☐ ☐
- Compares alternatives ☐ ☐
- Justifies behaviour ☐ ☐

UNDERSTANDS

- word ☐   letter ☐
- sound ☐   sentence ☐
- capital letter ☐   fullstop ☐

VISUAL SKILLS AND SEQUENCING

- 'Reads picture and sequences ☐
- Recognizes details in pictures ☐
- Suggests new ending for sequence ☐
- Draws inferences from pictures ☐
- Evaluates actions of characters ☐
- Sorts pictures and letter-shapes ☐

AUDITORY SKILLS

- Recognizes everyday sounds ☐
- Matches sounds with pictures ☐
- Identifies initial letter sounds ☐
- Identifies final letter sounds ☐
- Identifies medial letter sounds ☐

COMPREHENSION SKILLS

- Literal ☐
- Reorganization ☐
- Inference ☐
- Evaluation ☐
- Appreciation ☐
- Creative ☐

LIST OF BOOKS ATTACHED

READ ) 9+
READ TO)

READS FOR PLEASURE?  YES/NO

(1)

## PHONIC SKILLS

Matches and names symbol/sound
Consonants
Short vowels
Consonant digraphs
Final 'e'
Initial consonant blends
Final consonant blends
Vowel digraphs
Silent consonants

CONTEXT CUES

forward    backward
— | — |

BASIC WORD LIST?

## COMMUNICATION SKILLS

Reports
Expressive
Transactional
Poetic
Constructs flow diagrams

USE OF STANDARD ENGLISH

Plurals
Subject-verb agreement
Use of past tense

NOTES ON OTHER WORK COURSES

## HIGHER ORDER SKILLS

Alphabetical order
Contents table
Index
Dictionary
Encyclopaedia
Library system
Card index
Scans      Skims
Defines for purpose of reading
Forms questions for reading
Assesses reliability of books
Assesses suitability of books
Abstracts
Bibliographies
Strategies
Indexes
Stores
Notes

(2)

139

material is too difficult for him.  This is indicated by a word
recognition rate of 90 per cent or less (10 or more errors in
100 running words) and a comprehension ability of 50 per cent
or below.'  (para. 17.19)

Although this record was welcomed by some teachers
as a useful and comprehensive transfer document, it
has been criticized for including items which can
only be rated on a four-point scale with difficulty.
For instance, most teachers would find it impossible
to rate the item 'Expresses and recognizes tentativeness' on the given scale.  How could a pupil be said
to have reached instructional level for this item?

### GENERAL CONCLUSIONS

The examples of record keeping included in this chapter were chosen to indicate:

(1)   the different purposes for which records are
      used, e.g. admission, transfer;
(2)   the areas of the curriculum represented on
      records, e.g. mathematics, language, science;
(3)   the different school stages of the pupils,
      e.g. pre-reading records, transfer records;
(4)   the wide variation in record format, e.g.
      reading age graph, science flowchart;
(5)   the relationship between record keeping and
      assessment, e.g. Avon LEA's literacy record
      card.

Though there was a great variety of views about
what constituted a good record (and a bad record, for
that matter), the present examples have been selected
because they drew generally favourable comments from
the project teachers.  The teachers were particularly
attracted to simple yet well-designed formats which
had the following characteristics:

(1)   a clear layout;
(2)   distinct, stable printing that does not fade;
(3)   precise section headings;
(4)   the pupil's name and date of birth in promi-
      nent positions;
(5)   sufficient space for comments if required;
(6)   where necessary, a prominently placed key (or
      a user's handbook) to explain the use of
      abbreviations, symbols and criteria for the
      assessment of pupils.

Where content was concerned, once again there was

some confusion about what constituted relevance, although all teachers were quick to assess that relevance and lack of redundancy were the most important
criteria for record content. Nevertheless, the
following characteristics were agreed to be necessary
if relevant record keeping was to be achieved:

(1)   clear sequencing;
(2)   direct indications for future teaching;
(3)   clear distinctions between entries concerned
      with pupils' school experiences and those
      assessing attainment;
(4)   where information on assessment is presented,
      statements should be made about:
      (a)   the derivation of norms used when gra-
            ding or rating;
      (b)   the criteria used when deciding on pupil
            competence;
      (c)   details of any standardized tests used;
      (d)   details of other testing techniques used
            including 'home-made' tests.

## REFERENCES

1   E.g. 'Barbe's reading checklist and checklist for reading
    readiness', in *Individual Pupil Monitoring System:  Reading*,
    Boston, Mass.:  Houghton Mifflin, 1974.
2   S. Jackson, *Get Reading Right*, Glasgow:  Robert Gibson, 1971.
3   H. Fletcher *et al.*, *Mathematics for Schools*, levels I and
    II, Addison-Wesley, 1970—.
4   The project has produced the following materials under the
    series title *Match and Mismatch:  Raising Questions; Finding
    Answers*;  and an in-service group leader's guide, *Raising
    Questions:  Leader's Guide* with associated audiovisual mate-
    rials (Oliver & Boyd, 1977).  The project's final report, by
    John Elliott and Wynne Harlen, entitled *Portrait of a Project*
    was issued by the Schools Council (on request, 1980).
5   P. Rance, *Record Keeping in the Progressive Primary School*,
    Ward Lock Educational, 1971.
6   During the lifetime of the project the originators, Avon LEA,
    were further developing this record, and a revised version
    came into use in 1980.
7   Department of Education and Science, *A Language for Life*,
    report of Committee of Inquiry appointed by the Secretary of
    State for Education and Science under the chairmanship of
    Sir Alan Bullock [Bullock Report], HMSO, 1975.

# 6   Transfer records

The project team encountered a wide variety of record forms which were specifically designed to communicate information about pupils when they changed schools. For convenience, the team used two separate words for the kinds of pupil movement between schools which exist. These are:  (a) transfer, and (b) transition. The problems connected with these two kinds of movement are different.

*Transfer:*  This term has been used where an individual child moves to another school at the same educational stage for one of a variety of reasons, the most common one being a family move to another area.

*Transition:*  This term has been used to describe the movement of a whole year group of pupils from a lower to a higher stage of education.  A variety of instances exist:  infant to junior (where there are separate schools), first school to middle school, and primary, junior or middle schools to secondary grammar or comprehensive schools.

The basic difference between the two situations is the quantity of information which requires communication at a given time.  In the case of transfer, the amount of information sent to the next school was in some cases found to be quite detailed, but there was no problem for the receiving school since it was only necessary to assimilate information concerning one pupil.  In the case of transition, particularly to large comprehensive schools, information concerning up to 300 pupils has to be assimilated in a short space of time.  Even a moderate amount of data per pupil amounts to a sizeable quantity when multiplied by 100 or more.

Most of the LEAs visited provided an official record card for each pupil.  Some authorities were in the process of revising this at the time of the project.  Many revisions were the result of local government boundary changes.  In some cases, county boroughs had become part of a larger administrative area.  It was therefore possible to find several different LEA records in use within the same new authority.

   The project team found that the problems connected
with primary-secondary transition, particularly in
rural areas, had prompted some headteachers and
teachers from comprehensive schools and their feeder
primary schools to meet together and formulate a
common policy for communicating information about
pupils.   In urban areas, where pupils from a primary
school may go to one of several secondary schools in
the locality, this kind of policy may be difficult to
operate due to differing requirements of the secondary schools.   In the latter case headteachers tended
to rely on the LEA record card as a basis for communication plus additional information by letter where
primary headteachers felt this was necessary.
   The problems of primary-secondary transition, as
seen by the secondary school heads and teachers, seem
to stem from the variety of curricula followed in
primary schools.   For example, it was alleged that it
was often difficult to relate the stage reached by
one pupil in a school where scheme X was in use, with
that reached by a pupil from another school where
scheme Y was used.   Where secondary teachers wished
to compare pupils from different primary schools for
the purpose of 'setting' or ensuring a mixed-ability
grouping, they found that the subjective assessments
of primary teachers varied from school to school.
Consequently few useful comparisons could be based on
the transition records extant.
   The setting up of a liaison network between a comprehensive school and its feeder primary schools has
in some cases encouraged secondary teachers to visit
the primary schools on a regular basis and vice
versa.   Where this occurs, secondary teachers can see
at first hand what different primary teachers are
trying to achieve and also get to know the pupils who
will be transferring in the coming academic year.
Similarly, primary teachers can see at first hand
what will later be expected of their pupils.
   This form of liaison is not without its problems.
If the liaison procedure is not to be solely a banner
waving exercise for the secondary heads of first year,
a realistic amount of time must be allotted to it on
both sides of the transition.   Furthermore, subject
teachers need to be consulted over the kinds of information they wish to have about new pupils.   Quite
severe communication problems were found within large
comprehensive schools;   and perhaps as a consequence,
the notion of the 'fresh start' for new pupils was
fairly common.   Exactly what this means in terms of
the effect it has on the continuity of pupils' education is an open question.

ANALYSIS OF LEA RECORD CARDS

Interviews with teachers revealed deficiencies in
some official LEA record cards used for transfer and
transition.  With this problem in mind, the project
analysed the categories of information contained on
the LEA cards currently in use.  (Record cards from
66 LEAs were made available to the team.)

The number of items found on these cards varied a
great deal.  Some had over 70 categories whilst
others had as few as 10.  Overall, some 120 categories
were identified but, even within these, slight variations of wording existed between one authority and
another.  Table 2 (pp.145-148) shows these categories
and the percentage of authorities using them.

Many LEA records are marked *confidential* (77%);
of these, some clarifications are given as to the extent of restriction, e.g.

> (*A*)   'This card is confidential and may only be
> examined by an Officer of the County Council.'
> (*B*)   '... parents be allowed to inspect the card
> if that is their wish.  Extra care should,
> therefore, be taken in completion of the
> first page and centre pages.  The card con-
> tains a number of plain sheets with the
> headings - Infant, Junior and Secondary ...
> The content of these pages will naturally be
> confidential.'

*Format and design*

The size and layout of LEA records varied greatly,
from cards 120 × 210 mm to A4 size wallet/folders with
inserted sheets.  The following variants were in use
at the time of the survey (at the present time many
local authorities are reviewing and revising their
record systems):

> (1)   double-sided card or sheet (of various
> sizes)                                         27%
> (2)   folded, double-sided card                      21%
> (3)   double-folded (concertina) card,
> double-sided                                    6%
> (4)   booklet                                        10%
> (5)   folder or wallet with inserted sheets          17%

Of the records examined, only a third had any notes
for guidance and use mentioned on the card.  Of these,
several contained merely a note referring the user to
a set of notes separate from the card.

Table 2    Content categories used by LEAs in transfer and
transition record cards

| | Type of content | % use |
|---|---|---|
| | *Administrative data* | |
| 1. | Pupil's surname and forenames | 100 |
| 2. | Pupil's date of birth | 98 |
| *3. | Home address (including changes of address) | 93 |
| 4. | Home telephone number | 55 |
| *5. | Emergency contact address only, and address with telephone number | 29 |
| 6. | Emergency contact telephone number only | 6 |
| *7. | Parent's or guardian's name | 81 |
| 8. | Father's occupation | 24 |
| 9. | Father's place of employment | 16 |
| 10. | Mother's occupation | 23 |
| 11. | Mother's place of employment | 14 |
| 12. | Pupil's position in family | 53 |
| *13. | Family doctor's name, address and telephone number | 32 |
| 14. | Family doctor's name and address only | 24 |
| 15. | Name of school, and schools previously attended, with dates | 82 |
| 16. | Admission number of each school attended | 19 |
| +17. | EITHER | |
| | *Vital information:* health or physical factors of importance (placed in a prominent place on the record with a distinctive border) | 8 |
| | OR | |
| | This kind of information covered under the following headings: | |
| | (a)  *medical information* | 53 |
| | to include:   general health   19% | |
| | dates of medical examination   3% | |
| | glasses worn   6% | |
| | left-handed   3% | |
| | Mantoux test   2% | |
| | signal system to refer to further information   6% | |
| | parental permission for child to see school doctor or dentist   2% | |
| | (b)  *health and physical handicaps* which may affect child's progress | 56 |
| | personality factors affecting progress   6% | |

*    Some authorities expect this information to be kept on a
     separate file card.
+    Eleven per cent of authorities in the sample did not include
     categories for information under the headings in item 17 on
     the official record.

Table 2   (cont'd)

| | Type of content | | % use |
|---|---|---|---|
| 18. | Referrals to outside agencies: | | 29 |
| | (a) | their nature and result, with dates | |
| | (b) | results only as a comment | 2% |
| 19. | Remedial treatment | | 21 |
| | (a) | screening carried out | 8% |
| | (b) | learning difficulties specified | 2% |
| 20. | Home/family circumstances/background | | 56 |
| | (a) | non-indigenous parents | 9% |
| | (b) | child in care/fostered/adopted | 5% |
| | (c) | linguistic background | 5% |
| | (d) | religious denomination | 9% |
| | (e) | details of interviews with parents | 2% |
| | (f) | an *alert* - where special care record exists | 2% |
| | (g) | free meals | 2% |
| | (h) | attitudes of parents to the child | 5% |
| | (i) | attitudes of parent to the school | 11% |
| *21. | Sex of pupil | | 21 |
| 22. | Space for one or more photographs of pupil | | 24 |
| 23. | *Attendance* (usually recorded as a fraction) | | 71 |
| | +significant absences notes | | 56% |
| 24. | Any aspects of pre-school experience | | 16 |
| | (a) | report from nursery school (if attended) | 10% |
| | (b) | other pre-school experience | 6% |
| 25. | General aspects of primary education | | 16 |
| | (a) | number of terms spent in infant school | 4% |
| | (b) | details of dates and duration of primary education | 14% |
| | (c) | details of class size | 5% |
| 26. | *Attainment* | | 100 |
| | (a) | general comments only on all subject areas | 35% |
| | (b) | language/speech:  general comments on oral communication | 61% |
| | (c) | written language | 45% |
| | (d) | reading:  general comments | 45% |
| | | comments on facility/fluency | 10% |
| | | comments on comprehension | 14% |
| | | reading test results (reading age) | 34% |
| | | remedial help required | 6% |

\*   Many other authorities indicate this by colour coding their
    cards.
+   Some authorities issue a separate form for this information.

Table 2   (cont'd)

| | Type of content | % use | |
|---|---|---|---|
| 27. | Mathematics attainment | | 66 |
| | (*a*)   general comments only | 39% | |
| | (*b*)   concepts understood | 10% | |
| | (*c*)   specific concepts mentioned | 2% | |
| | (*d*)   computational skill:  general | 14% | |
| | (*e*)   specific computational rules | | |
| | mentioned | 2% | |
| | (*f*)   mathematics topics covered | 2% | |
| 28. | Schemes used for aspects of language and | | |
| | mathematics | | 10 |
| 29. | Other aspects of the curriculum | | 76 |
| | general comment only | 18% | |
| | *Specific mention of other curriculum areas* | | |
| 30. | Environmental studies | | 13 |
| | (*a*)   general comments only | 2% | |
| | (*b*)   specific comments or grades on: | | |
| | powers of observation | 6% | |
| | interest in the work | 3% | |
| | use of source material | 3% | |
| | ability to record/report | 3% | |
| 31. | Science/nature study | | 8 |
| 32. | Visual, musical arts | | 35 |
| | (*a*)   creative work:  general comments | 19% | |
| | (*b*)   specific comments on: | | |
| | materials used | 3% | |
| | movement ability - drama | 6% | |
| | musical ability | 10% | |
| | instruments played | 2% | |
| | co-ordination/manual dexterity | 11% | |
| | (*c*)   physical education/development | 16% | |
| | (*d*)   reasoning ability | 6% | |
| | (*e*)   noteworthy abilities | 13% | |
| | (*f*)   study skills | 2% | |
| 33. | *Information to be given on transfer or* | | |
| | *transition* | | 83 |
| | (*a*)   general comment/summary form | 16% | |
| | (*b*)   test results only | 8% | |
| 34. | *Test data given in some form on transfer or* | | |
| | *transition* | | 72 |
| | (*a*)   name of test | 63% | |
| | (*b*)   date of test administration | 60% | |
| | (*c*)   score on test | 64% | |
| | (*d*)   position/ranking | 10% | |
| | (*e*)   age at point of testing | 33% | |
| | (*f*)   comments from headteacher | 55% | |
| | (*g*)   additional recommendations | 5% | |

Table 2  (cont'd)

| Type of content | % use |
|---|---|
| 35. *Other categories of information sent on transfer or transition* | 34 |
|    (*a*) pupil's special interest and skills | 16% |
|    (*b*) special difficulties/remedial work recommended | 10% |
|    (*c*) pupil's special responsibilities | 6% |
|  *(*d*) pupil's personality and temperament: general comments only | 13% |
|    (*e*) specific comments/ratings: | |
|       adjustment to school life | 10% |
|       attitude to adults | 6% |
|       attitude to other children | 8% |
|       attitude to the environment | 2% |
|       attitude to discipline | 2% |
|       attitude to the property of others | 2% |

*Note:*  On the records using the above categories, most of the assessments were based on a 3, 4 or 5 point scale using criteria included in the record, e.g. *perseverance*:

1  very persevering and hard working
2  shows good application
3  usually works steadily
4  gives up rather easily
5  makes very little effort

| | |
|---|---|
| 36. A few LEA records contain information categories for age groups beyond the primary stage.  These include areas which have middle schools.  Among the categories are: | |
| Foreign/modern language | 19 |
|   primary French | 8% |
| Crafts/design | 2 |
| Home economics | 2 |
| Secondary school final examinations and forecast | 13 |

---

\*  One example included a signal system to denote that further information was available from the headteacher sending the record on, and that the receiving headteacher should make contact.

QUESTIONNAIRE FOR TEACHERS

Many of the records included were designed some fif-
teen to twenty years ago at the time of the previous
NFER survey.[1]   The team investigated the degree to
which these categories still represented the kinds of
information which teachers wished to receive about
new pupils.   A questionnaire was compiled using the
categories from the analysis above.   Items which
appeared to be duplicated were removed but provision
was made for teachers to add additional items which
they felt were important but had not been included on
the questionnaire.

Project teacher groups were asked to rate each
category of information on a four-point scale:

essential    I feel this to be important informa-
             tion;
desirable    I feel this information to be useful
             when it is available;
optional     I do not mind whether this information
             is given or not, even when available;
irrelevant   I do not feel this information to be
             of any value to me as a teacher.

Each teacher was asked to imagine that he/she has
received a new pupil and then to rate the categories
of information according to their perceived importance.

Table 3 (pp.150-154) shows the items in rank order
of importance over the complete set of categories.
This was done by ordering each category using the
*essential* rating first of all.   Where items were
given a tied ranking, the degree to which other
teachers considered the item *irrelevant* was taken
into account.   Where there was still a tie in the
ratings, the *desirable* and *optional* ratings were considered.   As the weighting on each rating is on a
nominal scale, other ways of ranking the items were
tried.   It was found that only for one or two items
was the rank order altered by plus or minus one position.

In summary, it can be seen that a certain amount
of information concerned with identification of the
pupil is regarded as essential;   though one may be
puzzled by the two respondents who rated pupil's
names (ranked 2 and 3) desirable rather than essential, and yet must have rated date of birth (ranked
1) as essential.

Next in order of importance are items concerned
with physical and health handicaps (10) as [p.154

Table 3   Categories of information on records, in rank order of
          importance ($n$ = 163)

| | Category | % of sample rating | | | |
|---|---|---|---|---|---|
| | | E | D | O | I |
| 1. | Pupil's date of birth | 100.0 | – | – | – |
| 2. | Pupil's surname | 98.5 | 1.5 | – | – |
| 3. | Pupil's forenames | 97.8 | 2.2 | – | – |
| 4. | Pupil's home address | 97.8 | 2.2 | – | – |
| 5. | *Vital information* - health or physical factors of importance | 92.6 | 5.2 | – | – |
| 6. | Person to contact in case of emergency | 92.6 | 4.4 | 0.7 | 1.5 |
| 7. | Parent's or guardian's name | 89.6 | 4.4 | 4.4 | 0.7 |
| 8. | Address of person to contact in case of emergency | 88.1 | 9.6 | 0.7 | 1.5 |
| 9. | Telephone number of person to contact in case of emergency | 84.4 | 13.3 | 0.7 | 1.5 |
| 10. | Health handicaps which may affect progress in school | 84.4 | 12.6 | 0.7 | 1.5 |
| 11. | Name of school attended at present | 84.4 | 11.9 | 0.7 | 1.5 |
| 12. | Quality of hearing (e.g. hearing loss) | 83.7 | 11.9 | 2.2 | 1.5 |
| 13. | Quality of sight (e.g. need for glasses) | 83.0 | 12.6 | 2.2 | 1.5 |
| 14. | Sex of child | 82.2 | 5.9 | 1.5 | 7.4 |
| 15. | Home telephone number | 81.5 | 15.6 | 3.0 | – |
| 16. | Learning difficulties specified | 74.8 | 19.3 | 3.0 | 0.7 |
| 17. | Results of referrals to other agencies | 73.3 | 19.3 | 5.2 | – |
| 18. | Oral language - any speech defects | 71.9 | 23.7 | 2.2 | 0.7 |
| 19. | Referrals to child/educational psychologist, with dates | 71.1 | 22.9 | 4.4 | 0.7 |
| 20. | Nature of any remedial treatment | 71.1 | 20.7 | 4.4 | 0.7 |
| 21. | Changes of home address | 70.4 | 17.0 | 8.1 | – |
| 22. | Child is 'in care' | 69.6 | 21.5 | 6.7 | 0.7 |
| 23. | Reading - stage reached on reading scheme(s) | 62.9 | 32.6 | 2.2 | – |
| 24. | Personality factors which might affect progress | 62.9 | 22.2 | 8.1 | 3.0 |

*Key:*   E = essential;   D = desirable;   O = optional;   I = irrelevant.
   * indicates that the percentage of teachers rating these
   items as *irrelevant* was equal to or greater than the percentage rating them as *essential*.

Table 3   (cont'd)

| Category | % of sample rating | | | |
|---|---|---|---|---|
| | E | D | O | I |
| 25. General note regarding referrals to other agencies | 57.0 | 28.9 | 8.9 | 0.7 |
| 26. Noteworthy disabilities (other than those covered in 10 and 24) | 56.3 | 37.0 | 3.7 | 1.5 |
| 27. Name of family doctor | 56.3 | 26.7 | 7.4 | 9.6 |
| 28. Child is fostered | 54.8 | 29.6 | 11.1 | 3.7 |
| 29. Names of schools attended previously | 53.3 | 34.0 | 11.9 | 0.7 |
| 30. Reading - remedial help required | 52.6 | 39.3 | 4.4 | 1.5 |
| 31. Child has free meals | 52.6 | 13.3 | 8.1 | 24.4 |
| 32. Mathematics - stage reached on mathematics scheme(s) | 51.9 | 39.3 | 6.7 | 0.7 |
| 33. Name of any tests given | 51.1 | 27.4 | 13.3 | 5.9 |
| 34. Telephone number of family doctor | 51.1 | 26.7 | 8.9 | 12.6 |
| 35. Educational screening has been carried out | 50.4 | 35.6 | 8.1 | 2.2 |
| 36. Address of family doctor | 48.1 | 27.4 | 12.6 | 11.1 |
| 37. General medical information (not covered in 5, 10, 12 and 13) | 47.4 | 40.7 | 5.2 | 6.7 |
| 38. Noteworthy abilities | 46.7 | 45.9 | 5.2 | 1.5 |
| 39. Mathematical concepts understood/mastered | 46.7 | 41.5 | 8.1 | 1.5 |
| 40. Reading test results | 44.4 | 45.2 | 8.1 | 1.5 |
| 41. Results/scores obtained on standardized tests (other than reading tests) | 44.4 | 31.9 | 16.3 | 5.2 |
| 42. Mathematics - computational skills mastered | 42.9 | 43.7 | 10.4 | 1.5 |
| 43. Reading - difficulties encountered | 42.2 | 43.7 | 11.9 | 0.7 |
| 44. Dates when standardized tests were administered | 42.2 | 33.3 | 16.3 | 4.4 |
| 45. Notes regarding significant absences | 41.5 | 45.9 | 8.9 | 2.2 |
| 46. Linguistic background (where English is a second language) | 41.5 | 35.6 | 13.3 | 5.9 |
| 47. Oral language - vocabulary and fluency | 40.7 | 39.3 | 11.1 | 2.2 |
| 48. Mother's place of work | 40.7 | 28.9 | 16.3 | 14.1 |
| 49. Child's position in family | 38.5 | 45.9 | 10.4 | 4.4 |
| 50. Signal indicating that further case records exist regarding the child | 37.8 | 34.8 | 15.6 | 8.9 |

Table 3   (cont'd)

| Category | % of sample rating | | | |
|---|---|---|---|---|
| | E | D | O | I |
| 51. Parental permission for child to see school doctor or dentist | 36.3 | 29.6 | 14.8 | 14.8 |
| 52. Child is adopted | 34.8 | 31.1 | 18.5 | 12.6 |
| 53. Dates of attending previous schools | 32.6 | 39.3 | 17.8 | 4.4 |
| 54. Reasoning ability - verbal reasoning | 30.4 | 43.7 | 22.9 | 1.5 |
| 55. Mathematical topics covered | 29.6 | 48.9 | 19.3 | 1.5 |
| 56. Reasoning ability - mathematical reasoning | 29.6 | 43.7 | 22.9 | 1.5 |
| 57. Home/family circumstances or background | 28.9 | 43.7 | 18.5 | 8.1 |
| 58. Attitude of parents to the child | 28.9 | 43.7 | 18.5 | 8.1 |
| 59. Comment on child's emotional maturity | 28.1 | 42.9 | 19.3 | 6.7 |
| 60. Attitude of parents to the school | 28.1 | 42.2 | 16.3 | 12.6 |
| 61. Father's place of work | 28.1 | 34.8 | 21.5 | 15.6 |
| 62. General comments on child's personal qualities | 27.4 | 53.3 | 11.1 | 2.2 |
| 63. Reading - comments on comprehension | 27.4 | 47.4 | 20.7 | 3.0 |
| 64. Comment on child's adjustment to school life | 27.4 | 45.9 | 18.5 | 5.9 |
| 65. Comment on child's attitude to other children | 26.7 | 47.4 | 17.8 | 5.9 |
| 66. Comment on child's self-confidence | 25.2 | 45.9 | 19.3 | 6.7 |
| 67. Comment on child's powers of concentration | 24.4 | 47.4 | 18.5 | 7.4 |
| 68. Comment on child's attitude to discipline | 23.7 | 48.9 | 17.8 | 6.7 |
| 69. Musical arts - musical instruments played | 22.9 | 50.4 | 21.5 | 4.4 |
| 70. Written language - imagination and creativity | 22.9 | 48.9 | 22.9 | 2.2 |
| 71. Written language - grammar and accuracy | 22.9 | 45.2 | 24.4 | 5.2 |
| 72. Comment on child's attitude to adults | 22.9 | 48.1 | 19.3 | 6.7 |
| 73. Comment on child's reliability | 22.9 | 48.1 | 19.3 | 7.4 |
| 74. Non-indigenous parents (country of origin, date of entry to UK) | 22.9 | 45.9 | 14.1 | 13.3 |
| 75. Written language - spelling accuracy | 22.2 | 46.7 | 23.7 | 5.2 |

Table 3    (cont'd)

| Category | % of sample rating | | | |
|---|---|---|---|---|
| | E | D | O | I |
| 76.  Comment on child's initiative | 22.2 | 48.1 | 20.0 | 6.7 |
| 77.  Dates of medical examination | 22.2 | 38.5 | 28.9 | 6.7 |
| 78.  Comment on child's perseverance | 21.5 | 48.9 | 20.0 | 7.4 |
| 79.  Child is right/left-handed | 21.5 | 37.0 | 25.2 | 16.3 |
| 80.  Record of attendance (as a fraction) | 20.7 | 47.4 | 22.9 | 6.7 |
| *81.  Mother's occupation | 20.7 | 31.9 | 25.9 | 20.7 |
| 82.  Comment on child's attitude to the property of others | 19.3 | 47.4 | 23.7 | 5.9 |
| 83.  Comments/ratings on child's interest in project/topic work | 19.3 | 43.7 | 31.1 | 4.4 |
| 84.  Details of interviews with parents | 17.8 | 42.9 | 25.9 | 11.9 |
| 85.  Comment on child's attitude to the environment | 17.0 | 40.0 | 30.4 | 9.6 |
| 86.  Written language - quality of handwriting | 16.3 | 43.7 | 28.9 | 8.9 |
| 87.  Reasoning ability - non-verbal reasoning (e.g. picture puzzles) | 16.3 | 39.3 | 35.6 | 5.9 |
| *88.  Father's occupation | 15.6 | 34.0 | 28.9 | 20.0 |
| 89.  General comments on tests taken (not covered by 40, 41 and 44) | 14.1 | 46.7 | 20.7 | 12.6 |
| 90.  Comments/ratings on child's powers of observation | 13.3 | 45.9 | 33.3 | 5.2 |
| *91.  Rank order/position of child based on test results | 13.3 | 20.0 | 23.7 | 39.3 |
| *92.  Religious denomination | 11.9 | 26.7 | 35.6 | 25.2 |
| 93.  Visual arts - comments on skills acquired | 11.1 | 40.0 | 40.7 | 7.4 |
| 94.  Physical education - child's interest in sport | 11.1 | 37.0 | 42.2 | 8.1 |
| 95.  List of topics covered in science, nature/environmental studies | 11.1 | 37.0 | 41.5 | 9.6 |
| 96.  Musical arts - comments on skills acquired (excluding those covered by 69) | 9.6 | 42.9 | 42.9 | 3.0 |
| *97.  Level to which topics in science, etc. have been studied | 9.6 | 29.6 | 40.0 | 14.1 |
| *98.  Space for one or more photographs of child | 9.6 | 29.6 | 40.0 | 14.1 |
| *99.  Drama/movement - comments on co-ordination | 8.9 | 39.3 | 40.7 | 8.9 |
| 100.  Physical education - comment on child's agility | 8.1 | 43.7 | 40.7 | 6.7 |

Table 3   (cont'd)

| Category | % of sample rating | | | |
|---|---|---|---|---|
| | E | D | O | I |
| 101. Study skill - ability to use reference library | 8.1 | 31.1 | 45.9 | 14.1 |
| 102. Physical education - games skills acquired | 8.1 | 31.1 | 45.9 | 14.1 |
| *103. Study skill - ability to use dictionary | 7.4 | 33.3 | 45.9 | 12.6 |
| *104. Study skill - ability to use card and book index | 7.4 | 25.9 | 48.9 | 17.0 |
| *105. Admission number at schools previously attended | 7.4 | 10.4 | 22.2 | 57.8 |
| *106. Visual arts - comments on creative work | 6.7 | 42.2 | 42.2 | 7.4 |
| *107. Drama/movement - comment on use of imagination | 6.7 | 33.3 | 48.9 | 8.9 |
| *108. Study skill - ability to prepare an outline before writing report | 6.7 | 28.1 | 46.7 | 15.6 |
| *109. Visual arts - comment on materials used | 6.7 | 28.1 | 46.7 | 15.6 |
| *110. Study skill - ability to use encyclopaedia | 5.9 | 33.3 | 46.7 | 13.3 |
| *111. Study skill - ability to make notes | 5.9 | 28.1 | 48.1 | 17.0 |
| *112. Study skill - ability to choose relevant details from references | 5.2 | 29.6 | 46.7 | 15.6 |
| *113. Study skill - ability to use non-book sources for information | 5.2 | 26.7 | 53.3 | 14.1 |

well as learning difficulties (16), referrals to
external agencies (19 and 25) and remedial recommendations (20).  The first items concerned with academic
attainment are the stage reached on a reading scheme
(23);  and information regarding remedial help with
reading (30).  The stage reached on a mathematics
scheme (32) is rated higher than any other item concerned with mathematics.

Data about standardized tests are given reasonably
high priority (33, 40, 41, 44) though the pupil's
rank order based on test results is given low priority (91).  Information on a pupil's personal characteristics is not highly rated, being just below half-
way down the list (62 and below), though 'Personality
factors which might affect progress' is rated more
highly (24).

Items concerned with parents' occupation are

ranked 81 and 88 as opposed to their places of work
which are ranked 48 and 61.  More importance is
placed on items which are of practical value, e.g.
place where parent(s) can be contacted in case of an
emergency, rather than on items which are of purely
sociological significance, e.g. parents' occupation.
Information concerned with other aspects of academic
development receives low rankings - handwriting 86,
visual arts skills 93, agility in PE 100, drama skill
99 and 107.  Study skills receive the lowest rankings
of all, 101 and below.

Further analyses were carried out on the data to
see if teachers' length and type of teaching experience led to differences of emphasis in the number of
categories considered to be essential.  There are
some slight indications (i.e. not sufficiently large
to be statistically significant) that less experienced teachers considered a larger number of categories to be essential than their more experienced
colleagues.  It must be pointed out that the teachers
who responded to the questionnaire were those who had
shown an interest in record keeping by attending project teacher groups or one-day workshops.  A considerable number of those in the sample were headteachers
or held senior posts of responsibility.  Such a
sample is probably not representative of the teaching
profession as a whole.

Teachers in the survey were asked what additional
categories of information they would consider to be
essential or desirable.  Few of the teachers considered the addition of categories to be important.
These mentioned the following extra categories:

(1)   home circumstances:
          two-parent family,
          parents separated,
          parents divorced,
          one-parent family,
          inconsistent partnership;
(2)   family on social security;
(3)   information about a child's pre-school or
      nursery school experience;
(4)   medical information:
          injections/vaccinations given (in particu-
              lar anti-tetanus, with date of last in-
              jection),
          allergies,
          essential medication - diabetes, epilepsy
              etc.;
(5)   guardianship - relationship of guardian to
      child.

The length of a teacher's professional experience
was considered worth noting by one of our respondents.
Items like this would need to be amended each year,
or at least accompanied by the date when the comment
was made if such information was to be kept relevant.
Several teachers mentioned the inclusion of samples
of pupils' work since 'actual specimens of child's
work in all basic skills (writing, mathematics, etc.)
are important to the next teacher so [he/she] can be
ready to carry on with the best education'.  Another
teacher considered that, for reading and comprehension ability, the use of reading quotient or reading
age would be sufficient, but samples of work were a
better indication of a pupil's ability in writing
creatively.  Samples of work taken yearly were seen
by yet another teacher as a useful way of presenting
a child's development and progress.

Procedures for transferring pupils' records at the
time of the survey were generally found to be hapha-
zard or non-existent.  Certain LEAs adopted the
following method.

(1)  Where pupils moved to another school in the
     same authority, their records were sent
     directly to the pupil's new school.
(2)  Where pupils moved to a different LEA, their
     records were held at a central office in the
     area from which they had moved until re-
     quested by the receiving local authority.
     *Eventually* the records were sent to the new
     school.

Variations of this practice exist.  Some authorities
do not permit official pupils' records from their
schools to be sent to other LEAs.

Whatever procedure was adopted, by far the most
frequent complaint heard from project teachers was
the delay experienced in obtaining the records of new
pupils.  Much of the academic information was soon
superseded and was therefore, by the date of the record's receipt, found to be obsolete or irrelevant.
Highly topical information, it was suggested, should
ideally accompany the pupil on his/her first day at
a new school.

One group of children for whom mobility is a way
of life are children of families in the armed services.  The Service Children's Education Authority
(SCEA), being aware of the problems related to pupil
mobility, has a standard record system for all service children.  A carefully documented procedure is
laid down for the transfer of records, which teachers

in service schools are expected to follow.  Break-
downs in this system occur mainly when a child moves
from a state school in the United Kingdom or moves
between state schools in the UK, since '... the
transfer of records then comes under the jurisdiction
of the relevant Local Education Authorities in the UK'
(see appendix E, para 1).  Since no set pattern of
transferring school records exists in England and
Wales, there is a consequential weakness in that
service children's records tend to be regarded in the
same way as the LEA transfer cards.  Many teachers in
England and Wales who have pupils from service families may be unaware of the SCEA procedure and hence
are unable to act appropriately.  The procedure is as
follows.

Throughout his school career, each child of school
age in a service family has a record folder and, at
the point of transfer, is issued with a transfer report.  The record folder (marked 'confidential') is
sent through the official channels to the headteacher
at the pupil's new school.  The transfer report,
which contains information of an academic nature, is
taken by the pupil, or his/her parents, directly to
the new school.  The advantage is that the very transitory information, mentioned earlier, is immediately
available to a new teacher.  For those not fully
aware of the SCEA procedure, the instructions are included as Appendix E.

A scheme for transferring records catering for the
children of 'travelling' families is in operation in
the West Midlands authority.  This is based on a
central co-ordinating office to which the school record of a child is sent when leaving a school.  The
child is given a card to deliver to the teacher at
his/her next school which indicates that the child's
record can be obtained from the co-ordinating office.

The problems of transferring information concerning children who change schools frequently will need
to be overcome if the continuity of pupils' education
is not to suffer.  In view of the findings above, the
following recommendations are made.

(1)   A common policy for transferring individual
      pupils' records both within and between local
      authorities would appear to be needed in
      order to simplify the present variety of
      practice.  Any revision of practice needs to
      take into account:
      (a)   the requirements by different personnel
            for information about pupils;
      (b)   the urgency with which information is

required, e.g. information of immediate
need to a pupil's new teacher could be
sent with the pupil on the first day at
his/her new school.

(2)   The more important items of information required by teachers, in order of priority,
appear to be:

(a)   pupil's names, date of birth, home
address;

(b)   vital information required for a child's
well-being;

(c)   person(s) to contact in emergency;

(d)   details of any handicaps, physical or
socio-emotional, which may affect progress in school;

(e)   details of any learning disabilities,
including spoken language;

(f)   details of referrals to psychologists,
reports from social workers, educational
welfare officers, school medical officers, etc.;

(g)   details of prescribed remedial treatment;

(h)   stages reached on reading, language and
mathematics schemes;

(i)   details of any screening or other tests
carried out;

(j)   other medical academic and personal information.

(3)   Secondary school teaching staffs and their
colleagues in feeder primary schools need to
meet, liaise and formulate a common policy
for the transfer of information about pupils.

(4)   Some cross-referencing work needs to be
carried out to enable teachers to relate the
stages pupils have reached on different
schemes.  This would be a very useful activity for locally based working parties.

(5)   Where assessment of pupils is carried out at
primary-secondary transfer, an agreed testing
programme would enable decisions to be made
on the basis of compatible data.

(6)   Different information about pupils is required depending on a recipient's position in
the secondary school organization.  Records
containing information for the school office
administration could well be separate from
those required by pastoral and subject tutors.

REFERENCE

1   A.S. Walker, *Pupils' School Records*, Newnes, 1955.

# 7 Record keeping and curriculum planning: aims, objectives and assessment

This chapter differs from others in the report in that it contains some material of a theoretical nature, discussed alongside project findings. The rationale for its inclusion can be summed up as follows.

(1)  Almost all school records, particularly those which are transferred to teachers in other schools, contain assessments of pupils' progress of one kind or another. The project teachers' many criticisms of records indicated a need to report assessment information in a more standard form.

(2)  The criteria by which teachers assess their pupils are frequently omitted from records or incompletely worded. There appears to be a need to identify which important items of information should be included on records if pupils' progress is to be communicated less ambiguously.

(3)  Record keeping as a topic for discussion cannot be divorced from the much wider area of curriculum planning and decision making.

According to interviews with teachers, record keeping was viewed with most enthusiasm when closely linked with curriculum planning, as frequently carried out during staff meetings. The practice of following a syllabus issued by the headteacher was considered to be too inflexible by many of the teachers with whom the project worked. In fact, where little or no consultation took place between headteachers and their staffs in the compilation of guidelines or syllabuses, such documents tended to remain in cupboards or desk drawers and seldom saw the light of day.

Many of the records seen by the project team were the culmination of hours of staff consultation. The degree of staff participation in the planning process seemed to be reflected in the degree to which records were used in the classroom. Records were seen to be

159

used both as curriculum guidelines and as a means of
checking what had been taught and learnt.   With all
this in mind, the project team produced two stimulus
papers for discussion in the project teacher groups:
'The need for aims and objectives', and 'Discussion
points on assessment'.   They were intended to serve
as a brief summary of a vast area of educational
technology and assessment literature.   Material from
these papers found to be most useful by teachers is
included here.

The first part of the chapter is devoted to a
brief review of the use of 'aims' and 'objectives' as
a means of clarifying teaching intentions, and as
criteria for the subsequent assessment of what has
been learned.   The second part presents project findings concerning the methods teachers employ in
assessing their pupils.

### AIMS AND OBJECTIVES

'If you're not sure where you're going, you're liable
to end up someplace else   -   and not even know it.'[1]

The terms 'aims' and 'objectives' have principally
been used by educational technologists, and not generally by teachers.   During the last few decades, the
production of teaching programmes for use in educational and training establishments has involved programme writers in stating instructional intentions
prior to writing and designing materials.   The statement of aims and objectives served three main purposes:   first, as a detailed plan for the writers and
designers of a programme during the production of
materials;   secondly, to inform the student what he
is expected to learn;   thirdly, as a set of criteria
against which it is possible to assess how well the
student has learnt the programme content and *pari
passu* ascertain the effectiveness of the teaching
materials.

The management of learning through the systematic
drawing up of learning objectives is generally regarded as an American educational phenomenon of the
1950s and 1960s.   Close acquaintance with it tends to
diminish its appeal, partly because of its mecha-
nistic nature and partly because it has lent itself
to excesses;   as was so eloquently stated by a leading British educationalist just prior to the
commencement of the project.

'But let there be no doubt whatever as to the objective of all
this.   It is to make the teacher accountable, and the Americans

are doing almost exactly what Robert Lowe, the famous exponent
of payment by results, did when he put into operation our
"Code" ... And let there be no doubt either that this disease
is coming our way. Accountability is now the "in" word and,
as they say in Dallas, "Schools are going to have to deliver
one year of educational growth for one year of instruction, no
matter what it takes".'[2]

   There do appear to be lessons to be learned from
any over-emphasis on 'blanket' testing (i.e. testing
every child at certain specified ages across a range
of skills) and the wholesale use of instructional
objectives. However, it would appear that an under-
emphasis in clarifying their intentions on the part
of teachers has, according to Bennett,[3] led to less
than satisfactory progress of pupils in schools.
   As in most things a compromise between the ex-
tremes of view is probably acceptable. This point is
brought out by Rowntree:

'To set the student off in pursuit of an unnamed quarry may be
merely wasteful but to grade him on whether he catches it or
not is positively mischievous. Do we sometimes appear to say
to students, "I can't say precisely what behaviour I want you
to acquire from this course, just do your own thing (guessing
what might come to mind) and I'll give you a grade according
to how I feel about it." If there really are behaviours that
cannot be spelled out reasonably clearly in advance (even after
we've observed such behaviour in previous students), let's not
belabour the students with them afterwards.'[4]

It must be admitted that a series of aims and objectives can be more easily drawn up for some subject
areas than others. For instance, it would be a comparatively simple task to produce a set of objectives
for mathematics as opposed to 'aesthetics'.
   So far in this chapter, no distinction has been
made between 'aims' and 'objectives'. Some confusion
was experienced on this point by teachers involved
with the project. The main difference between these
two terms lies in their scope.
   *Aims* are general statements of teaching intentions
to be followed over a long period of time. The wording used is relatively vague and hence it is well-
nigh impossible directly to assess a pupil's attainment in terms of aims. E.g. 'The child should be beginning to realize that he can play an important part
in his own development by, for example, recognizing
his strengths and limitations and setting his own
goals accordingly.'[5]

*Objectives* are precisely worded statements of what a pupil will be expected to do after following some form of instruction or after some specific experience. The criteria by which the pupil is to be assessed may also be included, thereby reducing as much as possible any ambiguity. E.g. 'The child will demonstrate recognition of the positive, comparative, and superlative forms of adjectives in selecting the correct form (all provided) of the same adjective.' (Competence might also be predefined, for instance, 90% accuracy.)

Once aims have been formulated, further detail planning is required to draw up a set of objectives which spell out in specific terms the intended route or routes towards the aims. *Aims should not therefore be maligned for their generality but should only be considered as starting points in the planning process.*

The following summary sets out the possible advantages of planning a primary school curriculum along a series of aims and objectives.

(1)  Both the pupil and the teacher can be aware of the kinds of performance expected at the end of a course of learning.
(2)  The stating of outcomes can provide a system for the diagnostic analysis of a pupil's strengths and weaknesses and degree of progress (as opposed to relative gradings).
(3)  This kind of approach can improve continuity and ensure that pupils and teachers are not working at cross purposes.[6]

From this it is but a short step to producing an assessment and record keeping appropriate to one's own requirement, with at the same time the enormous added advantage that such records could be passed on to other teachers and still be understood.

*Writing objectives*

From a quick survey of current literature, there appears to be agreement to subdivide human behaviour into three main areas:

(1)  activity of the 'mind' - knowing and thinking - *cognitive* behaviour;
(2)  attitudes and feelings - *affective* behaviour;
(3)  bodily co-ordination - *psychomotor* behaviour.

Most of the activities involving children contain

elements of these three areas in combination.  An
ability to learn depends on attitudes and physical
and mental capability to do so;  'motivation', 'learning set' and 'readiness' are terms used to describe
these states.

One of the most widely quoted theoretical frameworks used in education for the purposes of devising
assessment activities is the *Taxonomy of Educational
Objectives*.[7]  Details are included in appendix B.
These taxonomical classifications are based on a belief that learned behaviours can be categorized on a
hierarchical basis.  In the cognitive domain, for
instance, there are six levels:  knowledge, comprehension, application, analysis, synthesis and evaluation.  Recognition and recall of knowledge is considered to be the lowest form of cognitive activity
upon which the succeeding levels are built, evaluation being the highest level.

There are philosophical problems[8] and practical
difficulties in using this framework.  For example,
two children may operate at different levels when
asked to solve an identical problem.  A child who has
met a similar problem before needs only to recall (at
the knowledge level) his previous successful strategy
for solving it, whereas the child for whom the problem is unfamiliar may take longer to work out the
solution since he will need to recall relevant knowledge, comprehend the problem, apply relevant knowledge and rules and possibly analyse a totally new
situation.  A pupil's past experience would seem,
therefore, to be a better determinant of the level at
which he/she will operate, when solving a problem,
than the teacher's choice of the problem or test item.

The difficulties teachers experience in writing
objectives became apparent to the project team from
their examination of checklist records.  Items on
checklists may be regarded as 'objectives'.  Problems
which the teachers experienced in *using* checklists
will be dealt with later in the chapter (p.177);  one
major difficulty was vague language.  This made for
ambiguous, hence potentially inaccurate, interpretation of the records.  For this reason, writers on
educational objectives have stressed the need for a
precise use of language.

Concerning the choice of words,[9] the verbs listed
below cover nearly all the cognitive processes (i.e.
mental processes concerned with 'knowing' such as
perception, memory imagery, reasoning, etc.):

   (1)  *identify:*  point to, touch, mark, match, pick
        up;

(2)  *name:*  give orally, or in writing, a label/ word for an object;

(3)  *distinguish:*  pick out differences between, find similarities and differences between things;

(4)  *classify:*  put into, or mark, groups with common characteristics;

(5)  *describe:*  supply a verbal (oral or written) account that gives the essential properties, categories and relationships;

(6)  *order:*  list in order, sequence, rearrange, etc.;

(7)  *construct:*  make, draw, design, assemble, prepare, build;

(8)  *demonstrate:*  perform a set of procedures with or without verbal explanation.

The use of these words, together with others which accurately describe the behaviour observed, or to be observed, form the basis of criteria that can be used for assessment.  Such criteria are descriptions of 'competent' behaviour.

Project teachers had certain notions as to what constituted 'competence'.  In recognizing competence in pupils, they generally based their conclusions on 'professional judgement'.  Exactly what is meant by 'professional judgement' was not clear.  It seems that ideas about 'normal' behaviour are built up over years of experience, teaching many children.  This is of little help to the newly qualified teacher who is expected to judge competence.  Carefully written objectives could in some cases be of much assistance.

To say that a pupil is 'competent' in performing a task assumes that the assessor has predefined the characteristics which differentiate the competent from the incompetent.  Any definition of competence will be to some extent subjective and arbitrary, regardless of the method of assessment used.  Of critical importance will be what the pupil will be required to do at the next stage.

In order to clarify what are the essential components of an objective, the following summary is offered:

(1)  a *verb* to indicate the observable behaviour, e.g. point, label, underline, assemble, etc.;

(2)  a *verb* to indicate the mental activity implied, e.g. identify, name, discriminate, classify, generate, etc.;

(3)  an indication of the materials necessary for performance and any restrictions (e.g. time)

or other constraints;
(4)   an indication of the kind of product to be
      produced (when relevant);
(5)   the level of performance and accuracy recog-
      nizable as mastery of the objective (e.g.
      90%).[10]

The acid test for identifying a clearly written objective is:   'Can another competent person select
successful learners in terms of the objectives so
that you, the objective writer, agree with the selection?'[11]

If teachers specified everything taught in the
classroom in terms of such behavioural objectives,
life would be burdensome;   but the discipline is desirable when tests and records are being written.
The writing of objectives is time-consuming and may
only be considered worth while in so far as it helps
to focus attention on the purpose of one's own
teaching and assisting pupils to learn.

### RECORDS AND ASSESSMENT

Teachers are continually assessing their pupils' behaviour despite many emphatic comments to the contrary.   Pupils are judged informally on the basis of
how appropriate their behaviour is to the task in
hand or in relation to the expectations teachers have
in mind.   The keeping of records of pupils' attainment or achievement cannot be divorced from the
methods of assessment used.   The number of assessment
techniques which can be used depends on the amount of
time teachers are prepared to devote to assessing
their pupils in the formal sense.

Teachers are constantly engaged in questioning
pupils.   Many questions are used to test pupils'
learning and, from the answers given, assessments are
made and followed up by the provision of further information, guidance or practice.   Data obtained from
this kind of assessment would be too extensive to be
recorded in detail.   It is therefore necessary at the
curriculum planning stage to consider what 'mile-
stones' in pupils' learning *need* to be recorded.
From meetings with teachers, it appears that questions as to the amount of detail to be recorded are
very difficult to answer.   The quantity of recorded
information varies considerably and depends to some
extent on the capacity of teachers' memories, their
requirements for information, and the fact that
pupils with educational problems tend to generate
more record-worthy information.

Project teachers insisted that records should be easy both to fill in and to understand. This implies that information on school records needs to be written down in an abbreviated form and yet remain wholly comprehensible. Perhaps the simplest way of summarizing data is to use a numerical or alpha-numerical form; i.e. numbers and/or letters. On the records collected, such abbreviation of information was very common. Though the use of abbreviations reduces the clerical workload, the problem of interpretation is increased, particularly for teachers in other schools. This problem of interpretation is not restricted to marks and grades, since many of the phrases and words used by teachers on records and reports incorporate the same elements of ambiguity and imprecision, 'J- is consolidating his knowledge and is making slow progress.' Any person, parent or teacher, reading such a comment is given very little real information about J-'s present level of development, attainment and actual progress.

The following questions need to be asked if a fuller understanding is to be gained.

(1)   What *evidence* was used in order to conclude that the pupil was consolidating?
(2)   How was progress being *measured*?
(3)   If progress was considered to be slow, with what rate is the pupil being *compared*?
(4)   What is the *cause* of the slow progress:
    (*a*)   the need for a period of consolidation;
    (*b*)   illness, lassitude, frequent absence, etc.;
    (*c*)   underfunctioning;
    (*d*)   stress:   due to home circumstances, due to school situations, peer group pressures?

The evidence required to give a degree of objectivity to written comments such as the one above can be obtained in several ways:

(1)   standardized tests;
(2)   teacher-made tests;
(3)   observational techniques, including:
    (*a*)   observation of pupil's written work,
    (*b*)   unstructured observation - anecdotal records,
    (*c*)   structured observation using:
        checklists,
        rating scales,
        standardized attitude scales

(standardized projective techniques/
tests may only be conducted by
trained personnel).

   Methods of collecting information by testing and/
or observing must be related to the kind of assessment
being carried out and the kinds of pupil performance
under examination.  For instance, it would be inappropriate to give a pencil-and-paper test to gather information about a pupil's social behaviour;  observation would be more sensible.

   Three main decisions need to be made when assessing pupils;  these concern the purpose of the assessment, its nature, and the basis for interpreting the
results.

(1)  *Purpose of the assessment*
   (*a*)  *Placement:*  Screening and readiness
         tests used for determining what a pupil
         can already do prior to selecting new
         learning material at an appropriate
         level, e.g. placing a child on a reading
         scheme.
   (*b*)  *Formative:*  Tests or observations used
         to obtain information during a pupil's
         progress through a scheme or course.
         Information is gathered to indicate to a
         pupil how well he is learning and giving
         an early warning of any errors or miscon-
         ceptions, e.g. marking of written exer-
         cises;  using the error analysis charts
         in an SRA *Reading Laboratory*.[12]
   (*c*)  *Diagnostic:*  Where a pupil has been
         making persistent errors, or appears un-
         able to cope with the tasks given, a
         variety of information can be gathered
         to determine the cause of the learning
         difficulty.
   (*d*)  *Summative:*  At the end of a scheme or
         course of study, tests or examinations
         may be given to find out how much a
         pupil has learned.  Marks or grades are
         frequently allotted as a summation or
         summary of progress.
(2)  *Nature of the assessment*
   (*a*)  What a pupil can do when put in a test
         situation designed to elicit maximum
         performance.
   (*b*)  What a pupil does under natural condi-
         tions, typical behaviour exhibited with-
         out the constraints of a test situation.

(3)   *Interpretation of results*

(*a*)   *Relative:* Information from tests can be treated statistically to establish how each pupil's score is related to the average score of a group of pupils. Interpretation carried out on this basis is known as *norm-referencing*, since each score is given in relation to the norm or average of the reference group, i.e. class group, school group, national group.

(*b*)   *Relative to task:* The pupil's attainment is compared with a specified standard or criterion of competence. Interpretation on this basis is known as *criterion-referencing*.

Both interpretations are relative but they are relative to different things:

(i)   to the group of pupils being tested,
(ii)   to the standard of competence.

Grades or ratings on three, five or more points on a scale may be allotted relative to the number of pupils attaining a certain range of scores. Grades or ratings used this way indicate the number of pupils at each level and not the quantity of learning. Ausubel gave a warning in connexion with marks or grades allocated this way:

'... test scores and school marks often become ends in themselves, displacing in importance and presumed validity the knowledge, competencies, and scholastic achievement they are intended to sample and represent ... society places greater weight on a test score or on a diploma from a prestigious institution than on intrinsically more valid long-term evidence of scholarship and fitness to practice a profession. This perversion of the nature and function of measurement is in a sense inevitable in a complex society where the meaning and purpose of symbols tend to get lost in time ...
The tendency to regard test scores as ends in themselves and as more important than the knowledge they represent is much more a *reflection* of undesirable social attitudes about the real value of scholarship than a cause of such attitudes or an inevitable product of measurement and evaluation.'[13]

Despite this, from the evidence, particularly on transfer record cards (see chapter 6), grades or ratings are frequently allotted on a percentage of the group basis regardless of the actual abilities of pupils, e.g.

| Grade | A | B | C | D | E |
|-------|---|---|---|---|---|
| % of group | 5 | 20 | 50 | 20 | 5 |

Grades can, however, be allotted on a criterion-referenced basis, each grade being keyed to a performance objective indicating the quality of a pupil's learning, e.g.

A  Has made no errors in the work on ———.
B  Has made a few errors in the work on ——— but was able to correct them without further prompting.
C  Has made several errors in the work on ——— and has been unable to correct the work without teacher help.

or:

1  Skill well developed, good proficiency.
2  Skill developed satisfactorily, proficiency could be improved.
3  Basic skill developed, low proficiency, needs additional practice.
4  Basic skill not acquired.

*These ratings need to be related to a performance objective if they are to have any substance.*

Once the purposes for assessing pupils have been clarified, the next step is to select an appropriate *method* of collecting information.  The various methods available, listed earlier in the chapter, will be explained in conjunction with some examples of their use in schools included in the survey. Table 4 gives a summary of assessment purposes and techniques.

ASSESSMENT METHODS

*Standardized tests*

The project found widespread use of standardized tests in schools.  Despite their prevalence, however, teachers' interpretation of results quoted on records is still fraught with difficulty because of the wide variety of different tests used (see Table 5, listing tests in use, p.181).  This problem arises where tests from different sources are standardized in different ways, producing scores which are presented in different forms and are not directly comparable. For instance, teachers may well be puzzled by having to compare scores on a test recorded in the form of

Table 4  Summary comparison of basic types of classroom testing*

|  | Placement testing | | Formative testing | Diagnostic testing | Summative testing |
|---|---|---|---|---|---|
|  | Readiness pretest | Placement pretest |  |  |  |
| Focus of measurement | Prerequisite entry skills | Course or unit objectives | Predefined segment of instruction | Most common learning errors | Course or unit objectives |
| Nature of sample | Limited sample of selected skills | Broad sample of all objectives | Limited sample of learning tasks | Limited sample of specific errors | Broad sample of all objectives |
| Item difficulty | Typically has low level of difficulty | Typically has wide range of difficulty | Varies with segment of instruction | Typically has low level of difficulty | Typically has wide range of difficulty |
| When test administered | Beginning of course or unit | Beginning of course or unit | Periodically during instruction | As needed during instruction | End of course or unit |
| Type of instrument | Typically is criterion-referenced mastery test | Typically is norm-referenced survey test | Typically is criterion-referenced mastery test | Specially designed test to identify learning errors | Typically is norm-referenced survey test |
| Use of results | Remedy entry deficiencies or assignment to learning group | Instruction planning and advance placement | Improve and direct learning through ongoing feedback | Remedy errors related to persistent learning difficulties | Assign grades, certify mastery or evaluate teaching |

* Reproduced from N.E. Gronlund, *Measurement and Evaluation in Teaching*, New York: Macmillan, 3rd ed. 1976, table 6.1. This table was adapted from P.W. Airasian and G.F. Madaus, 'Functional types of student evaluation', *Measurement and Evaluation in Guidance* 4, 1972, 221–33.

reading ages with another test where scores are presented in terms of a reading quotient, and yet another with results in the form of standardized scores.

It is useful to consider briefly how standardized
tests[14] are constructed.   The development of these
tests follows a well-established pattern involving
field trials on a representative sample of children
numbering between 2000 and 25 000.   Test items or
questions are selected for their ease or difficulty
and how well they discriminate between the able and
less able child.   Tables of standardized scores are
provided so that an individual score can be compared
with a *national* peer group.

Standardized tests are checked for validity, that
is, that they are testing what they purport to test.
Various factors affecting the validity of a test are
illustrated in the section on 'Teacher-made tests'
(see below).   The reliability of a standardized test
is an important factor, particularly when important
decisions are to be based on the results.   Reliability,
usually expressed as a correlation coefficient (e.g.
0.96)[15] indicates to what degree pupils would obtain
the same, or nearly the same, score on being re-tested.

Readers interested in the details of standardization procedures should refer to textbooks on educational measurement.[16]   Table 5 at the end of this
chapter (pp.181-182) gives a list of standardized
tests used by teachers in our survey.   What to look
for in a standardized test is covered as appendix C.

*Teacher-made tests*

Many teachers met during the project used standardized
tests in order to obtain data which were reliable and
seemingly objective, frequently without considering
whether data of this kind were helpful to them in
making decisions about pupils' future learning.   Tests
made by teachers themselves were often seen to be much
more relevant to this latter purpose.

The following questions should be borne in mind
when devising a test for pupils.   (The term 'test' can
include a range of techniques from pencil-and-paper
tests to informal observation of pupils during normal
activities in school.)

(1)   Why are you constructing a test?   The reasons
      may be various and are presented in table 4,
      p.170.   (Tests have been given purely to
      occupy children quietly for a short time!)
(2)   What are you expecting your pupils to be able
      to do, or 'know', as a result of your teaching,

for which you are setting the test?

(3)   What kinds of activities or behaviours are you asking of your pupils when taking the test?

(4)   What kind of test would be most appropriate for gathering information on the activities selected for examination?

Unless the four questions above are considered before devising the test, the results obtained may be in- valid.  Of the two concepts, validity and reliability, mentioned in connexion with standardized tests, validity is the more important for a teacher-made test.

A vital factor to be considered by teachers, when devising questions in either oral or written form, is the choice of words.  Lack of precision in using vocabulary may lead to a pupil misunderstanding what is required of him.  So, if a pupil gives a 'wrong' answer it may be that he is answering a different question from the one his teacher is asking.  Points made earlier in the chapter concerning the wording of objectives are pertinent to the writing of test questions, since ambiguity can affect the validity of tests.

Some factors to be considered in relation to vali- dity are probably best illustrated by listing the most common faults in question construction:

1.   Unclear directions as to the kind of pupil response required.

2.   Reading vocabulary and sentence structure too difficult for pupils to comprehend.

3.   Inappropriate level of difficulty of test items.

4.   Poorly constructed test items.  Unintentional clues given either within the test item, or a series of items, will reduce the validity.

5.   Ambiguity - leads to misinterpretation and confusion, frequently amongst the more able pupils (brighter pupils frequently see more possibilities in the range of answers to a question).

6.   Test items inappropriate for the outcomes be- ing quantified.  The test attempts to measure higher order reasoning by using wording and question form which is suitable mainly for measuring factual knowledge.

7.   Test too short.  There is an insufficient quantity of items sampling a particular skill or behaviour, or an insufficient sample of

behaviours represented in the test.
8.  Improper arrangement of items.  Items are
    usually placed in order of difficulty.  Diffi-
    cult items early in a test can deter the less
    able pupil and also use up time for trying
    easier questions later on.[17]

Other factors to be considered:

(i)   When objective tests are being constructed,
      one needs to try and avoid identifiable
      patterns of answers emerging.  (Such tests
      have answers - true/false - or a multiple
      choice format.)  Faults in this category
      are similar to (4) above.
(ii)  The use of negative words and phrases can
      make it harder to understand a question.
      As well as any other skills being tested,
      all test questions given in a written form
      will demand a certain level of reading and
      comprehension skill before a pupil can
      respond.
(iii) Where a response in written form is requi-
      red from a pupil, handwriting capabilities
      will to some extent affect his test scores.
      Research studies in the field of examina-
      tions have pointed to the considerable
      effect pupils' handwriting can have on the
      way examiners allocate marks to essays,
      regardless of the quality of knowledge and
      reasoning content.[18]

Should any of these factors be overlooked, the
validity of the test will be reduced.  The degree to
which teachers can ignore the concept of test reliability will depend on the importance placed on the
results and the weightiness of decisions likely to
be based on them.  For general classroom purposes,
where erroneous decisions can be speedily rectified,
the reliability of teacher-made tests is not so critical.
Records which are used for transfer and transition
of pupils were heavily criticized by project teachers
for the difficulties of interpretation which they
presented.  The interpretation of teacher-made test
results which appeared on such records could be
greatly assisted by the inclusion of the following
additional information:

(1)  the range of scores (marks) obtained by the
     class on each test;

(2)   some information on how grades or ratings
      were allocated: what criteria (or guidelines)
      were used in deciding the cut-off points be-
      tween each grade;
(3)   a copy of the test (where possible) and some
      details of the conditions under which the
      pupil was examined or observed;
(4)   (and perhaps) the conversion of raw test
      scores into $z$-scores (see appendix D).

*Observational techniques of assessment*

Many of the comments written on records by teachers,
particularly those concerning pupils' personal,
social and emotional development, are based on casual
observations over a lengthy period.  The evidence for
these comments and the situational context within
which they were made, were generally not included on
the record or report.
   Many of the project teachers expressed suspicion
about 'subjective' comments.  Others tended to avoid
reading them least their own perceptions became pre-
judiced!  For these reasons it was frequently found
that comments on a pupil's personal development would
be put aside for about a month during which time the
new teacher had time to form his/her own opinion.
Conversely, the recipients of transfer and transition
records complained frequently that information on a
pupil's personal and social development was not included.  (From the survey and questionnaire on transfer record content, and from informal contacts at
project workshops, it was evident that teachers in
secondary schools or who had secondary school experience considered this category of information more
important than did their primary teacher colleagues.)
   Since many teachers appeared to devote considerable time to writing about the personal, social and
emotional development of their pupils, it is worth
while considering the aspects of these records to
which many of the project teachers objected.  Consider the following hypothetical, though possibly
typical, example as a basis for criticism:  'T— does
not work as hard as he should, though he seems a
bright child when he tries hard.  He can be annoying
in class.'
   Three main points emerge:

(1)   There is little factual and useful informa-
      tion contained in this statement.
(2)   The teacher shows some dissatisfaction with
      this pupil's work and also some indication

is given of the teacher's perception of him.
(3)   Evaluations of this kind are often based on
imperfect memories and may be a summary of a
few atypical but memorable incidents.
Comments of this kind are frequently written
as end of term or year reports at a time when
teachers are suffering from fatigue.

This type of summary record was frequently found in
infant schools where they were called 'profiles' or
'pen portraits (or pictures)'.
    When writing down observations as opposed to
opinions, there is a need, then, to consider the
following features, identified by Gronlund[19] as cha-
racterizing a good anecdotal record.

1.   It provides an accurate description of a
     *specific* event.
2.   It describes the setting sufficiently to give
     the event meaning.
3.   If it includes interpretation or evaluation by
     the recorder, this interpretation is separated
     from the description and its different status
     is clearly identified.
4.   The event it describes is one related to the
     child's personal development or social inter-
     actions.
5.   The event it describes is either representa-
     tive of the typical behaviour of the child or
     significant because it is strikingly different
     from his usual form of behaviour.  If it is
     unusual behaviour for the child, the fact
     should be noted.

    The following advice, synthesized from project
teacher group deliberations, is also offered to
teachers wishing to improve their observation of
children.

(1)   Determine in advance what to observe but be
      alert for unusual behaviour.
(2)   Observe and record enough of the situation to
      make the behaviour meaningful.
(3)   Make a record of the incident as soon after
      the observation as possible.
(4)   Limit each anecdote to a brief description of
      a single specific incident.  (Limiting each
      description to a single incident simplifies
      the task of writing, using and interpreting
      the records.)
(5)   Keep the factual description of the incident

and your interpretation of it separate. (Use only non-judgemental words in the description. Avoid words such as: lazy, unhappy, shy, hostile, sad, ambitious, persistent, etc.) Interpretations of an incident should be expressed in tentative terms.

(6)   Record both negative and positive behavioural incidents.

(7)   Collect a number of anecdotes on a pupil before drawing inferences concerning typical behaviour.[20]

The writing of good anecdotal records appears to require a great deal of practice and skill.

In contrast to the unstructured nature of observations and their summary in anecdotal records, there are occasions where more systematic observations are called for. Amongst the records collected, two main techniques were found for assisting teachers in structuring observations. Both rating scales and checklists were used widely for assessing pupils' social/personal development.

Rating scales
A carefully produced rating scale can be a useful way of structuring one's observations. Such a scale comprises a list of personal characteristics or qualities that are to be judged and some type of scale for indicating the degree to which each attribute is present. These are the main advantages of using this technique.

(1)   It directs observation toward clearly defined behaviours.

(2)   It provides a common frame of reference for appraising all pupils on the same set of characteristics.

(3)   It provides a convenient method for recording the judgements of several observers.

The judgements of the observer can be presented numerically on a scale, e.g. 1-5 or 1-7, etc. A verbal description is usually given to each point on the scale, e.g.

5   outstanding
4   above average
3   average
2   below average
1   unsatisfactory

Categories such as these were found frequently on records but, to avoid the vagueness of such terms, more specific criteria could be used, e.g. for *co-operation*:

1  refuses to co-operate - usually passive
2  co-operation short-lived, poor concentration
3  co-operates willingly as a rule
4  sometimes offers extra help and assistance
5  wishes to please people and is most willing

Judgements can also be presented graphically and can allow for a greater degree of freedom in assessing behaviours, as in Fig. 4, for *plays with other children*.

never          seldom          occasionally          frequently          always

Fig. 4  Graphical scale for rating behaviours for the item: *plays with other children*. A mark is put along the line according to one's judgement. As in the previous example, more descriptive categories could be used.

Checklists
These are similar to rating scales except that the kind of judgement required tends to be of the *yes/no* variety. One is asked to judge whether a characteristic is present or absent at the particular time when an observation is made. Unless a checklist is extremely lengthy, the number of behaviours included merely represent a sample of those on which a teacher wishes to focus attention (see comments on checklists made earlier in relation to objectives, p.163). This method of assessment was found frequently in infant schools in the form of a 'pre-reading record' and follows a similar pattern to informal reading inventories.[21]
The checklist may be used as a framework for assisting teachers to focus on particular pupil behaviours, traits or development. Whether or not it can be used as a record to communicate meaningfully to other teachers depends greatly on the kind of wording used and the frequency of entries made. Many of the checklist records seen by the project team were criticized by other teachers on the following grounds.

(1)  They were too lengthy and detailed.
(2)  There was a lack of criteria on the record to explain what a *yes/no* or a tick actually re-

presented.
(3)   The instability of assessments (a pupil may
      be able to perform a task one week but unable
      to do the same the following week).

Though teachers who had *devised* checklists generally praised their usefulness, teachers who had *received* them from other schools expressed their preference for a summary comment.  This preference high-
lights the degree of perceived uncertainty in the
interpretation of assessments on checklist.  As mentioned in chapter 4, many teachers tried to overcome
this uncertainty by using a three-category system in
conjunction with their checklist.  The following
example was frequently found:

√  has been introduced to
×  has had satisfactory practice in
*  fully understands this work

Despite this refinement, other teachers criticized
the last two categories for their relative vagueness.

The recognition by many teachers of the limitations of checklists prompted frequent questions to
the project team on how matters could be improved.
We found no simple answer, unfortunately, despite
some searching amongst assessment literature.
Assuming that teachers wish to continue with this
approach to assessment, improvement may only be
effected through the careful use of words and general
agreement on meanings.  Euphemisms in use today originally had, perhaps, more specific meanings.  However, the common use of 'good', 'poor', 'improving'
and 'unsatisfactory' on records and reports weakens
this form of recording due to the wide interpretations possible.
Imprecision can be illustrated by two examples
taken from checklists collected in our survey:

(1)   has a concept of conservation of number;
(2)   knows terms - bigger, smaller, more, less.

The words 'has concept of', 'knows' and 'understands'
are usually reserved for general aims or goals but
have little use in the writing of objectives.  Without wishing to dwell again on the minutiae of objective writing, it is perhaps obvious that the examples
above give little in the way of qualitative information about pupils' attainments.  The following versions give some concrete information as to the form

of assessment used.

   (1)   The pupil can demonstrate with a group of objects his ability to conserve a numerical quantity.

   (2)   The pupil can use the words 'bigger', 'smaller', 'more', 'less' appropriately when comparing groups of objects.

Despite the improvement, there is still no indication of criteria by which a pupil could be judged competent. The number of correct answers or allowable errors remains unclear in these examples. This illustrates the difficulties encountered when assessments are made on a criterion-referenced basis. The lengths one has to go to in making criteria precise enough to avoid ambiguity may not be worth the time and effort spent.

In most of the checklists seen by the project team, several of the important elements, such as competence level, were not made explicit and therefore remained as mere assumptions in the minds of the teachers who compiled the records. When these records were read by teachers from other schools, interpretation of the content was (obviously) found difficult.

Generally, the teachers with whom the project worked found checklists to be a useful way of focusing attention when observing pupils' characteristics. The teachers who had received checklists from other schools expressed the view that, without additional information such as indicated above, this kind of record was of doubtful value. It appears, therefore, that checklists are more successful in communicating the work and topics which a pupil has attempted and experienced than in providing assessment data about achievements.

It was by no means clear what use was made of test results, apart from their being entered on records. It was impossible in the time available to investigate how far teachers habitually diagnosed pupils' learning difficulties from analyses of pupils' responses or behaviours. Most of the project teachers agonized about 'labelling' children, and it would therefore have been interesting to know how results of standardized tests affected teacher expectations of their pupils. In particular, the widespread use of intelligence quotient (IQ) labels may predetermine pupils' futures. It has been suggested that IQs are more often used as excuses by teachers and psychologists for pupils' poor educational performance rather than as an indication perhaps of poor teaching.  Neisworth, writing about the irrelevance of IQ in education, suggests that conventional intelligence tests:

'... can provide fair predictions of school success, assuming we do nothing exceptional to help or hinder certain students and thus destroy the prediction.  Prediction *per se* is of little use since we do not use intelligence tests to make selection decisions.'[22]

'One off' sampling of a pupil's performance in making a diagnosis can be likened to relying on a dipstick reading when finding the general running state of a car.  Accurate diagnosis of pupils' learning difficulties demands observation and perhaps testing over a wide range of activities.

To sum up:  designing and compiling record-keeping systems should come at the final stages of a planning process once answers have been found to the following questions.

(1)  'What am I expected to teach, and in what order?'
(2)  'What educational purposes is my teaching to serve?  What teaching methods are known to achieve these purposes?'
(3)  'What standards of achievement am I expected to aim at?'
(4)  'How will I discover whether the course I've been teaching has been successful or not?'
(5)  'What can I usefully be told about the abilities, interests and attitudes of the pupils I am to teach?'[23]

Table 5 lists the tests that were used in schools visited or contacted by the project.  The tests were used as part of the assessment procedures adopted by teachers, and provided data for ongoing record keeping.

Table 5   Percentage use of tests found in schools visited or
contacted by the project (*n* = 192)

| | % use |
|---|---|
| READING TESTS | |
| *Graded Word Reading Test* (by F.J. Schonell): | |
| Oliver & Boyd | 32 |
| *Reading Tests* A, AD (by A.F. Watts), BD:   NFER | 17 |
| *Standard Test of Reading Skill* (by J.C. Daniels | |
| & H. Diack):   Chatto & Windus | 17 |
| *Neale Analysis of Reading Ability* (by M.D. Neale): | |
| Macmillan Education, also NFER | 17 |
| *Burt (Rearranged) Word Reading Test* (by C. Burt): | |
| Hodder & Stoughton Educational | 13 |
| *Group Reading Test* (by D. Young):   Hodder & Stoughton | |
| Educational | 12 |
| *Holborn (Sentence) Reading Scale* (by A.F. Watts): | |
| Harrap | 11 |
| *Silent Reading Tests* A, B (by F.J. Schonell): | |
| Oliver & Boyd | 7 |
| *Word Recognition Test* (by C. Carver):   Hodder & | |
| Stoughton Educational | 6 |
| *Reading Comprehension Test* DE (by B. Barnard):   NFER | 5 |
| *Southgate Group Reading Tests* 1, 2 (by V. Southgate): | |
| Hodder & Stoughton Educational | 5 |
| *Wide-Span Reading Test* (by M.A. Brimer & H. Gross): | |
| Nelson | 4 |
| *Get Reading Right* (by S. Jackson):   Robert Gibson | 4 |

OTHER READING TESTS USED BY A FEW SCHOOLS
*Edinburgh Reading Tests* (sponsored by Scottish
   Education Department and Educational Institute of
   Scotland):   Hodder & Stoughton Educational
*Crichton Vocabulary Scale* (by J.C. Raven):   NFER
*English Picture Vocabulary Test* (by M.A. Brimer &
   L.M. Dunn):   Educational Evaluation Enterprises
*Group Reading Assessment* (by F. Spooncer):   Hodder &
   Stoughton Educational
*Aston Index* (by M. Newton):   Learning Development
   Aids
*Reading Level Tests* (tests of known readability,
   using *cloze* technique which systematically deletes
   words from passages):   NFER
*Framework for Reading:* checklists for diagnostic
   purposes (by J. Dean & R. Nichols):   Evans
*Swansea Test of Phonic Skills* (from Schools Council
   Compensatory Education Project):   Blackwell
*Reading and Remedial Reading:* screening procedures
   (by A.E. Tansley):   Routledge

Table 5   (cont'd)

|  | % use |
|---|---|
| **ENGLISH LANGUAGE TESTS** | |
| *English Progress Tests* (various authors):  NFER | 12 |
| *Graded Word Spelling Test* (by P.E. Vernon):  Hodder & Stoughton Educational | 6 |
| *Bristol Achievement Tests: English Language* (general editor: M.A. Brimer):  Nelson | 2 |
| *Tests of Proficiency in English:*   listening, reading, speaking, writing: NFER | 1 |
| *An English Language Scale* (by F.J. Watts):  Harrap | 1 |
| **VERBAL REASONING TESTS** | |
| *Verbal Tests* BC (by D.A. Pidgeon), C, CD (by V. Land), D (by T.N. Postlethwaite):  NFER | 26 |
| *Non-verbal Tests:  Picture Test A* (by J.E. Stuart), *Non-verbal Tests* BD (by D.A. Pidgeon), DH (by B. Calvert):  NFER | 10 |
| *Essential Intelligence Tests*:  Forms A, B (by F.J. Schonell & R.H. Adams):  Oliver & Boyd | 3 |
| *Deeside 7+ Picture Test*  (by W.G. Emmett):  Harrap | 2 |
| *Moray House Picture Intelligence Tests* (by M.E. Mellone):  Hodder & Stoughton Educational | 2 |
| *Oral Verbal Intelligence Test* (by D. Young):  Hodder & Stoughton Educational | 2 |
| *Non-readers Intelligence Test* (by D. Young):  Hodder & Stoughton Educational | 1 |
| *Coloured Progressive Matrices*, sets A, Ab, B (by J.C. Raven):  H.K. Lewis, also NFER | |
| **MATHEMATICS TESTS** | |
| *Mathematics Attainment Tests* A, B, Cl, C3, DEl, DE2:  NFER | 30 |
| *Basic Mathematics Tests*:  NFER | 7 |
| *Bristol Achievement Tests:  Mathematics* (general editor:  M.A. Brimer):  Nelson | 2 |
| *Mathematics Grading Tests*:  Schofield & Sims | 2 |
| *Nottingham Number Test* (by W.E.C. Gillham & K.A. Hesse):  Hodder & Stoughton Educational | 1 |
| **OTHER TESTS IN USE** | |
| *Richmond Tests of Basic Skills* (by A.N. Hieronymus *et al.*):  Nelson | 5 |
| *Bristol Social Adjustment Guides* (by D.H. Stott, N.C. Marston & E.G. Sykes):  Hodder & Stoughton Educational | 1 |

See also appendix C, 'What to Look for in a Standardized Test'

REFERENCES

1 R.F. Mager, *Preparing Instructional Objectives*, Palo Alto, California: Fearon Press, 1962, p.vii.
2 A. Clegg, 'Battery fed and factory tested', *Times Educational Supplement*, 11 July 1975.
3 N. Bennett, *Teaching Styles and Pupil Progress*, Open Books, 1976.
4 D. Rowntree, *Educational Technology in Curriculum Development*, Harper & Row, 1975, p.38.
5 P. Ashton *et al.*, *Aims into Practice in the Primary School: a Guide for Teachers* (from the Schools Council Aims of Primary Education project), University of London Press (now Hodder & Stoughton Educational), 1975, aim 45, p.21. The project's list of 72 aims also appears in the companion report by Ashton *et al.*, *The Aims of Primary Education: a Study of Teachers' Opinions* (Schools Council Research Studies): Macmillan Education, 1975.
6 See N.E. Gronlund, *Stating Behavioral Objectives for Classroom Instruction*, New York: Macmillan (UK: Collier-Macmillan), new ed. 1978.
7 *Taxonomy of Educational Objectives: the Classification of Educational Goals:* Handbook I, *Cognitive Domain*, ed. B.S. Bloom, Longmans, 1956; Handbook II, *Affective Domain*, by D.R. Krathwohl *et al.*, Longmans, 1964. A.J. Harrow, *A Taxonomy of the Psychomotor Domain: a Guide for Developing Behavioral Objectives*, New York: McKay, 1972.
8 H. Sockett, 'Bloom's Taxonomy: a philosophical critique', *Cambridge Journal of Education* 1 (Lent), 1971, 16-25.
9 H.J. Sullivan, 'Objectives, evaluation, and improved learner achievement', in *Instructional Objectives*, by W.J. Popham *et al.* (American Educational Research Association monograph 3), Chicago: Rand McNally, 1969. The version of the list included here closely follows that in Gronlund (see note 18), p.68.
10 R.M. Gagné and L.S. Briggs, *Principles of Instructional Design*, New York: Holt, Rinehart, 1974.
11 Mager (see note 1), p.12.
12 Science Research Associates, *Reading Laboratory* series, Henley-on-Thames: SRA, 1973—.
13 D.P. Ausubel, *Educational Psychology: a Cognitive View*, New York: Holt, Rinehart, 1968, p.571.
14 Nationally standardized tests are produced commercially by test publishing agencies such as NFER-Nelson (former NFER tests and former Nelson tests such as *Bristol Achievement Tests*, general editor: M.A. Brimer; *Richmond Tests of Basic Skills* by A.N. Hieronymus *et al.*), Hodder & Stoughton Educational (*Moray House Tests* by G.H. Thomson *et al.*), etc.
15 For some information on reliability and standard error of measurement, see for instance the general information

section at the beginning of the NFER-Nelson *Catalogue of Tests for Educational Guidance and Assessment*.

16  A useful *free* booklet is available from NFER-Nelson.

17  Based on N.E. Gronlund, *Measurement and Evaluation in Teaching*, New York:  Macmillan (UK:  Collier-Macmillan), 3rd rev. ed. 1976, pp.98-9.

18  P. Hartog and E.C. Rhodes, *The Marks of Examiners*, Macmillan, 1936.  (Other references show that unreliability of essay markings can be linked with further factors such as marker fatigue.)

19  See Gronlund (see note 17), p.432.

20  Abridged from Gronlund (see note 18), pp.433-5.

21  See e.g. R. Strang, *The Diagnostic Teaching of Reading*, New York:  McGraw-Hill, 1969.

22  J.I. Neisworth, 'The educational irrelevance of intelligence', in *Teacher Diagnosis of Educational Difficulties*, ed. R.M.E. Smith, Columbus, Ohio:  Merrill, 1969, p.45.

23  P.H. Taylor, *How Teachers Plan their Courses:  Studies in Curriculum Planning*, Slough:  NFER Publishing Co., 1970, p.72.

# 8    Confidentiality

Consideration of this topic may well best be introduced by looking at two recent and wholly contradic-
tory statements.

'Confidentiality is not sinister but is designed to protect the
very pupils on whom records are made.'
                    (meeting of National Union of Teachers, May 1977)

'One is surprised that teachers who are themselves parents have
not long ago revolted against this pernicious and wholly
immoral practice [the keeping of confidential records].'
                    (letter to *The Teacher*, 10 November 1972)

Concern about who should have access to school records has been expressed to the project team more
often than about any other issue connected with record keeping.  Whilst most LEA records are still
labelled 'confidential' and internal records are implicitly assumed to be so, an increasingly vocal
campaign has been mounted to 'open' school records to
parents.
     This chapter is divided into two parts.  The first
briefly describes the background to the confidentiality controversy and will give some indication of
the range of views held by teachers interviewed in
the earlier stages of the project.  The second part
of the chapter suggests possibilities for future
policy, since it is the outcome of developmental work
of one of the project teacher groups and its production of guidelines for teachers in the way they should
deal with 'sensitive' information.

### BACKGROUND TO THE CONFIDENTIALITY ISSUE

Until quite recently it was generally accepted that
keeping comprehensive and detailed school records was
part of the primary teacher's professional commitment
and that such records should only be accessible to
those of similar professional occupation.  Many teachers interviewed by the project team subscribed to

this view and most LEAs also appeared to be quite
satisfied with this policy.

A survey of school records in 102 LEAs in England
and Wales instigated in 1975 by *Where*,[1] the journal
of the Advisory Centre for Education, indicated little
change in LEA policy since the NFER survey findings
published in 1955.[2]   The 1955 report stated that
three-quarters of LEAs would in no circumstances
allow parents either to see the children's records or
be informed in detail of their contents.   Two decades
later, *Where* reported that of the 88 LEAs which had
replied to the questionnaire, only one had formally
given parents full permission to see the records of
their children and twelve, at the head's discretion
only.[3]   The *Where* survey also reported that over half
the LEAs were in the middle of reviewing their record
systems and were considering policy changes.

Many teachers interviewed by the project team
linked the keeping of confidential records with professionalism.  'Record cards are confidential.  Their
contents are intended as an aid to diagnosis and to
treatment and are of necessity recorded in somewhat
technical terms.  They are like the case-books of the
physician and like them, they require for their interpretation, the skilled judgement of the expert.[4]  This
view had the support of the main teacher unions.  Of
those who were in favour of keeping confidential records, three main opinions linking confidentiality to
professionalism predominated:

(1)   Records are solely concerned with the passing
      on of information to other professionals -
      they have nothing to do with parents.
(2)   As the headteacher is responsible for the
      school, she/he should choose what information
      should be disseminated and to whom.  As a
      professional, the head reserves the right of
      control over records.
(3)   Teachers have professional responsibilities
      in the same way as doctors, lawyers and social
      workers;  therefore as professionals they are
      entitled to keep their own records.  Confiden-
      tiality is part and parcel of professionalism.

There is some support for these views in law, since
it is recognized that the recipient of confidential
information has a general duty not to disclose it to
'unauthorized' persons without the consent of the individual concerned.  There is also an implied right
to disclose confidential information to colleagues
where, at the professional discretion, say, of the

teacher and in accordance with the practice in the
profession, it is proper to do so.  It is also well
established in law that confidential reports are the
property of those who prepare them (and in the last
instance their employers) and not of parents or
guardians of the children about which the reports are
made.  In fact parents have *no* legal right of access
to their children's records.

Therefore, in the eyes of the law, unless specifically instructed to do so by his/her employer, a
teacher is entitled to refuse to disclose confidential information concerning a pupil.  Furthermore,
the passing on of such confidential information to
those in his/her profession who have a professional
interest in receiving it, is justified in legal
terms.[5]  For example, a teacher is legally entitled
to refuse a request for information from parents and
is also able to pass on information about pupils to
other people within the educational service without
the knowledge or consent of their parents.

In addition to the professional/confidentiality
link, teachers gave other reasons for restricting
access to school records.

(1)   If records are seen by parents, useful but
      potentially embarrassing information may be
      omitted or 'driven underground'.
(2)   The confidential nature of most record cards
      ensures that an honest and frank account of
      pupil progress and development is made.
(3)   Often school records are far too technical
      and jargonistic for parents to understand.
      If parental access is granted, records may,
      as a result, be misinterpreted or misunder-
      stood.

A further point, made in a report of one of the
numerous LEA working parties considering record
keeping, is that some recorded information, though
useful as a background to providing effective help
for a child, would be hurtful to parents if seen and
therefore should be withheld from them.[6]  This consideration was frequently mentioned in teacher group
discussion.

There was a great deal of support among teachers
for retaining the right to keep confidential records
on school pupils.  However, the research team also
found considerable support for the opening of school
records to parents, and found that access to school
records was often equated with moves towards parental
involvement in school activities and growing concern

about 'secret' records in general.

Anxiety has been expressed about the possible erosion of freedom caused by the expanding use of computers and other advanced technology in processing information about the individual. 'Government information concerning individuals the accuracy of which cannot be determined or corrected by the individual concerned, is subject to no external control. The dangers to personal privacy and personal right have been highlighted by the advent of the computer.'[7]

On both sides of the Atlantic, moves have been made to check collection and storage of personal information. The United States Congress ratified an Act concerning the privacy of the individual in 1974 which states the following.

'Sec. 2(a) the Congress finds that:

1. the privacy of an individual is directly affected by the collection of, maintenance, use and dissemination of personal information by Federal (State) agencies
2. the increasing use of computers and sophisticated technology ... has greatly magnified the harm to individual privacy
3. in order to protect the privacy of individuals ... it is necessary and proper ... to regulate the *collection, maintenance, use and dissemination* of information of such agencies.'[8]

The Act further sought to provide safeguards for the individual to determine 'what records pertaining to him are collected, maintained, used or disseminated ... to prevent records pertaining to him to be used or made available ... without his consent, ... to permit (him) ... to gain access to information pertaining to him ...'[9]

A United States statute more specifically concerned with national rights and standards regarding the use of school records, the Family Educational Rights and Privacy Act (known as the Buckley Amendment) was also passed in 1974. It contains several important features including guaranteeing to parents or guardians the right to inspect their child's records; it protects the confidentiality of student records, i.e. to check the unnecessary spread of information, and it provides procedures through which parents can challenge questionable recorded information.

In this country in 1977 a Private Member introduced into Parliament the Freedom of Information and Privacy Bill. This was not, in fact, based on the US Privacy Act (1974) but took as its underlying premise the

principle already in operation in the Swedish consti-
tution - that all official information should be
openly accessible (with certain categories of information excepted).[10]

In addition to this, Government White Papers have
been published on the subject of computers and privacy. The right of the individual not to have information concerning him or her spread to those who have
no right to know it has now been agreed upon, but no
recommendation concerning that individual's right to
inspect, and where necessary correct, such information has yet been made. The following extract, from
the 1975 Government White Paper entitled *Computers
and Privacy*, gives recommendations for good computer
practice. The points were selected for their relevance to record keeping in schools.

(1) Information should be regarded as held for a
    specific purpose and not be used, without
    appropriate authorization, for other purposes.
(2) Access to information should be confined to
    those authorized to have it for the purpose
    for which it was supplied.
(3) The amount of information collected and held
    should be the minimum necessary for the
    achievement of a specified purpose.
(4) There should be arrangements whereby the sub-
    ject could be told about the information held
    concerning him.
(5) In the design of information systems, periods
    should be specified beyond which the informa-
    tion should not be retained.
(6) Data held should be accurate. There should
    be machinery for the correction of inaccuracy
    and the updating of information.
(7) Care should be taken in coding value judge-
    ments.[11]

Worry about the proliferation of secret records in
schools led to the formation in 1976 of a pressure
group, The Campaign Against Secret Records on School
Children, and at about the same time the Confedera-
tion for the Advancement of State Education (CASE)
called on schools to grant parents access to all profiles and records concerning their children.

Though no legislation in this country has yet
granted parents legal access to records in the same
way as the US Buckley Amendment prescribes (see
above), many parents and teachers argue that parents
have a *moral* right to see their children's records
and, what is more, that there are practical disadvan-

tages to keeping confidential school records.

'1 - teachers who use them know that they cannot be held account-
    able for anything which is recorded in them.
 2 - children whose records contain inaccurate or imprecise in-
    formation are denied any real hope of redress.
 3 - [where records play an important part in decisions on the
    future of the child] child and parents are shut out from
    any real knowledge of the evidence on which these deci-
    sions are taken.[*]
 4 - a certain relationship exists between teachers and parents.
    By and large it is one of mutual trust and co-operation.
    By using these secret records, teachers are putting that
    relationship at risk.'[12]

The team found that teachers who favoured parental
access to school records saw no great problem in
adopting an open record policy.  They argued that, if
schools were interested in involving parents in educational decisions and activities, an open record
policy was inevitable, and gave the following reasons
for schools adopting such a policy.

(1)   Since all records kept by the school are and
      should be factual, there can be no objections
      to records being open.
(2)   Teachers should be prepared to show internal
      records to parents and discuss the contents
      with them.  If parents do not understand what
      is written, teachers should explain where
      possible.  Teachers have a professional
      responsibility to be frank with parents.
(3)   The possibility of the abuse of records by a
      minority of teachers should be avoided.
(4)   Where parents are able to see the school re-
      cord, they are in a position to check that
      background information is accurate and up to
      date.

With reference to the last point, many teachers
cited personal experience of some kind of error given
permanent credence by being written on the school
record card.  The point made was that, where a closed
record system operated, no means existed by which an
information error could be formally checked and
corrected, e.g. a father was described on the record
as being out of work and in trouble with the police;

* Teachers are strongly urged to consult with their Chief Education Officer about problems related to court orders over
  custody and evidence required in similar litigation.

in fact he had been on sick leave and had committed a
parking offence.  This error was discovered only when
another teacher, who happened to know the man in
question, saw the record by chance and was able to
put the matter right.  Examples of record keeping
abuses were quoted in *Where*.

'A teacher wrote "dirty sexual habits" into a 10-year old boy's
record after one incident.  (Kent)

A primary schoolgirl had "vicious tendencies" according to one
teacher.  Her next teacher failed to find them ...

... an entry on a girl's record said she came from a very free-
thinking family "because her parents had taken her to an anti-
nuclear demonstration".'[13]

Most teachers, whether for or against confidential
records, would undoubtedly disapprove of the above
comments.  However, it was frequently pointed out
that it is only when parents are given formal permission to check the records of their children that
abuses such as these can be recognized.  Further reference to accuracy in record keeping is made later
in the chapter.
     An additional point made by one teacher was that
the responsibility for accuracy of information
written on the school record differs according to LEA
record policy.  Where records are available for
parents to see, accuracy is the joint responsibility
of the teacher and the parents.  Where the record
system is closed, accuracy is the sole responsibility
of the teacher, who often only sees the pupil in the
school context and therefore has no means of checking
background information.
     In visits to schools in LEAs operating an open re-
cord policy, two salient points emerged.  First, the
amount of information actually written on the records
was greatly reduced.  Secondly, several headteachers
drew attention to the fact that the proportion of
parents actually requesting to see the records of
their children was minimal.  Headteachers, in fact,
deliberately pass on certain information to parents
orally.
     Whilst the team found that teachers were very con-
cerned about the issue of confidentiality, no one
view predominated and the attitudes of teachers towards this issue ranged widely, from vehement opposition to open records, to enthusiastic support.  Many
teachers were in two minds, feeling that, though parents needed to be kept closely informed about the
academic progress of their children, some information

was perhaps better withheld.

The following comments were typically made by teachers holding this middle-of-the-road view.

(1)   Perhaps the only record which should not be revealed to parents is that containing information on the personality and social background of the child.

(2)   Perhaps records should only be shown to parents in the presence of the head or class teacher, who could then explain any misconception or misunderstanding.

(3)   If the headteacher is not prepared to show school records to parents, at least she/he should be prepared to quote appropriate passages from the record.

One headteacher said that school records should be made available to nine-tenths of parents and seemed to see no problem in how the 'approved' parents should be selected.

In summary, whilst teachers were very concerned about the relationship between record keeping and confidentiality (and often argued very cogently from one view point or another), there was little agreement except in very general terms, i.e. that the interests of the child must be respected at all costs.

One of the six project teacher groups, working very closely with the research team, chose to examine in depth the issue of confidentiality and the next part of the chapter shows how this particular group of teachers sought to provide a code of conduct for teachers in their treatment of information on school records.

POSSIBILITIES FOR FUTURE POLICY

The main task of the group was to review the whole debate on the keeping of 'secret' records and to make recommendations. Increasingly the group became aware of the need to identify where the roots of the controversy lay. Early on in the discussion it became apparent that the opening of school records, say to parents, rarely arouses much response where only academic information is concerned. However, when other, more 'sensitive' kinds of information are recorded, such as home background or pupil personality traits, the reaction is often far stronger.

In the light of the consensus of the group, it was with certain sensitive information that the defenders and detractors of secret and open records were prin-

cipally concerned.  Guidelines were developed for the
use and protection of this sensitive information.  It
is not possible to give a permanent solution to the
problem but the following is an honest attempt to
give help.

*Guidelines on recording sensitive
information on school records*

The following factors should be considered when using
or writing records or reports which contain 'sensitive' information.

I     What do we mean by 'sensitive' information?
(1)   Any information
      (*a*)  which may be seen as being hurtful and/or
            embarrassing if divulged to the parent or
            pupil who is the subject of the record;
      (*b*)  which may adversely affect the future (in
            or out of school) of the child.  This may
            include home background, parental attitudes,
            certain medical information, personal quali-
            ties of the child, e.g. honesty-dishonesty.
(2)   Any communication from an external supporting
      agency should be treated as sensitive unless
      otherwise stated.  By external supporting agen-
      cies is meant educational or child psychologists,
      members of the educational welfare and school
      medical services, social workers.

II    Types of records kept in school
(1)   *The official permanent record* (OPR) supplied by
      the LEA for the purpose of communicating informa-
      tion about pupils at the point of transfer to
      other schools.
(2)   *Records and reports* to and from external welfare
      agencies (see I.2) and to parents.
(3)   *Internal formal school records*, e.g. checklists,
      schemes of work, samples of work.
(4)   *The teacher's own private day-to-day notes*,
      which may contain marks, jottings or anecdotes
      about a pupil's development.  This private record
      is not generally passed on to other colleagues.
      The contents may however be used as a basis for:
      (*a*)  discussion with colleagues,
      (*b*)  completing internal school records and the
            OPR,
      (*c*)  writing reports to parents or officers of
            the supporting welfare agencies.
(5)   For the purposes of guidelines, when we refer to
      school records, it will be in relation to the

types II.1 to II.3 and will exclude the teacher's day-to-day notes (II.4).

III Purpose of recording sensitive information
(1) Information of a sensitive nature is often kept in schools to enable teachers to provide appropriately for, and deal sympathetically with, children in their care. Much information may also be kept to give a clear indication of a pupil's current stage of development.
(2) Only facts which the teacher perceives as relevant *for the ultimate benefit of the child*, should be written down.

IV Responsibility (usually of the teacher) in recording and using sensitive information
(1) On the permanent record, all entries containing information of a sensitive nature should be dated and signed by the teacher and/or headteacher. Any person adding information to the record should similarly accept responsibility for what he/she writes.
(2) Sensitive information should be communicated where possible on a face-to-face basis -- where the recipient makes a written note of the communication, the reading back of the notes to the donor can highlight any inaccuracy or misunderstanding.
(3) Where information is sought by telephone, the credentials of the inquirer and the purpose of the inquiry should be checked. If doubts arise, the inquirer should be referred to the Chief Education Officer or the legal department of the LEA.
(4) Teachers receiving information should verify it prior to entry on the appropriate record. The purpose and method of entry should take into account the permanent or transitory nature of the information and the possible need to qualify or update the entry (see section V).
(5) Where a parent or parents volunteer information 'in confidence' concerning their child, they should be made aware that other supporting agencies (see I.2) may request information from the permanent record. Where parents object to certain information being divulged, their wishes should be respected if possible. In cases where the restriction of information may adversely affect the child, such objections may be overridden.
(6) Agencies or individuals supplying information to

schools should:
- (a)   state the purpose for passing on the information to the school;
- (b)   be informed of the LEA policy towards parental access to records, i.e. whether or not
parents are allowed to see the official
permanent record;
- (c)   in the light of (b), state whether this information be attached to the OPR.

V   Procedure for updating/deleting and protecting
sensitive information
(1)   School records should be regularly reviewed
(annually at a minimum) and updated where
necessary (see also IV.4).  Out-of-date or irrelevant information should be qualified or
altered but not erased.
(2)   Where information from the permanent record is
passed on to supporting agencies, the validity
of the information should be reviewed prior to
communication.
(3)   Records containing sensitive information should
not be left unattended for the casual observer
to see or in a place where they could fall into
the hands of unauthorized or irresponsible
persons.
(4)   Conversations concerning sensitive information
on pupils should be avoided in places where they
might be overheard.

VI   Access to school records
(1)   Where an LEA has a policy of *open* records, this
generally means that parents are allowed to see,
if they wish, the official permanent record of
their children.  Additionally parents may be
allowed to see the internal formal records of
their children.
(2)   Where an LEA has a policy of *confidential* records, this generally means that access to these
records is restricted to the schools' psychological service, educational administration and
the educational welfare and medical services.

VII   General principles for recording sensitive
information
(1)   Whether the policy of the LEA is open or closed,
certain criteria need to be considered.
- (a)   In all situations particular attention
should be paid to regularly checking and
validating information written on records.
- (b)   All entries on the record need to be made

accurately and as objectively as possible. In general, facts rather than opinions should be noted.
(c) Access to school records should be restricted to those directly responsible for the child and to the head. Other people actively responsible for the welfare of the child may be allowed to see the record subject to permission of the head.

These guidelines may prove helpful to teachers and policy makers who are concerned about the content, organization and ethics of current school recording practice. However, teachers should be aware of the possibility of abuse, misunderstanding and error in record keeping, and must be prepared to accept responsibility for what they write, that parents' wishes should be respected, and that school records should be regularly reviewed and updated.

## REFERENCES

1  Advisory Centre for Education, 'The *Where* survey of school records', *Where* 109, October 1975, 261-5.
2  A.S. Walker, *Pupils' School Records*, Newnes, 1955.
3  Since 1975, several more authorities, e.g. ILEA, Clwyd, have opened their official cards to parents.
4  C.M. Fleming, *Cumulative Records* (Educational Research Pamphlets, 1), University of London Press, 1945.
5  For further information, see J.D. McLean, *The Legal Context of Social Work*, Butterworth, 1975, pp.15-16.
6  Hampshire LEA, *Report of the Working Party on Pastoral Care Arrangements in Secondary Schools*, June 1975.
7  A. Lewis, MP, 'The right to know', *Sanity*, 1978, p.4.
8  United States Congress, Privacy Act 1974 (88 Stat. 1 896, 5USC 552a note).
9  Ibid., Sec. 2 (b).
10  If this had been passed, decisions would have been needed on whether the term 'official' should include *internal* school records.
11  Government White Paper, *Computers and Privacy*, Cmnd 6353, HMSO, December 1975, Table 1, 'The Younger Committee's principles'.
12  P. McNamee, 'School records on pupils:  secret from parents - open to abuse?', *Where* 109, October 1975, p.259.
13  Ibid., p.260.

# 9    Open plan study

This particular study was not part of the original
research proposal;  it was undertaken as a result of
classroom observation and interviews with teachers in
the initial research phase.  As has been mentioned
earlier in this report (p.16), several incidents
occurred which caused the researchers to question
whether school records performed different or more
complex functions in open plan schools as compared
with traditionally organized classrooms.

Thus the open plan study was initiated to find
out:

(1)    what kind of records were being used in
       schools designated as 'open plan';
(2)    the major considerations and problems of
       keeping records in open plan schools;
(3)    whether the functions and systems of recor-
       ding differed according to teaching style,
       e.g. co-operative[1] or independent teaching.

The team wanted to find out if it was really
the case that:

'In a team teaching situation, keeping records will become
more complicated.  Each record will have to serve the requirements of a number of teachers ... the various aspects of a
child's progress will be recorded by different teachers and
this will mean that a child's record must always be kept up to
date if the most suitable type of work is to be prepared for
the child.'[2]

This chapter is divided into three sections.  The
first briefly describes the general background to
open plan schools;  the second describes the study
and the overall results;  and the third section considers the record keeping implications for co-operative teaching.  This last section also includes
examples of records used by teachers adopting a co-
operative teaching style.

BACKGROUND TO THE STUDY

It is fairly difficult to pinpoint the exact reason
for the emergence of open plan schools in the late
1960s and early 1970s.  Some will argue that this form
of school building was designed to provide a more
flexible teaching and learning environment, whereas
others will recognize economic restrictions as the
fundamental reason for open plan development.  (The
Plowden Report[3] noted that there were considerable
economic advantages to the design of compact schools.)

Whatever viewpoint is seen as most likely, there
are now more than 1500 schools which have been designated by their LEAs as 'open plan', most of which
have been built since 1970.  However, though the
schools share the same designation, they vary considerably in almost every other way.  'Schools included
in this category vary enormously in basic design, in
the type and orientation of space and in size of
space, in addition to the enormous variety of
teaching approaches found within them.'[4]

Neville Bennett found, in a survey carried out in
1975,[5] that the definitions of 'open plan' schools
given by individual LEAs differed considerably.  Of
thirteen different definitions the three most popular
were as follows.

'An Open Plan school is one which facilitates joint use of space
and resources leading to co-operation between teachers and flexible grouping of children.'  [15 authorities]

'An Open Plan school is one in which the teaching area is not
divided into classrooms as such, but which provides home bases
together with joint general purpose and specialist areas.'
[11 authorities]

'An Open Plan school is one which consists of varied and flexible interconnecting units with some type of moveable parti-
tions, to facilitate different teaching styles.'  [10 authori-
ties]

Though LEAs differed in their emphasis on co-
operative teaching approaches in relation to open
plan schools, when comparisons were made between open
plan and traditional schools, the most distinguishing
feature was in building design.  Bennett and his team
thus focused on school architecture when formulating
a classification system.  They adopted the teaching
unit rather than the school as a basis of a three-
dimensional classification:  the number of teachers
for whom the unit was designed (two, three, four or
more);  the type of shared space, i.e. were there

shared teaching spaces, practical wet areas, etc.;
and the number of enclosures, e.g. quiet areas, class
bases.  Preliminary research findings showed that
paired units were most popular and also that there
was considerable variation in the number, kinds and
sizes of enclosures.[6]

In addition to the information given above, the
Schools Council project, Open Plan Schools:  an
inquiry (directed by Bennett), provided the project
team with the names and addresses of the schools from
which a sample was drawn, and it is to the study of
record keeping in open plan schools that we now turn.

RECORD KEEPING IN OPEN PLAN SCHOOLS

The open plan project team were helpful to the record
keeping researchers in two ways.  First, care was
taken to include items on record keeping in questi-
onnaires sent nationally to the headteachers of all
open plan schools and to the teachers in a third of
those schools.  Information was thus received from a
national sample on the kinds of record kept, the type
and frequency of recording, recent school-based innovation in record keeping, and the proportion of
schools sending written reports to parents.

Virtually all teachers kept some form of school
records (less than 1% kept none at all) though, not
surprisingly, more of those exclusively teaching
juniors (43.5%) and teaching the general primary
range (31.8%) perceived record keeping as a collaborative activity - i.e. records were kept by both
teachers and pupils - than did infant teachers (15.9%).

A pattern emerged when type and frequency of
record keeping were examined.  Records in basic
skills were kept either daily or weekly;  records in
project or topic work, though not kept by all
teachers, were usually completed weekly or at the end
of each term;  and social-personal and physical
skills records were mainly filled in at the end of
each term or year.

In response to questions about whether or not parents were kept informed by written report, whereas
more than four-fifths of junior teachers indicated
that a written report was sent to parents, the percentage fell to 29% of infant teachers (Table 6).

When headteachers were asked whether there had
been recent developments in record keeping in their
school, nearly three-quarters (73%) indicated that
record keeping changes had been made in the area of
basic skills and nearly half (44%), in the area of
social-personal record keeping.  (For further details

Table 6   Percentages of teachers in open plan schools making
written reports to parents

| Frequency | Age range taught | | |
|---|---|---|---|
| | Primary | Exclusively junior | Exclusively infant |
| Once yearly | 52.7 | 60.2 | 24.3 |
| Twice yearly | 8.6 | 19.4 | 3.7 |
| Three times yearly | 0.4 | 1.3 | 0.9 |
| No report | 38.3 | 19.1 | 71.1 |

see appendix F.)   As many of the schools had, however,
been in existence for five years or less, a high incidence of recent record development is not surprising.
The second way in which the open plan team helped
was by asking headteachers to indicate in the
national questionnaire whether they personally were
willing to provide information specifically for the
record keeping project.   The six hundred headteachers
who indicated willingness to co-operate were contacted and asked to provide a copy of any school-based
record currently in use, a brief description of their
school record system, and information about any problems, specific to open plan schools, experienced in
setting up a record keeping system.
Over half the headteachers (317) replied, though
52 declared their interest in the work of the project
but had no wish to become directly involved.   Some 30
or 40 were too late in replying for inclusion in the
study.   The letter sent to the schools was deliberately open-ended, so that the replies might show up
as wide a range of record keeping activities (and
problems) as possible.   Though the researchers found
initial difficulties in collating widely differing
forms of data and description, patterns soon emerged
which made data analysis fairly straightforward.   The
replies were analysed in terms of type of school
(e.g. infant, primary, middle);   the types of record
kept (e.g. phonics, science, transfer);   the organizational factors specifically related to open plan
schools (e.g. predominant teaching style);   and problems or special factors connected with record keeping
in open plan schools.

*Types of school*

There were more primary and infant schools in the
sample than any other school type.   Junior and middle
schools were somewhat under-represented compared with

other types (Table 7).   However, as we were dependent
for our sample on headteachers' willingness to work
with the project and as there was insufficient time
to recruit other schools to the study, we were unable to correct the bias of the sample.

Table 7   School types in the sample
of open plan schools

| Type | No. | % |
|------|-----|---|
| Primary | 90 | 45.5 |
| Infant | 50 | 25.3 |
| First | 18 | 9.1 |
| Junior | 28 | 14.1 |
| Middle | 5 | 3.0 |
| Other | 2 | 1.0 |

*Types of record kept*

The research team decided to categorize the types of
records according to labels used by the headteacher
respondents rather than by fitting them into a theoretical framework formulated by the project.   This
decision was made because, for this study, the team
wanted to have as little influence as possible on the
kinds of information sent in by the headteachers.
Hence 45 kinds of school record were identified.
These included subject-based records (e.g. reading,
science), 'functional' records (e.g. summary or
transfer), and administrative records (e.g. card index, admission forms).
   Over 80% of all schools in the sample kept some
kind of record of language development.   Individual
reading records, kept by 63% of the schools, were far
the most common, with phonics (11%) and traditional
grammar (9%) coming a weak second and third.   Most of
the schools kept records of mathematical development
(over 80%), usually in the form of concept or topic
checklists.   Infant and first schools were particularly mathematically oriented;   over 90% of these
schools kept some kind of mathematics record.   An
indication of the emphasis being placed on continuity and transfer record procedures by LEAs is
that official transfer record cards were compulsory
for nearly half the sample schools (43%).
   Handwritten profiles (i.e. unstructured comments)
were the next most popular type of record, kept by
35% of all schools - rather more so in infant schools
(54%) than primary (28%) or junior (28%).   Also,

nearly a third of the sample schools (29%) used
itemized summary records with headings such as
'mathematics', 'language', 'personality', usually
filled in termly or yearly.

A way of recording emerged which had not seriously
been considered earlier in the work of the project
but which apparently appeals to many open plan
schools;   a quarter of all schools collected either
typical (23%) or significant (2%) samples of pupil
work.   More middle (60%)[7] and primary (29%) schools
used this form of record keeping than any other
school type;   however, infant (22%) and junior (14%)
were well represented in this category.

Other types of records kept by teachers in open
plan schools included admissions forms (25% of the
sample), standardized test scores (17%), reports to
parents (20%) and day-to-day record books (24%).
Only 2% of sample schools considered it necessary to
keep records on either physical or scientific development.

The project was particularly interested in finding
out whether methods of recording which might be considered especially appropriate to co-operative
teaching in open plan schools would be substantially
represented.   In fact this was not the case.   Records
which could be thought of as useful in team teaching,
e.g. assignment sheets (records kept by pupils), were
used in very few of the schools.   Twelve per cent of
all the schools in the sample kept records on work
covered by a group;   9% of the sample kept topic or
thematic records;   9% formally allowed pupils to keep
their own records (usually in the form of daily or
weekly assignment sheets) and only 8% recorded the
work undertaken by each pupil.

This apparent lack of use of records which could
be regarded as particularly appropriate to co-
operative teaching in open plan schools, led the project to make an additional small study of the
differences in patterns of record keeping (if any)
existed) between those open plan schools employing
predominantly traditional classroom-based teaching
styles, those in which the predominant mode of
teaching was co-operative and in those which used
both methods in fairly equal proportions.   The findings of this study are reported later in the chapter
(p.204).

The total number of records kept by each school
ranged from a single (5% of sample) record to 13 records per pupil (1% of sample).   As can be seen from
Table 8, most schools regarded between 3 and 7 records (average 5) for each child as sufficient.   How-

Table 8  Total numbers of records kept by open plan schools

| School type | No. of records kept | | | | | | | | | | |
|---|---|---|---|---|---|---|---|---|---|---|---|
| | 1 | 2 | 3 | 4 | 5 | 6 | 7 | 8 | 9 | 10 | 13 |
| | % | % | % | % | % | % | % | % | % | % | % |
| Primary | 1 | 7 | 12 | 20 | 13 | 19 | 9 | 4 | 7 | 3 | 1 |
| Infant | 6 | 2 | 12 | 18 | 24 | 18 | 12 | - | 2 | 2 | - |
| First | 5 | 11 | 17 | 22 | 5 | 17 | 17 | 5 | - | - | - |
| Junior | 7 | 11 | 11 | 21 | 21 | 4 | 11 | 11 | - | 4 | 1 |
| Middle | - | - | 20 | - | - | - | 40 | - | - | 20 | - |
| All schools | 5 | 7 | 12 | 20 | 16 | 16 | 11 | 4 | 4 | 3 | 1 |

ever, several schools kept as many as 10 separate records and two as many of 13.

*Organizational factors specifically related to
open plan schools*

In describing the organization of their schools,
headteachers in our sample mentioned teaching style
and regular consultation with staff as having most
impact on the way they kept school records.  Headteachers from 88 schools referred to the predominant
teaching style in their schools, of which 48% were
mainly class-based using traditional class teaching
methods;  31% generally used co-operative teaching
methods;  and 22% used both teaching styles.  Staff
meetings and consultations as a feature of record
keeping were mentioned by 15% of all the headteachers
in our sample.

*Problems or special factors connected with
record keeping in open plan schools*

The record keeping problem most frequently mentioned
in open plan schools was that of optimal size and
scope of recording.  Nearly two-fifths of sample
headteachers (37%) wrote of the difficulty of making
their system of record keeping sufficiently comprehensive and detailed and yet, at the same time,
keeping recording to the minimum so as not to make it
too consuming of teacher time.  Other difficulties
included problems of staff agreement in devising a
standard school record system (11%) and concern about
who should have access to school records (10%).  However, 14% of the headteachers stated that they could
see no record keeping problems particularly specific
to open plan schools.

*Small study - comparison of record systems*
*in schools with different teaching styles*

The purpose of the overall study was to find out
whether school records have a different or additional
function for co-operative or team teaching.  However,
the data analysis yielded very little which indicated
that record keeping was more complex in team teaching
situations.  As this was at odds with the experiences
of the researchers in the first phase of the project,
it was decided to look more closely at the information sent in by those headteachers who had specifically commented on teaching style;  and identify any
differences in patterns of record keeping.  They
formed a subsample of 88 of which, as previously mentioned, 42 (48%) used mainly class-based methods, 27
(31%) were organized for team teaching and 19 (22%)
used both teaching methods.  Table 9 shows the dis-
tributions of school type in each category.

Table 9   Percentages of school types using different teaching
styles

| School type | Teaching style (%) | | |
| --- | --- | --- | --- |
| | Traditional/class-based ($n$ = 42) | Mixed ($n$ = 19) | Team teaching ($n$ = 27) |
| Primary | 54 | 32 | 38 |
| Infant | 29 | 42 | 19 |
| First | 2 | 11 | 4 |
| Junior | 12 | 11 | 19 |
| Middle | - | - | 11 |

There was little difference between the three
teaching styles in the proportion of mathematics and
language records used except that rather more team
teaching schools (15%) than class-based schools kept
traditional English or grammar records!  There was
also little difference between the categories for
transfer records;  however, where itemized summary
records were concerned, fewer of these were used in
team teaching schools (22%) than in traditional (33%)
or mixed style schools (37%).
Quite significant differences were found in the
proportions of schools in each category using handwritten profiles and samples of pupil work as forms
of record keeping.  Nearly half (48%) of the team
teaching schools used handwritten profiles, compared
with less than a third of the traditional schools
(31%) and nearly half (48%) the team teaching schools

kept folders of pupil work samples, compared to 31%
of the traditional schools.

Once again, as with the main sample, the records
associated with team teaching (e.g. assignment sheets)
were not used to any extent by the schools in the subsample.  However, rather more team teaching schools
(22%) kept records of work undertaken by each pupil
than did the more traditional ones.  Also substantially more team teaching schools (37%) sent written
reports to parents than did the other schools (20%),
and they also kept more records on each pupil.  An
average total of six records per pupil were used in
team teaching schools whereas the more traditional
schools used between four and five.  Perhaps team
teaching schools are more concerned about their
public image than schools organized on more traditional lines.

With regard to problems or special factors connected with record keeping, team teaching schools were
relatively more concerned with problems of 'minimal
yet comprehensive record keeping' (quote from headteacher) and, as table 10 indicates, more team
teaching schools saw the principal function of record
keeping as charting individual pupil progress;  more
team teaching schools were concerned about the issue
of confidentiality and surprisingly more of these
schools stated that they had few or no problems with
school records and that they could see no major difficulties in keeping records in open plan schools.

Table 10   Percentages of school types identifying problems and
          special factors connected with record keeping in
          open plan schools

| Problem/special factor | Traditional | Mixed | Team teaching |
|---|---|---|---|
| Few or no record keeping problems | 14 | 11 | 22 |
| Problems of size and scope of recording | 33 | 26 | 48 |
| Record keeping mainly for checking on pupil progress | 24 | 32 | 37 |
| Concern about confidentiality | 10 | 5 | 26 |

*Record keeping implications and recommendations*

Our open plan study suggests that record keeping in
open plan schools is, typically, fairly recently
evolved amidst a great deal of staff discussion about

which kinds of information would most appropriately provide a picture of the 'whole' child, and yet not be too time-consuming in administration.  There are about five records kept for each child, including a reading record, a mathematics checklist, an admissions and/or transfer sheet, and either a record of overall pupil progress freely written or termly/yearly summaries itemized under three or four headings, e.g. language, mathematics, creative activities, social and personal.  An individual folder of samples of pupils' work is also kept.

For most of the teachers, the importance of recording is in the information it provides which will actively benefit the quality of teaching and learning in school.

'It provides us with a system (of recording) which will:

   (*a*)   help the teacher to follow pupil development and so provide experiences which the child needs to help his progress;
   (*b*)   help to highlight gaps and other weakness in learning;
   (*c*)   help the teacher to form an all round picture of the child and his development.'

(primary headteacher)

Records as a means of passing on information to other teachers, to the LEA or to parents received low priority compared with school records as a means of improving the quality of teaching and learning.  We tentatively suggest that this is a major difference between record keeping in open plan and traditional schools.

Many of the teachers in our sample viewed record keeping as an exercise in staff collaboration and curriculum planning and saw their own chosen recording system as principally geared to a particular school organization.

'[The records] are the result of long discussion and have been amended and refined to their present state as situations and experience have determined.  They will very likely be altered in the future if we feel it necessary.'

(Manchester junior headteacher)

Many headteachers are aware of the necessarily flexible nature of school records and the need to review and update on a yearly basis.

*Examples of records*

We received a large number of samples of records
currently being used in open plan schools.  Many of
the records were fairly typical of those seen by the
research team on earlier project visits, good
examples of which may be seen and are discussed in
greater detail in chapter 5.  We concentrate here
on methods of record keeping preferred by team-
teaching schools, i.e. handwritten profiles and
samples of work.  We also look at examples of records
which we associate with team teaching in open plan
schools, e.g. assignment sheets kept by pupils, group
and topic records, records of work undertaken by individual pupils.  It is quite possible that the low
incidence of these records is due not to any lack of
interest in keeping records in this manner but to
lack of knowledge about their formulation and use.

Handwritten profiles or comments
Over a third of all the schools and half of the team
teaching schools in our subsample used this method of
recording individual pupil progress.  Some teachers
kept their records entirely in this way and at the
end of each week or month, made brief comments across
a wide range of subjects.  For example, a Midlands
junior school used a small exercise book to record,
at monthly intervals, individual pupil progress under
headings of 'reading' (this includes list of books
read and reading age), 'language and topics', 'mathematics', 'child development' (comments on social
development), and 'humanities' (integrated studies
including history, geography, science).
    In our visits to schools and at teacher group
meetings we have had a great deal of discussion about
the value of such records.  Criticisms have been made
about the subjectivity of many of the comments, the
lack of skill with which many of them are written and
difficulties of interpretation by receiving teachers.
However, despite these detractions, they are preferred by many because teachers consider that they
are able to describe personality and progress of
pupils more fully and interestingly by using handwritten profiles than with other recording techniques.
We recommend their use, not as an exclusive method of
school recording but in *conjunction* with other, more
specific, subject records.
    The following are two typical and generally infor-
mative examples of handwritten profiles and then two
typical (unfortunately) less helpful comments.

*Example 9.1*   'Stephen attends school in the mornings only at the moment.  He was a little unsettled at school during the first few weeks and he found it difficult to form friendships with other children.  He is a very sensitive child who lacks confidence in his work and needs much encouragement from the teachers.'
[Signed and dated (reception class)]

*Example 9.2*   'Bernice is a very *talented* girl - all her school work is of a high standard and she excels at sports, games and in musical activities. She is enthusiastic in all her subjects sometimes becoming over-confident and adopting a superior attitude towards other children.  Sometimes her attitude costs her popularity - which results in "snooty" moods.' [Signed and dated (junior class)]

*Example 9.3*   'Robin has made progress this term. He has a good idea of number.'
[Signed and dated (infant class)]

*Example 9.4*   'Tony is still rather a baby at times.  He has so much energy he doesn't know what to do with it all!!  Can be very noisy.'
[Signed and dated (infant class)]

All comments written on school records should be signed and dated.  Examples 9.1 and 9.2 are preferable to 9.3 and 9.4, since they are more precisely evaluative and more competently written.  An analysis has been made of *unacceptable* statements found on records.  Although it is American in origin, it is applicable to teachers in this country.

*'Categories of Unacceptable Statements*
(1)   Libelous unverified statements regarding the student.
(2)   Unverified statements regarding parents, family and home.
(3)   Ambiguous, opinionated, subjective statements of the students.
(4)   Factual but biased statements with negative implications.
(5)   Factual but inconsequential statements that add nothing to understanding the student.
(6)   Inferential statements with negative implications that may or may not be verifiable.'[8]

Do any of the four examples selected fall into one or more of these categories?

Samples of work
This recording method, used by a quarter of the whole
sample and nearly half the team teaching schools, has
much to commend it since it is first-hand - i.e.
original pupil work rather than tests or comments on
it, non labour-intensive and interesting to the
pupil, and progress and improvement over several
years shows up very clearly.  (Each piece of work
needs to be accurately dated to be of any value.)
However, receiving teachers who often have more than
thirty folders of such work to read at the beginning
of each year may find them less than welcome.  Also,
the bulk of material can make storage difficult.
Samples of work can be collected at significant
stages in a child's progress, e.g. the first painting,
the first story, or may be examples of typical work,
i.e. the average product of a child.
     All the examples of work included here were selec-
ted by teachers - however, it has been suggested that
pupils should also be allowed to select their own.

Assignment sheets kept by pupils
Most of the assignment sheets (about a dozen) we received were used in junior schools or departments.
Pupils were required to write far more on some assignment sheets than on others but, apart from that, the
sheets included very similar categories and content.
All the sheets allocated spaces for the date and the
specific subject/learning category;  many allocated
spaces for the marks and task completion;  a few
allowed for comments from the teachers.  (Example
9.5, p.210, shows an assignment sheet, chosen for its
simplicity and practicality rather than originality.)

Individual work records
This kind of record differs from the assignment sheet
since it is a record of work done by each child
filled in and stored *by the teacher* rather than the
pupil.  Where large numbers of children are involved,
as in team teaching, teachers keep an individual record for each child so that no child is overlooked or
'missed in the crowd'.
     Most of these records are kept on a weekly or
monthly basis, and very often complex symbol systems
and instructions are evolved for their maintenance.
For instance, a diagonal line may be used to indicate
the beginning of a task, a cross for completion and a
dot when a pupil is not required to do a particular
piece of work (Midlands primary).  Example 9.6 (p.212)
is an instance of this kind of record incorporating a
simple symbol system.

Example 9.5  Pupil's assignment sheet (2pp)

Your name .................  Class .................  Month .................

|  | 1st week | 2nd week | 3rd week | 4th week |
|---|---|---|---|---|
| Reading<br>Book, page |  |  |  |  |
| Creative writing |  |  |  |  |
| Daily diary |  |  |  |  |
| English individual work<br>Exercises |  |  |  |  |
| Dictionary<br>Use and spelling |  |  |  |  |
| Library |  |  |  |  |

Handwriting

Spelling

Poem, play

Group work

Mathematics
1. Exercises and problems

2. Number bonds

3. Practical maths

HAVE YOU HAD YOUR WORK MARKED THIS WEEK?
MARK X IN THE BOXES WHEN THIS IS DONE

Example 9.6   Individual work record

## Child's name

| DATE | | | | | | | | | | | | | | |
|---|---|---|---|---|---|---|---|---|---|---|---|---|---|---|
| Writing | | | | | | | | | | | | | | |
| News | • | | | | | | | | | | | | | |
| Story | | | | | | | | | | | | | | |
| Library | | | | | | | | | | | | | | |
| English | | | | | | | | | | | | | | |
| Sounds | | | | | | | | | | | | | | |
| Maths envelope | | | | | | | | | | | | | | |
| Fletcher | ✓ | | | | | | | | | | | | | |
| Number | | | | | | | | | | | | | | |
| Tables | | | | | | | | | | | | | | |
| Starting points | | | | | | | | | | | | | | |
| Craft | | | | | | | | | | | | | | |
| Painting | | | | | | | | | | | | | | |
| Free choice | | | | | | | | | | | | | | |
| Comprehen | | | | | | | | | | | | | | |

Child brings assignment card to teacher after each topic

Key:   • to start;   ✓ when finished

Records of group work
Most of the records submitted under this category
were based on group or class lists and were records
of work experience rather than levels of attainment.
Class records of a similar kind are often used in
more traditional classrooms.

Only two records were received which indicated in
any detail the extent of the work of a group of children as a whole.  One (example 9.7, p.215) simply
showed a ten-part division of the school curriculum
around which comments were written at the end of each
week.  The other informally listed, under two
headings 'Subject' and 'Record of work', the topics
which the group as a whole had undertaken and any
clarification in the form of comments.  We suggest
that this kind of record is not particularly helpful
except as a means of keeping the headteacher or a new
teacher informed about curriculum coverage.  For the
individual teacher, a list of topics and children's
names in matrix form (example 9.8, p.216) may be of
more use.

Topic records
Work experience rather than attainment is, as with
records of group work, the major criterion of the
topic record.  Topic records sent to us were generally divided into three sections.  Spaces were allocated:

   (1)  for the starting and finishing date of the
        topic;
   (2)  for a brief description of the topic or
        project;
   (3)  for teacher comments on the quality of the
        work undertaken.

Several topic-specific records (i.e. designed specifically for use with particular topics) were received,
one entitled 'Potato workshop'.  Others listed study
skills appropriate to the kind of investigation
usually associated with topic or project work, e.g.
reference and precise skills.  A rather more complex
example of a topic record is given in example 9.9
(p.217).  We suggest, once again, that these records
have a limited value except in terms of keeping headteachers, new members of staff and parents informed
of the range of curriculum activity covered.

SUMMARY

The open plan record study indicated that, in general, there is little difference between traditional and open plan schools in their use of school records. Basic skills are well represented on record cards as is social and personal development. Records logically thought to be associated with co-operative teaching are used by very few schools.

When different teaching styles are compared, however, some difference in practice is indicated. In an effort to avoid complexity in record keeping, many schools using team teaching methods favour handwritten, open-ended profiles and samples of pupil work rather than more structured checklists and forms. As a solution to 'the tail wagging the dog' situation, i.e. difficulties in record keeping in co-operative teaching circumstances that might lead to the abandonment of team teaching, schools using this teaching style seem to have opted for *simpler* rather than more complex recording techniques.

REFERENCES

1  The researchers adopted the following definition of team (or co-operative) teaching:  'A form of teaching organization in which 2 or more teachers have the responsibility, working together, for all the teaching of a given group of pupils in some specified area of the curriculum.' (K. Lovell, *Team Teaching*, University of Leeds Institute of Education, 1967, p.5).
2  P. Rance, *Record Keeping in the Progressive Primary School*, Ward Lock Educational, 1971, p.19.
3  Central Advisory Council for Education (England), *Children and their Primary Schools* [Plowden Report], 2 vols, HMSO, 1967.
4  S.N. Bennett, 'The organisation of teaching and curriculum in open plan schools', *Aspects of Education* 21, 1978, 35-49.
5  S.N. Bennett et al., *Journeys into Open Space*, University of Lancaster, 1975, p.1.
6  Bennett (see note 4).
7  This percentage is far lower than earlier figures have suggested (e.g. those of Neville Bennett). Quite possibly many teachers do not regard reports to parents as school records and may therefore not have included them in their lists of records.
8  C.D. Wilhelm and M. Case, 'Telling it like it is: improving school records', *School Counselor* 23, 1975, p.85.

Example 9.7    Group work record

RECORD FOR WEEK ENDING ...................
(To be read in conjunction with maths, English, reading and assignment cards)

1.    Centre of interest, child-orientated work, etc.


2.    Other activities


3.    Environmental study


4.    Music and movement


5.    PE/games


6.    Story/poetry/drama


7.    Religious instruction


8.    Singing/counting games, etc.


9.    Handwriting/sounds


10.   Creativity


      NOTES

Example 9.8 Matrix type of group topic list

✓ started set work
✗ completed set work

| | Number bonds 1-10 | Number bonds to 20 | Addition (vertical form) | Addition (horizontal form) | Subtraction | Multiplication | Division | Place value | Tens & units | Hundreds, tens & units | Thousands | (etc.) |
|---|---|---|---|---|---|---|---|---|---|---|---|---|
| Alan M | | | | | | | | | | | | |
| Brian G | | | | | | | | | | | | |
| Colin H | | | | | | | | | | | | |
| Donald P | | | | | | | | | | | | |
| Garry J | | | | | | | | | | | | |
| Keith W | | | | | | | | | | | | |
| | | | | | | | | | | | | |
| | | | | | | | | | | | | |
| | | | | | | | | | | | | |

(etc.)

Example 9.9   Individual topic record

Name of child ........................    Date of birth .................

Class ......................    Educational year ..............

------------------------------------------------------------------------

Give brief notes on the topics undertaken, whether class, group or
individual.  Comment on how work was tackled, its presentation,
creativity and originality, and how books and other resources were
used.  Make notes on artistic, musical, dramatic and PE abilities.

Write up at the end of each half-term.  Sign and date.

| Date | Topics | Comments |
| --- | --- | --- |
| | | |

# 10 Case study: record keeping innovation and development in a primary school

Throughout the period of the project, the team were continually reminded of the practical ambience of the project work. Whilst teachers in the groups were sometimes interested in the theoretical issues of record keeping, they consistently asked for information on record keeping practices in other local authorities and for examples of school records.

With these considerations in mind, the team decided to make a case study of record keeping in a school which was in the process of reformulating its own record system, in order to illustrate the relationship between school records and classroom activities. Whereas much of the work of the project was concerned with specific issues, e.g. record format, record content, access to records, the researchers felt that focusing on the record keeping of an individual school would give greater significance to the specific issues (as mentioned above) because they were placed in the context of school practice.

Information for the case study was obtained in a number of ways.

(1) The major issues of record keeping were discussed at formal, taped interviews.
(2) Written statements of background and method were submitted by the teachers.
(3) Formal staff meetings on record keeping were tape-recorded.
(4) Informal discussions took place between the teachers and researchers.
(5) Observations and documentation of classroom activities were carried out by the research team.
(6) Samples of school records were collected.

This chapter is divided into two sections; the first describes the background of the school and the context in which innovation in record keeping arose. The second section considers the record keeping system in operation.

THE SCHOOL CONTEXT

'Brewers Lane' school is situated in a largely resi-
dential multiracial inner city area where the majority
of people live in either very old or new council
dwellings.  Two or three of the blocks of flats nearest the school serve as 'accommodation for problem
families' (headteacher) and hence the school has an
increased pastoral responsibility for the children of
these families who attend.  It is situated in a de-
clining industrial area of high unemployment with only
one major employer, which is a large brewery.
(Recently it too has been 'laying off' workers.)
    The school has a staff of 13 (including nursery and
'opportunity' class teachers) who teach about 320
pupils between the ages of 3 and 11 years in classes
of just under 30 in size.  We would suggest that this
school is a particularly appropriate choice for a case
study since it shares many of the problems of other
such schools and yet is striving to overcome them
through curriculum improvement and critical analysis.
    About three years ago* the infant and junior de-
partments, until then operating as two separate
schools, were amalgamated under a junior head who had
little infant experience and who has since retired.
A new head has been appointed very recently and this
is how he describes the situation he met.

'My initial impression of the school was very favourable.  However, on closer inspection I found that this, in the junior department, was a reflection of individual isolated competence on
the part of most of the teachers, but the department as a whole
lacked applied experience, co-ordination, schemes of work and
an allied record keeping system.
    The infant department, however, was alive to educational
developments and consequently working as a team with a combined
curriculum as an integrated whole.  There was a comprehensive
well constructed reading scheme with an attendant reading record card for each child.'


    Although the two schools had officially combined,
there was little evidence of co-operative activity
between the two departments.  The head regarded a review of record keeping within the school as a means
of building up co-operation and continuity of work
between them.

* As at the time the report was completed in draft (i.e. 1975).

'It is my intention as headmaster, to use the strength of my
infant teacher colleagues to build upon our work with record
keeping and curriculum development, so that it is gradually
extended upwards through the school, to provide an ongoing
and consistent policy for all the school in the main area of
primary school work.'

Thus, though all of the work described in this
chapter was carried out in the infant department, it
received the support of the head partly because it
offered solutions to the problem of staff unity and
co-operation.  Towards the end of the project's involvement with the school, all the infant teachers had
adopted a similar system of record keeping and several
junior teachers were expressing interest.  (Progress
has, however, been made since then;  at a subsequent
staff meeting, the infant teachers outlined and explained their system of recording to the rest of the
staff.  As a result the whole of the school agreed to
adopt the infant system of recording at the start of
the next academic year.)

The headmaster's interest in record keeping as part
of curriculum development was principally for organizational and administrative reasons.  However, the
teachers were involved at a much more practical level.
They adopted a new system of keeping records because
they were dissatisfied with former procedures (or lack
of them).

'There was no record keeping at all, only the red [LEA] record
book and that wasn't filled in every year either.  Just when
the children transferred to the junior school, one record was
filled in for them ...  There was a complete gap in [recording]
the child's education or development from the nursery up to top
infants.'

Dissatisfied at the lack of a generalized system with
'everyone doing their own thing' and at having no
guidance on how to keep records, they began to co-
ordinate their record keeping at first to 'fill the
gaps' and then later for considerations of a more professional nature.  'About a year ago, we started to
use reading record cards which you fill in as the
child reads to you and add some sort of qualitative
statement about how he's doing it.'

Having achieved a degree of success with the reading cards, the teachers went on to develop a rather
more complex and systematic method of recording which
included flow diagrams, tabulations, summary records
and the collection of samples of work.  When asked
why they recognized the need for a new system of re-

cording, the teachers gave six main reasons:

(1)  to identify difficulties, problems, successes
     with individual children;
(2)  to enhance the teacher's observation of indi-
     vidual children;
(3)  to identify children's strategies of learning
     so that they could be developed to provide
     the framework for success on an individual
     basis;
(4)  for diagnostic purposes, to indicate appro-
     priate action and method at an early stage,
     enabling problems to be recognized and likely
     successful action to be taken;
(5)  to give the teacher further understanding of
     the cognitive development of each child in
     attaching importance (by recording) to pupil
     experiences, concepts, understanding and
     skills;
(6)  for communication:  both for the child and
     for the teacher, between the class teacher
     and the head, and for other colleagues who
     will deal with these pupils in the future.

(Many points reiterated here were made in phase 1 of
the project - see chapter 3.)
     After considering the main purposes and possible
benefits of a new record system, the teachers then
turned to the practicalities of devising one.  The
following quotation illustrates the principles which
they thought necessary to incorporate:


'The main points that we considered were:  that [the system of
recording] had to suit the way in which we teach, it had to be
flexible;  the actual recording had to be ongoing alongside
the child and also the tabulation [evaluation and recording of
classroom activities] had to be an ongoing thing with the
teacher so that, at the end of term, she wasn't faced with a
massive recording exercise.  It should be capable of providing
the "what" statement, the "how" statement and the implications
to be derived from them.  The system should be sensitive to
the interests of the children.'


Thus the record system had to satisfy several criteria.

(1)  It should reflect the educational philosophy
     and approach of the teachers, i.e. a child-
     centred, integrated, structured environment
     with areas of activity and inquiry essential

to pupil development.
(2)   It should be flexible in order to provide for
      the teachers' intentions and the child's
      interest.
(3)   It should be capable of providing both quanti-
      tive (what is done) and qualitative (how it is
      done) statements of pupil development.
(4)   It should be sensitive to the interests of
      children so that appropriate experiences
      could be provided.

A NEW SYSTEM OF RECORDING

This part of the chapter describes the record system
now in operation in Brewers Lane school.  There are
five main components:

(1)   flow diagram - a plan of topic work;
(2)   tabulation - the monitoring and evaluation of
      work done, related to the flow diagram;
(3)   the official LEA record book
(4)   pupil's individual reading record card;
(5)   pupil's individual file.

*(1)  Flow diagram*

The teachers use the flow diagram as a means of
planning the term's work flexibly and at the same
time linking classroom activity with the environment
and available resources.  The flow diagram is deliberately constructed to include the essential elements
of the infant school curriculum though the teachers
allocate only about half the school day to 'flow'
activities.  Thus, the flow included here (example
10.1, p.224) is a diagrammatic representation of
careful curriculum planning using broad goals and
aims.  It includes work in number, language, science,
history, craft and social development.
   The broad aims and objectives of this particular
flow diagram were outlined in some detail:

*(a)  Aims:*  To capitalize on children's natural en-
      thusiasm in telling the teacher and each other
      about the presents they had for Christmas.

*(b)  Main goals*
      (i)   To develop children's understanding of
            money value and time with a toy shop.
      (ii)  To develop children's understanding of
            number, shape and speed in transport,
            particularly cars and bicycles.

(iii)  To extend children's knowledge of family
       structure and names.

(c)  *Secondary goals*
     (i)   To extend children's knowledge of the
           history of the bicycle.
     (ii)  To develop children's understanding of
           cogs, electricity and batteries.
     (iii) To extend children's experience of sets.
     (iv)  To encourage awareness of word families.

Teachers' views
Whilst this was considered to be a reasonable approach
to recording, the teachers were quite frank about
their own shortcomings when first confronted with a
new way of working: 'I think I made a mistake when I
first used the flow diagram, in that I wasn't flexible
enough.  I got a bit bored with what I was doing and
so did the children.'  However, having overcome initial difficulties, they found much to commend this
kind of planning: 'The flow gives you a sense of
direction and you are able to pinpoint areas where you
know the children need extra experience.'
    The opportunity to look ahead, organize any extra
equipment which might be needed in the future, and
provide guidance for new or supply teachers were all
cited as advantages of this system.  The need for
flexibility in record keeping was frequently mentioned: 'I virtually planned [the flow diagram] on
working with cars.  But we've gone on to bicycles ...
so in fact I did develop a whole new piece of flow,
because it is bicycles in which [the children] are
really interested and not cars.'  Thus, the choice of
flow diagram technique as a means of classroom
planning was made to combine the interests and motivation of pupils and the teachers' educational intentions.

*(2)  Tabulation*

The tabulation indicates the way in which work related
to the flow diagram is organized and evaluated.  The
record is divided into six main columns:

(a)  *display:*  a description of how work has been
     displayed;
(b)  *added provision:*  extra materials supplied by
     the teacher or the pupils;
(c)  *children involved:*  names of children who
     participate in each activity;
(d)  *practical:*  a note is made of any practical

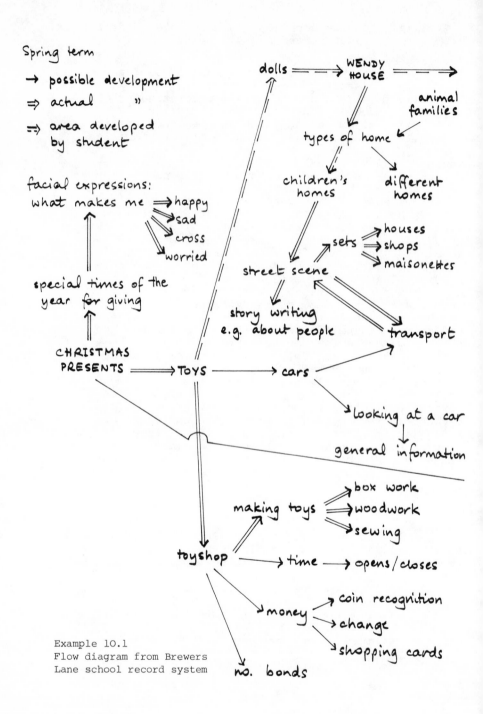

Spring term

→ possible development

⇒ actual        "

⇒⇒ area developed
   by student

facial expressions:
what makes me ⇒⇒ happy
              sad
              cross
              worried

special times of the
year for giving

CHRISTMAS
PRESENTS ⟹ TOYS ⟶ cars

dolls ⟶ WENDY HOUSE ⟶

animal families

types of home

children's homes      different homes

houses
sets ⟹ shops
maisonettes

street scene

story writing
e.g. about people

transport

looking at a car

general information

making toys
box work
woodwork
sewing

toyshop ⟶ time ⟶ opens/closes

money
coin recognition
change
shopping cards

no. bonds

Example 10.1
Flow diagram from Brewers
Lane school record system

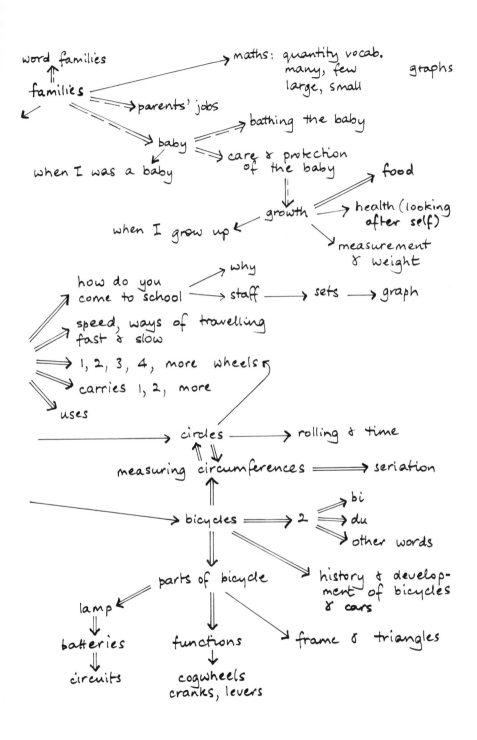

word families

families

→ maths: quantity vocab.
many, few
large, small

graphs

→ parents' jobs

→ bathing the baby

baby

→ care & protection
of the baby

when I was a baby

→ food

growth → health (looking
after self)

when I grow up ←

→ measurement
& weight

how do you
come to school

→ why

→ staff → sets → graph

speed, ways of travelling
fast & slow

1, 2, 3, 4, more  wheels

carries 1, 2, more

uses

→ circles → rolling & time

measuring circumferences → seriation

→ bicycles → 2

→ bi
→ du
→ other words

parts of bicycle

→ history & develop-
ment of bicycles
& cars

lamp

batteries

circuits

functions

cogwheels
cranks, levers

→ frame & triangles

Example 10.2   Tabulation from Brewers Lane school record system

| DISPLAY | ADDED PROVISION | CHILDREN INVOLVED | PRACTICAL |
|---|---|---|---|
| Models made by children displayed on table against wall- see plan | | Those wishing to make models of Christmas presents they received Zev Keith Sam Kay Kelly Children suggested they wrote stories about toys Sam Kay Kelly | Children made box work models either painted or collaged Kelly sewed teddy bear |
| | | Children who had bicycles for Christmas Sam Kerry Children wishing to write for class book - 1 bike each Kerry Kelly H Kay Individuals wished to make own bikes on development of bicycks. Able to write fairly well on own but benefiting from extra practice despite rep. see above. Sam Kelly P Kelly H Kay Joanne Tina C Julian Tristan | Large, accurate painting of chopper bicycle |
| | | Children wishing to do work + those writing 1 or 2 sentences on own Tristan Kelly P Jyoti Narindir Kerry Julian | Cards designed to make people happy for various occasions |
| | | Children copying under writing needing simple reading material+ Zev Scott Jamie Fahriada Keith David Arshad Lee Children wishing to write Tina Chimos, Joanne Children writing 1 or 2 sentences needing help with resources Tina Tristan Jyoti Narindir Children needing practice + reading material Arshad David Lee Darren Keith | |
| | | Children needing reinforcement no. 2. Scott Lee Jamie Naveed Arshad David Zev Keith — practice + simple reading material | |
| | | Children requiring reinforcement + practice Kay Kelly Sam Julian Kerry | |
| | | Children capable of work & increased vocab. Sam Kay Kelly Kerry Kelly Julian | |

| LANGUAGE | COMMUNICATION LITERACY | | NUMERACY |
| | READING | WRITING | |
| --- | --- | --- | --- |
| | | Stories about toys made into book displayed by models ← | |
| Names of parts + functions discussed with class. Group discussion with older chdn. Early bikes + development. Aiming for reasons why & consequences of certain developments – brakes pedals, moveable gears wheels etc. | Parts of bicycle labelled. Work made into book – displayed in book corner | Picture + writing – des. of bikes + developments. | |
| Class discussion – why Christmas presents – other times of year – to make people happy | | One or two sentences as to why – displayed over table with pics | |
| Discussion – difference between cross + sad | Work displayed by display table – what makes me happy. Read with group + other individuals – very simple book – language directed. What makes you sad What makes you cross How do you make people cross | Children copied over & under writing —— makes me happy  Children either wrote on own or copied according to ability – not as structured in language | |
| | Work made into book 2 —. — drew 2 —. Book of pairs made a pair of shoes etc. | | Children collecting and recording 2 of objects ← 2 — Pairs |
| | | | Counting in lots of 1 elephant has 2 ears 2 elephants have 4 etc. Made into flipover book. |
| Discussion with gp. ^ bi-words mainly coming from tchr. bi-lingual, bi-ped etc. Chdn. said bi meant 2, added bi-plane Connection between bi-ped, pedals, sent. parts noted by chdn. du-words added. —→ Other 2 words | Made into flipover book. Matching words in pockets by side word lists. | Children drew pictures & wrote definitions | |

activities, e.g. model making, painting;
(e)   *communication:*   this section is subdivided into language, reading, and writing and describes the work carried out in these areas;
(f)   *numeracy.*

The tabulation record contains statements (see example 10.2, p.226-7) of what has been attempted.   It does not contain qualitative evaluations about the level of pupil response.   Qualitative statements about each child's performance in activities related to the flow are recorded in the red record book (see below).

*(3)   Red record book*

This LEA official book is intended to be passed from teacher to teacher at the end of each year.   The teachers in Brewers Lane school have adapted this record book to fit in with their other modes of record keeping.   The beginning of the book is meant to serve as a section in which teachers record marks, grades and the results of tests.   The remaining pages are numbered to correspond with the number of pupils and are designed as individual records.   Each page is subdivided into five sections:

(a)   general personality sketch;
(b)   particular abilities;
(c)   special needs;
(d)   language;
(e)   mathematics.

The teachers at Brewers Lane school have altered sections 4 and 5 into three columns (see example 10.3, opposite).

'In sections 4 and 5, rather than writing across the page [on language and mathematics] we have divided 4 and 5 into three sections.   To make the link between the flow diagram and the red record book, the middle section contains qualitative statements about what happened with a particular child in a particular part of the flow diagram activity.'

The other two columns contain evaluative statements about number and language.   It is intended that comments made on the individual record should be specific, precise and descriptive.

Example 10.3   Page in red record book from Brewers Lane school
record system

---

**2·2**   [denotes extent of schooling]

NAME                                                    DATE OF BIRTH

CRAIG SMITH

Autumn ½ term

1.   Craig has formed a close relationship with Mina this term
and as Mina was unable to speak English, Craig
acquired a sense of responsibility which has
helped him to be less immature [ finds it easier
to leave his mother in the mornings ]
His co-ordination ( pencil ) is much improved.

2.

3.

4.

| Has conservation of number − 7. ✱ | jobs − phonic work is now beginning to hear initial sounds. offered word FACTORY for f sound. 1 2 3 + away − seriation houses good, representation good. used tallest 2nd tallest but last tallest instead of shortest. daff's setting − things growing counted 10 in 1 set + 9 in other told me that 1st one had ✱ more. | Is beginning to recognise sounds and collect words Is making progress with flash cards and with lots of practice should soon have a reading book ( f/c introd ). |
| --- | --- | --- |
| 5. | | |

Pupil 11

*(4)   Reading record card*

This was the first record devised by the teachers.
Each child is given a 'zig zag' (concertina) reading
card on the front of which is displayed the child's
name, address, date of birth and the number of terms
or years so far spent in school (example 10.4a).   The
centre sheets of the card are divided into three
columns (example 10.4b).   Included on the back of the
card are two phonic lists which are ticked off or
filled in, either by the teacher or by the pupil, to
indicate progress in phonic knowledge (example 10.5).
   This reading card is an ongoing record and is
filled in each time a pupil reads to his or her
teacher.   This may be every day, several times a week
or once a week, according to the teacher's view of
the individual need of the child.   On this record are
written evaluative statements about how well a pupil
is able to read, statements about where a child is on
the reading scheme and comments on phonic skills.

Example 10.4a   Front of reading record card from
Brewers Lane school record system

2·2 yrs

Craig   Smith
14  Hardy  Court
Keir  Street
New  Town
Upshire

January 19..

Example 10.4b   Centre sheet of reading record card from
Brewers Lane school record system

| DATE | TASK | COMMENT |
|---|---|---|
| March 1st | Red Platform II  123 Away<br>Jennifer and the Little<br>Black Horse  ✓ | Check upper and lower case<br>Uu; Nn; Qq; |
| 9th | The Old Red Bus ✓ | Is beginning to use initial consonant<br>blends. When applied to text - copes<br>well. Now needs to apply to his<br>written work - less confident. |
| 14th | Billy and Percy Green ✓ | |
| 15th | Roger Rings the Bell ✓ | |
| 16th | Mr. Brown's Goat ✓ | bl —) |
| 21st | Tom and the Monster ✓ | sh —} with known word endings<br>ch —} e.g. ack<br>br —)     op<br>            ick<br>            ock etc. |
| 22nd | 123 Away<br>Cat's Dance<br>P.8. | |
| April 11th | p.18. | Has more difficulty with,  sp<br>word collections made.       st<br>                                       sm<br>                                       sn. |
| 12th | Reading with Rhythm<br>The Old Kettle ✓ | Used apparatus for initial consonant |
| 17th | p.11 ✓ | blend with familiar word endings<br>making own words. Successfully<br>completed. |
| 18th | Trog and His Axe ✓ | |
| 19th | Trog and the Fire ✓ | Needs to look closely at words |
| 20th | Trog makes a Trap ✓ | like it's, can't, don't, I'm, won't. |
| 24th | Grandpa has a swim ✓ | — occurring frequently in these books. |
| May 3rd | p.11 ✓ | |
| 9th | Roderick the Red<br>p.25 ✓ | |
| 17th | Gregory the Green | |

*(5)  Pupil's individual file*

Pieces of work by pupils, which are recognized by the
teacher as indicating a particular stage of their development, are dated and placed in an individual file.
Each child has one which also contains all completed
work books and any work which has been displayed in
the classroom.  'This starts from the first drawing
they do when they come in - so that over the three
years, a complete picture of their work has been
built up.'
   Thus, a typical file of a child who has been in
the school for three years may include two completed
reading cards, three story books, two number books,
one phonic book, one 'busy' (rough work) book and

Example 10.5   Phonic lists in reading record card
               from Brewers Lane school record system

| Before | Letter | After |
|---|---|---|
| bl, br | b | |
| cl, cr, ch | c | ch, ck, tch |
| dr | d | d, ed, end, and |
| fl, fr | f | |
| gl, gr | g | |
| | h | |
| | j | |
| | k | nk, ck |
| | l | ll, ble, ple, lt |
| | m | |
| | n | nk, nd, nt, ng |
| pl, pr, ph | p | |
| | qu | |
| | r | er, ar, ir, or, ur |
| squ, scr, st, sp, sn, sm, sl, sk, sc, shr, sh | s | |
| thr, tw, tr, th | t | th |
| | v | |
| wr, wh | w | |
| | x | |
| | y | y, ly |
| | z | |
| au, ai | a | ar, ad, and, ag, an, ap, at, all, ay-e |
| el, ea, ee | e | er, ed, eck, eg, en, ep, et, ell, ew |
| ir, ie | i | ir, id, ick, in, ip, it, ill, ing, ian, ide, ig |
| or, oi, ou, oa, oo | o | or, og, on, ock, op, ot, oll, ow, ous, out |
| ue, ur | u | ur, ug, un, ut, uck, ull |

Aa Bb Cc Dd Ee
Ff Gg Hh Ii Jj
Kk Ll Mm Nn Oo
Pp Qq Rr Ss Tt
Uu Vv Ww Xx Yy
Zz

eleven dated pieces of display work (mathematics,
language and topic) including one long story.  The two
samples in example 10.6, from the file of the same
child, give some indication of state and scope of progress in reading and writing over one and a half
years.
   These files are kept for a number of reasons.  They
are passed on to future teachers, who are able to see
rate of progress as well as scope of work;  they are
seen by the pupils, who are often 'amazed when they
look back and see the progress they have made';  and
they are seen by parents at parent-teacher interviews.

   FURTHER DEVELOPMENT

Whilst the teachers at Brewers Lane school regard
their present system as detailed, comprehensive and
workable, they are not totally satisfied with it and
see it as only partly developed.  'The next thing we
have to start thinking about is how we can pass on to
other teachers the collection of information from the
"flow", the red record book and the reading zigzag in
a reduced and acceptable form.'
   The main problems the teachers have found with
their new record system are:

   (1)   a continual need for updating - a flexible
         ongoing system of recording necessitates con-
         tinual modification according to pupil inter-
         ests and resources available;
   (2)   duplication:  teachers sometimes find that
         they are duplicating comments on different
         records;
   (3)   difficulty in summarizing accumulated infor-
         mation to pass on to future teachers.

They do not, however, feel that their method of record keeping is too time-consuming.  '... we only record a little bit each night or a bit every few days
- so that it is not a big exercise to be coped with
at the end of term - anyway it's part of our teaching
as we go along.'
   In conclusion, Brewers Lane school was selected
for the case study not for the general applicability
of its system of record keeping to other schools, but
for the *manner* in which its teachers themselves have
approached the tasks of converting an unacceptable
method of record keeping into a highly appropriate
one.

234

Example 10.6 Two samples of one child's work, 1½ years apart, from Brewers Lane school record system

Once upon a time there was a motorcycle. he was a nice motorcycle but he didn't start well so his owner took him

to the snap yard and left him. he got very sad. but one

day a boy came to play he saw the motorcycle and so he got on just then he shot off and out of control skided

and went for fense hit it.

went over and went for the garage. he was mended. after

that he was taken to the boys house and lived happyliy ever after.

March 78

A long time
A long time

was a
was a

there
there

King and a
King and a

princess and
princess and

Sept 76

# 11 Summary, conclusions and recommendations

OVERVIEW OF THE REPORT

The purpose of this report is to help teachers in
primary schools to keep better records of the progress
and development of the children in their care. The
Schools Council project on which it was based started
in the autumn of 1976 and lasted for two years. Its
brief was:

(1)  to collect information about the ways in which
     school records were being kept by primary
     schools;
(2)  to collate and analyse this material;
(3)  to evaluate the collated material in collabo-
     ration with teachers in six regional groups;
(4)  to develop with these groups of teachers ways
     of improving record keeping practice.

The collection of information about what primary
schools record, and how they record it began in fact
before the project officially started. A letter was
sent to the Chief Education Officer of every LEA in
England and Wales telling of the forthcoming project
and asking each for the nomination of up to half a
dozen schools known to keep systematic records, or
where innovatory systems were being tried. This resulted in the nomination of over 200 schools. The
sample from which the information was drawn was thus
*not* a random one. A letter was sent to the head of
each school asking for information about the school
and the records kept and, on the basis of the replies,
visits were arranged to see as wide a variety of
practice as possible. Specimens of the systems in
use were collected at the time of the visit and by
post from the schools not visited.
This wealth of material was collated and analysed
for later use by the six regional teacher groups.
The visits, collation, analysis of this material, and
the arrangements for the teacher groups at Slough,
Reading, Birmingham, Cardiff, Haverfordwest and Whitby

(and an 'associate' group at Newbury) were completed
by Easter 1977, six months into the project.

The teacher groups met regularly over the next
year.   Each had the general task of deriving broadly
acceptable principles and practices for the keeping
of school records.   In addition, several groups developed interests of a more specific kind.   As a result of these general and special interests, the project team were asked to provide further information
in the form of papers on a number of topics, some of
a theoretical nature.   Some of these are incorporated
into chapter 7 of this report (see p.159).   Others
are included as appendix F.   They are not put forward
as authoritative 'final' statements on these complex
issues, but rather as simple introductions.   It is
hoped that readers will treat them as such and will
find them interesting and of use.

The summer term of 1978 was spent in writing this
report (first draft).   A more detailed description of
the two-year project is given in chapter 2.

Chapter 1 describes the context - educational,
political, and social - in which the project took
place.   It is characterized as one of increasing
pressure on education to render an account of itself,
and to do so openly.   These issues have been labelled
'accountability' and 'confidentiality'.   The former
pervades the whole report in spirit, but is specifically discussed only in chapter 1.   The latter has a
chapter (8) devoted to it later in the report.   Both
range far beyond the sphere of education and seem
likely to endure as issues of public concern.   They
have political and technical attributes;   *who* should
render account and to whom;   *who* should have access
to information;   *how* should account be rendered;   *how*
should information be efficiently disseminated to
those who have a right to know while at the same time
reasonable privacy is ensured for the individual.

Following discussion of the context and the working
of the project, teachers' views about the purpose and
functions of school records are presented in chapter
3.   It is perhaps notable that a substantial minority
saw thorough and systematic record keeping as serving
essentially defensive ends;   possibly a response to
the climate of accountability referred to in chapter
1.

The records collected by the project during its
first phase of operation (p.10) were divided into two
kinds by the function which they seemed designed to
fulfil:

(1)   records used mainly within a school;

(2)   records used mainly for transferring information to other schools.

Records in the latter group, generally of local
authority official design and (in conformity with
tradition) coloured pink and blue, are discussed in
chapter 6.  It is interesting to note that project
teachers' views of what was important in terms of
content were somewhat at odds with those of the originators.  Project teachers criticized the general
lack of instructions as to how these records should
be completed by originating teachers, and interpreted
by recipients.  They were also critical of the lack
of direct reference *on the actual record* to such instructions, when they did exist.  Without access to
the assumptions on which such records had been completed, the information transmitted was considered
at best ambiguous.  For transfers within a given LEA,
these criticisms still applied but obviously to a
lesser degree.
    Records used mainly within a school were examined
in minute detail (reported in chapters 4 and 5), and
it is from this critical examination of a rich variety of practical material that the general principles
for the improvement of record keeping mainly derive.
As the process of evaluation described in chapter 5
developed, however, the lack of an adequate framework
of a more theoretical nature was increasingly felt,
and the project team were asked to attempt to provide
one.  Two stimulus papers were produced, and chapter
7 is the synthesis of these papers, interspersed as
appropriate with examples drawn from the practical
substance of the previous two chapters.  In order to
illustrate the relationship between curriculum
planning and record keeping - the alpha and the omega
of the matter - a case study in chapter 10 describes
the experience of the staff of one school which em-
barked on this process of self-reappraisal.
    In the research team's search for factors likely
to influence record keeping practices, that of school
organization appeared initially to offer a fruitful
line of inquiry.  The initial survey of school records
included a wide variety of schools:  those built on
traditional classroom principles as well as more recent buildings of an open plan nature.  However, a
particular study of practices in open plan schools
(chapter 9) revealed that record keeping differed
little from that in more traditionally built schools.
Organizational differences tended to be reflected in
different patterns of recording, the tendency being
for teachers operating in team teaching situations

to favour handwritten open-ended profiles rather than
structured checklists, and also to keep samples of
pupils' work.  Simplicity of recording techniques
appeared to be an overriding factor in team teaching.
Records also seemed to reflect the degree to which
teachers managed their pupils as individual learners
rather than the school building in which the learning
took place.

The confidential nature of many school records was
an issue frequently raised during the lifetime of the
project (1976-8).  It would be naive to imagine that
any final solution to the problem of restriction of
access can be suggested, since different circumstances
demand different solutions.  The research team, together with a group representing the professions with
a concern over pupils' education and welfare, examined
some of the major problems facing teachers when handling 'sensitive' information about pupils and their
background.  The group set about formulating a set of
guidelines for teachers suggesting how 'sensitive' information should be collected and used (chapter 8).
Five main points covered in the guidelines are:

(1)   a definition of 'sensitive' information;
(2)   types of record containing sensitive infor-
      mation;
(3)   the reason for recording sensitive informa-
      tion;
(4)   teachers' responsibilities when recording and
      using sensitive information;
(5)   procedures for protecting and updating sensi-
      tive information.

### DISCUSSION

When the project was being planned, and in its early
days, the possibility of producing a system, or
systems, of record keeping which would have fitted all
primary schools was considered.  This notion was
abandoned as unworkable for two reasons.  The first
was very practical, and concerned the rich variety of
experience offered to children in the primary years.
Each school visited offered a curriculum which subtly
differed from the next, in the context of a different
pattern of organization.  Curriculum content, sequence
and depth were clearly determined by essentially *local*
considerations;  pupils' abilities and aptitudes,
teachers' interests and specialisms, the kind of
school building, and its environment.  The priorities
and values of each school reflected those of its
headteacher and, perhaps to a lesser extent, his

staff.  A single unified system or systems that could
encompass all possibilities would either have had to
be vast and, in regard to any single school, full of
redundancy, or else would have had to be expressed in
such broad and general terms as to be of little value.
It seems probable that the latter is true of LEA
official records, and accounts for teachers' lack of
enthusiasm for them, generally and specifically, as
implied in the evaluation reported in chapter 6.
The second reason was rather one of principle.  It
was noticed repeatedly that the record keeping systems
being used thoroughly, even with enthusiasm, by the
teachers within a school were ones which were:

(1)   of comparatively *recent* origin;
(2)   the product of a *collaborative* exercise in-
      volving the teachers as a whole.

At first, it was thought that the popularity of these
record systems was due to recency and a sense of participation, but later an alternative, fuller, explanation emerged.  Record keeping represents the last
stage in the process of teaching, not the first.  To
set up a record keeping system, then to decide what
to teach, in what sequence and how, is to get the
process back to front;  a case of 'the tail wagging
the dog' with a vengeance.  Such a way of working can
only have two outcomes:  either the record keeping
system atrophies, being used half-heartedly once in a
while, or worse, it stands as an inadequate statement
of the curriculum, becoming increasingly moribund as
time passes.
The rich variety of teacher-produced records
gathered from schools in the project's first phase,
analysed in chapter 4, and exemplified and evaluated
in chapter 5, are the true reflection of teachers'
endeavours.  As they stand, they tend to be of value
only to their originators because the *assumptions* of
what has been expected by teachers, and the assessment of children's response, are seldom made sufficiently explicit to convey information adequately to
anyone else.  For this reason chapter 7 has a central
importance to this report, since it attempts to present, in simple and condensed form (as presented to
the teachers who collaborated with the project team),
systematic ways of first deciding what is appropriate
for the children in terms of their ages, aptitudes,
abilities, and environment;  specifying in more detail
what is to be expected of them;  assessing how far
they have progressed;  and finally recording all of
these in such a way that they are conveyed unambigu-

ously to other teachers in other places or stages in education.

CONCLUSIONS AND RECOMMENDATIONS

When producing records, the following synthesis of the collective views of the team and the project teachers should be kept in mind.

*Design*

Record should have:

(1)  a clear layout;
(2)  clear, stable printing that will not fade;
(3)  clear section headings;
(4)  the pupil's name in a prominent position (official forms generally use the top right-hand corner of a sheet);
(5)  sufficient space provided for comments;
(6)  a prominently placed key (or a user's handbook) to explain the use of abbreviations, symbols and criteria for the assessment of pupils.

*Content*

Record content should:

(1)  be relevant to the purpose of the record;
(2)  be clearly sequenced;
(3)  give direct indications rather than implications for future teaching;
(4)  give a clear distinction between entries concerned with pupils' school experiences and those which are assessments of attainment;
(5)  clearly present assessment information, *stating*:
 (*a*)  the derivation of norms used when grading or rating,
 (*b*)  the criteria used when deciding on pupils' competence,
 (*c*)  details of standardized tests used as a basis for grading or rating,
 (*d*)  details of other testing techniques used,
 (*e*)  teacher-made test marks *in a standardized form*, possibly as standardized $z$ scores (see appendix D) to indicate the range and distribution of scores. (This is particularly necessary where sets of marks from different sources have to be compared.)

The following *general* recommendations are also made.

(1)  *The formulation of records should always be a collaborative exercise involving all the teachers within a primary school.*  The discipline imposed on teachers by the act of examining their aims, objectives and assessments is a very valuable one in its own right.  A case study (chapter 10) has been included to illustrate this process.  The experience of one such school is hardly likely to be typical of all schools making such an attempt, but it provides useful pointers along the way for those wishing to follow.  Satisfaction with, and systematic, even enthusiastic use of, record keeping systems seemed to be guaranteed only in those schools which had produced a record system as a collaborative exercise involving all the staff.  Clearly this cannot be a once-and-for-all event.  New teaching priorities emerge, and teachers come and go, and the process needs thus to be a dynamic one with the systems produced seen as in a state of continual evolution.

(2)  When records are also intended to communicate information to the next stage in education, *the scope of the collaboration should extend to the recipients*.  All too often during the course of project activities, the team met with the bland rejection of primary school records, by secondary colleagues, on the grounds that much of the information offered was not what was wanted and that, where the information was potentially of a useful nature, comparability between different 'feeder' primary schools was impossible.  Surprisingly, the same criticism was often voiced at the infant-junior interface, where these were separate schools, in spite of the fact that generally only one of each was involved.

(3)  Much valuable first hand information about pupils and their learning habits is lost since time is not immediately available for teachers to make the necessary notes in sufficient detail.  Therefore, if record keeping is to be rather more than an end of day or weekly activity, and seen as part of the process of teaching, then *teachers need to be freed of many of the non-teaching and supervisory activities commonly a part of primary school life*.  Without time being made available at the point when important observations are made, record keeping of pupils' progress will remain somewhat sketchy.  Without time being made

available the process of curriculum planning of
which record keeping is merely the final stage
cannot be undertaken as a collective staff exercise.  Without time being made available, the
inter-school visiting and collaboration so important to ensuring continuity in the curriculum
between stages of education and the creation of
a system of records which communicate meaningfully across the 'transition barrier' cannot be
achieved.

# Appendix A
# Recommended reading and additional information

The following publications and comments may be useful in the formulation of school records.

*Reading - general*

Dean, J., *Recording Children's Progress*, Macmillan Education, 1972. Also included in Anglo-American Primary Education Project, *British Primary Schools Today*, vol. 3, Macmillan Education, 1972.

Dean, J., and Nichols, R., *Framework for Reading*, Evans, 1974.

Cohen, L., *Educational Research in Classrooms and Schools: a Manual of Materials and Methods*, Harper & Row, 1976 (contains section on 'Readability measures for use by teachers', pp.240-51).

Downing, J.A., and Thackray, D.V., *Reading Readiness*, University of London Press,* 2nd rev. ed. 1975.

Gilliland, J., and Merritt, J., *Readability*, University of London Press,* 1972.

Goodacre, E.J., *Hearing Children Read: Including a List of Reading Schemes and Other Materials*, Centre for the Teaching of Reading, University of Reading, rev. ed. 1974.

Goodacre, E.J., Dean, J., and Root, B., *Teaching Young Readers*, BBC Publications, 1977 (booklet accompanying programme).

Tansley, A.E., *Reading and Remedial Reading*, Routledge, 1967, new ed. 1972.

*Vocabulary lists*

Dolch, E.W., *The Basic Sight Word Test*, Champaign, Ill.: Garrard Press, 1942.

Edwards, R.P.A., and Gibbon, V., *Words Your Children Use*, Burke (for Leicestershire Education Committee), 2nd rev. ed. 1963.

Gates, A.I., *A Reading Vocabulary for the Primary Grades*, New York: Columbia University Press, 1935.

* Now Hodder & Stoughton Educational.

Fry, E.B., 'Teaching a basic vocabulary', *Elementary English* 41, April 1960.

McNally, J., and Murray, W., *Key Words to Literacy and the Teaching of Reading*, Schoolmaster Publishing Co., 2nd rev. ed. 1968.

*Graded book lists*

Atkinson, E.J., and Gains, C.W., *An A-Z of Reading and Subject Books*, Stafford:  National Association for Remedial Education, 1973.

Moon, C., *Individualized Reading*, Centre for the Teaching of Reading, University of Reading (updated twice yearly).

Mugford, L., 'A new way of predicting readability', *Reading* 4 (2), 1969, 31-5.

*Phonic lists*

Cotterell, G., *Diagnosis in the Classroom*, Centre for the Teaching of Reading, University of Reading, 1974.

Jackson, S., *Get Reading Right*, Glasgow:  Robert Gibson, 1971.

National Association for Remedial Education, *Class Phonic Skills Chart*.  Available separately from NARE; also included as Table 5 in Herbert, D., and Davies-Jones, G., *A Classroom Index of Phonic Resources*, Stafford:  NARE, 1976.

*Miscellaneous reading topics*

Goodman, Y., and Burke, C., *Reading Miscues Inventory*, New York:  Macmillan, 1970.

Melnik, A., and Merritt, J., *Reading:  Today and To-morrow*, University of London Press* in association with Open University Press, 1972.

Melnik, A., and Merritt, J. (eds), *The Reading Curriculum*, University of London Press* in association with Open University Press, 1972.

Strang, R., *The Diagnostic Teaching of Reading*, New York:  McGraw-Hill, 1969.

Vincent, D., and Cresswell, M., *Reading Tests in the Classroom*, Slough:  NFER Publishing Co., 1976.

*Oral language*

Clift, P.S., *Word Study* (a phonics teaching programme), Bell and Howell, 1969.

Crystal, D., *Child Language, Learning and Linguistics: an Overview for the Teaching and Therapeutic Professions*, Edward Arnold, 1976.

* Now Hodder & Stoughton Educational.

Crystal, D., Fletcher, P., and Garman, M., *The Grammatical Analysis of Language Disability*, Edward Arnold, 1976.

Department of Education and Science, *A Language for Life*, report of Committee of Inquiry appointed by the Secretary of State for Education and Science under the chairmanship of Sir Alan Bullock [Bullock Report], HMSO, 1975.

Schools Council Communication Skills in Early Childhood Project (director Y.J. Tough), *Talking and Learning: a Guide to the Fostering of Communication Skills*, Ward Lock Educational in association with Drake Educational Associates, 1977.

*Written language*

Berse, P., 'Criteria for the assessment of pupils' compositions', *Educational Research* 17 (1), 1974, 54-61.

*Spelling*

Livingstone, A., 'A study of spelling errors', in Scottish Council for Research in Education, *Studies in Spelling*, University of London Press,* 1961. Reprinted in B. Wade and K. Wedell (eds), *Spelling: Task and Learner* (*Educational Review* Occasional Publication 5), University of Birmingham School of Education, 1974.

Peters, M.L., *Spelling: Caught or Taught?* Routledge, 1967.

Peters, M.L., *Success in Spelling: a Study of Factors Affecting Improvement of Spelling in the Junior School*, Cambridge Institute of Education, 1970.

Peters, M.L., 'The significance of spelling miscues', in B. Wade and K. Wedell (see under Livingstone, above).

The following framework based on work by Peters (1974) and by Livingstone (see spelling references above) suggests ways of assessing a child's strengths and weaknesses in spelling by carrying out an analysis of errors and miscues. Certain questions need to be asked if a sound diagnosis of poor spelling is to be made.

    (1)   Is the child verbally intelligent?
    (2)   Is his visual perception of 'word form' adequate?

* Now Hodder & Stoughton Educational.

(3)   Is he a careful child?  (Can be assessed by
      observing other areas of a child's activities,
      and can be rated:  careless/casual/adequate/
      careful/pedantic.)
(4)   Is the child suitably 'set' to learn words as
      he meets them (i.e. can he make a determined
      attempt at learning words which cause some
      difficulty)?
(5)   Does the child see himself as a good speller?

Specific difficulties
(1)   Does the child experience difficulties in
      writing at school?
(2)   Does the child find difficulty in discrimina-
      ting similar sounds?
(3)   In reading, does the child use phonological
      (sound) cues rather than syntactic and seman-
      tic (grammatical meaning) cues?
(4)   Does the child have difficulty in remembering
      words or phrases which are momentarily shown
      on a flashcard (quality of short-term memory)?

Spelling errors
(1)   *Reasonable phonic alternatives*
      (*a*)   Homophones, e.g. hole-whole, wile-while,
             were-wear-ware, too-two, stairs-stares.
      (*b*)   Insertions, e.g. take*i*ng, thin*c*k,
             fairl*e*y, wa*r*ter.
      (*c*)   Transpositions, e.g. twink*el*, parc*le*,
             fie*r*s, fre*i*nd, s*i*ad.
      (*d*)   Omissions, e.g. goin(going), wen(when),
             sord(sword).
      (*e*)   Confusions, e.g. leftenent (lieutenant),
             paggages (packages).
(2)   *Phonic alternatives* not *conforming to a
      spelling precedent*
      (*a*)   Transpositions, e.g. St*au*rday, Mr*a*ch,
             p*a*lying, ashoe*r*.
      (*b*)   Omissions, e.g. mking (making).
      (*c*)   Confusions, e.g. carst (carrots),
             aspeshyl (especially).
(3)   *Random words*
      Confusions, e.g. beabiad (decided), croilfid
      (qualified).
(4)   *Perseveration* (repetition of syllables), e.g.
      uncon* onon*scious.

Many of the errors in category (1) are due to over-
generalization of spelling rules.  Similar over-
generalization of grammar rules produces the following examples of generating past tenses:

go-goed, wented;
hear-haw (as in 'see' and 'saw'), -heared, -herd
   (categorized as a homophone).

Memorizing homophonic parallels is a form of special
remedial help which may be used to reduce such errors.
Children making this kind of error will learn to discriminate more carefully as the rules are applied
more frequently.
   Errors made in category (2) may be due to a
child's lack of attention to detail and/or failure to
analyse what has been written.  When errors such as
these are pointed out, some children will correct
them with little or no further help.  A failure to
correct these despite help may indicate perceptual
difficulties.
   Errors in category (3) also indicate perceptual
difficulties.  Remedial spelling programmes are
needed in such cases.
   Errors in category (4) indicate motor deficiencies.
A remedial handwriting course is required to remedy
persistent errors of this kind.

*General learning problems*

Frostig, M., and Maslow, P., *Learning Problems in the
   Classroom:  Prevention and Remediation*, New York:
   Grune & Stratton, 1973.
Illingworth, R.S., *The Child at School:  a Manual for
   Teachers*, Oxford:  Blackwell Scientific, 1975.
Johnson, D.J., and Myklebust, H.R., *Learning Dis-
   abilities:  Educational Principles and Practices*,
   New York:  Grune & Stratton, 1967.
Smith, R.M. (ed.), *Teacher Diagnosis of Educational
   Difficulties*, Columbus, Ohio:  Charles E. Merrill,
   1969.

*Conceptual skills development*

Ausubel, D.P., *Educational Psychology:  a Cognitive
   View*, New York:  Holt, Rinehart, 1968.
Beard, R., *An Outline of Piaget's Developmental Psy-
   chology*, Routledge, 1969.
Bruner, J.S., Goodnow, J.J., and Austin, G.A., *A
   Study of Thinking*, New York:  Wiley, 1956.
Bruner, J.S., Olver, R.R., and Greenfield, P.M.,
   *Studies in Cognitive Growth*, New York:  Wiley, 1966.
Flavell, J.H., *The Developmental Psychology of Jean
   Piaget*, New York:  Van Nostrand, 1963.
Fogelman, K.R., *Piagetian Tests for the Primary
   School*, Slough:  NFER Publishing Co., 1970.
Gagné, R.M., *The Conditions of Learning*, New York:

Holt, Rinehart, 2nd ed. 1970.
Green, D.R., Ford, M.P., and Flamer, G.B. (eds),
   *Measurement and Piaget*, New York:  McGraw-Hill,
   1971.
Kamii, C., and Derman, L., 'The Englemann approach to
   teaching logical thinking:  findings from the administration of some Piagetian tasks', in Green *et al.*,
   1971 (above).
Russell, D.H., *Children's Thinking*, Ginn, 1956.

(Books on conceptual development are legion.  The
above list is neither exhaustive nor necessarily includes the best, but rather those found to be of
interest to members of the project team.)


*Mathematics*

Glenn, J.A. (ed.), *Teaching Primary Mathematics:
   Strategy and Evaluation*, Harper & Row, 1977.
Fogelman, K.R., *Piagetian Tests for the Primary
   School* (see under 'Conceptual skills', above).
Krutetskii, V.A., *The Psychology of Mathematical
   Abilities in Schoolchildren* (ed. J. Kilpatrick and
   I. Wirszup, trans. J. Teller), University of
   Chicago Press, new ed. 1978.
Nuffield Mathematics Project, various guides for
   teachers (*Introductory Guides, Teachers' Guides,
   Weaving Guides*) and *Checking Up*, I-III, W & R
   Chambers/John Murray, 1967-73 (now generally out of
   print).
Skemp, R.R., *Psychology of Learning Mathematics*,
   Penguin, 1971.
Williams, E.M., and Shuard, H., *Primary Mathematics
   Today*, Longman, metric ed. 1976.

Diagnostic format
Fig. 5 (p.252) shows a grid sheet from the NFER's
*Basic Mathematics Test B* (see p.41), illustrating how
test results presented in grid form can provide
nostic information.

Learning errors
This list of errors and/or habits made by pupils in
mathematics learning provides information for
teachers rather more valuable than gradings or
ratings.  It is confined to the basic four rules but
could be adapted to other areas of mathematics (see
comments on mathematics records, chapter 4, pp.36-
42).

TYPES OF ARITHMETIC HABITS OBSERVED IN ELEMENTARY SCHOOL PUPILS*

### Addition [addition, bonds]

Errors in combinations[+]
Counting
Added carried number last
Forgot to add carried number
Repeated work after partly done
Added carried number irregularly
Wrote number to be carried
Irregular procedure in column
Carried wrong number
Grouped two or more numbers
Split numbers into parts
Used wrong fundamental operation
Lost place in column
Depended on visualization
Disregarding column position
Omitted one or more digits

Errors in reading numbers
Dropped back one or more tens
Derived unknown combination
  from familiar one
Disregarded one column
Error in writing answer
Skipped one or more decades
Carrying when there was nothing
  to carry
Used scratch paper [for working
  out]
Added in pairs, giving last sum
  as answer
Added same digit in two columns
Wrote carried number in answer
Added same number twice

### Subtraction

Errors in combinations[+]
Did not allow for having borrowed
Counting
Errors due to zero in minuend
Said example backwards
Subtracted minuend from subtrahend
Failed to borrow; gave zero as
  answer
Added instead of subtracted
Error in reading
Used same digit in two columns
Derived unknown from known combi-
  nation
Omitted a column
Used trial-and-error addition
Split numbers

Deducted from minuend when bor-
  rowing was not necessary
Ignored a digit
Deducted 2 from minuend after
  borrowing
Error due to minuend and sub-
  trahend digits being same
Used minuend or subtrahend as
  remainder
Reversed digits in remainder
Confused process with division
  or multiplication
Skipped one or more decades
Increased minuend digit after
  borrowing
Based subtraction on multipli-
  cation combination

* Reproduced from G.T. Buswell and L. John, *Diagnostic Chart
  for Fundamental Processes in Arithmetic*, Indianapolis,
  Indiana: Bobbs-Merrill, 1925. Quoted in R.M. Smith (ed.),
  *Teacher Diagnosis of Educational Difficulties*, Columbus,
  Ohio: Charles E. Merrill, 1969, pp.168-9

+ 'Combinations': nearest English equivalent is number bonds,
  e.g. $4 + 2 = 6$    $4 \times 2 = 8$
       $4 - 2 = 2$    $4 \div 2 = 2$

## Multiplication

Errors in combinations[+]
Error in adding the carried number
Wrote rows of zeros
Carried a wrong number
Errors in addition
Forgot to carry
Used multiplicand as multiplier
Error in single zero combinations, zero as multiplier
Errors due to zero in multiplier
Used wrong process - added
Error in single zero combinations, zero as multiplicand
Confused products when multiplier had two or more digits
Repeated part of table
Multiplied by adding
Did not multiply a digit in multiplicand
Based unknown combination on another
Errors in reading
Omitted digit in product
Errors in writing product
Errors in carrying into zero
Counted to carry
Omitted digit in multiplier
Errors due to zero in multiplicand
Error in position of partial products
Counted to get multiplication combinations
Illegible figures
Forgot to add partial products
Split multiplier
Wrote wrong digit of product
Multiplied by same digit twice
Reversed digits in product
Wrote tables

## Division

Errors in division combinations[+]
Errors in subtraction
Errors in multiplication
Used remainder larger than divisor
Found quotient by trial multiplication
Neglected to use remainder within problem
Omitted zero resulting from another digit
Counted to get quotient
Repeated part of multiplication table
Used short division form for long division
Wrote remainders within problem
Omitted zero resulting from zero in dividend
Omitted final remainder
Used long division form for short division
Said example backwards
Used remainder without new dividend figure
Derived unknown combination from known one
Had right answer, used wrong one
Grouped too many digits in dividend
Error in reading
Used dividend or divisor as quotient
Found quotient by adding
Reversed dividend and divisor
Used digits of divisor separately
Wrote all remainders at end of problem
Misinterpreted table
Used digit in dividend twice
Used second digit of divisor to find quotient
Began dividing at units digit of dividend
Split dividend
Counted in subtracting
Used too large a product
Used endings to find quotient

[+] 'Combinations':  see note on p.249.

*Study skills*

A. Kravitz, 'Teaching the essential reading skills in
   social studies', in J.A. Figurel (ed.), *Forging
   Ahead in Reading*, Newark, Delaware, International
   Reading Association, 1967.  Quoted in Melnik and
   Merritt, *The Reading Curriculum* (reference under
   'Miscellaneous reading topics', p.244).

The following comprehensive checklist of study skills
is given by Kravitz (Melnik and Merritt, reference
above, pp.49-51).

'1 *Selection and evaluation*
   Can the student do the following?
   *a*  recognize the significance of the content
   *b*  recognize important details
   *c*  identify unrelated details
   *d*  find the main idea of a paragraph
   *e*  find the main idea of larger selections
   *f*  locate topic sequences
   *g*  locate answers to specific questions
   *h*  develop independent purposes for reading
   *i*  realize the author's purpose
   *j*  determine the accuracy and relevancy of information
 2 *Organization*
   Can the student do the following?
   *a*  take notes
   *b*  determine relationship between paragraphs
   *c*  follow time sequences
   *d*  outline single paragraphs
   *e*  outline sections of a chapter
   *f*  outline an entire chapter
   *g*  summarize single paragraphs
   *h*  summarize larger units of material
 3 *Location of information*
   Can the student do the following?
   *a*  find information through a table of contents
   *b*  locate information through the index
   *c*  use a library card catalog to locate materials
   *d*  use the *Reader's Guide to Periodical Literature* to
        locate sources of information
   *e*  use an almanac to obtain data
   *f*  understand and use various appendices
   *g*  use glossaries [and dictionaries]
   *h*  use encyclopedias to locate information
 4 *Following directions*
   Can the student do the following?
   *a*  see the relation between the purposes and the
        directions                                    [p.254

Fig. 5 Grid sheet for test results, reproduced from NFER
*Basic Mathematics Test B* (1969)

NAME ..............................

| Page | R | W |
|---|---|---|
| 1 (7) | | |
| 2 (5) | | |
| 3 (8) | | |
| 4 (5) | | |
| 5 (6) | | |
| 6 (6) | | |
| 7 (3) | | |
| TOTAL (40) | | |

| SCORE BAND |
|---|
| — |

| AGE | | RAW SCORE |
|---|---|---|
| years | months | |
| | | |

Signature of marker _____     Date _____

| | a | b | c | = | + | − | × | ÷ | d | e | f | g | h | i | j | k | l | m | n | p | q |
|---|---|---|---|---|---|---|---|---|---|---|---|---|---|---|---|---|---|---|---|---|---|
| 1 | | | | ● | | | | | | | | | ● | | | | | ● | | | |
| 2 | | | | ● | ● | | | | | | | | | | | | | | | | |
| 3 | | | | ● | ● | | | | | | | | | | | | | | | | |
| 4 | | | | | | | | | 1 | | | | | | ● | | | | | | |
| 5 | | | | | ● | | | | | | | | | | | | | | | | |
| 6 | | | | ● | | | | | | | | | | ● | | | | | | | |
| 7 | | ● | | | | ● | | | | | | | | | | | | | | | |
| 8 | | | | ● | | | | | | | | | | ● | ● | | | | | | |
| 9 | | ● | | | | | | | | | | | | | | ● | | | | | |
| 10 | | ● | | | | ● | | | | | | | | | | | | | | | |
| 11 | | ● | | | | | | | 2 | | | | | | | | | | | | |
| 12 | | | ● | | | | | | | | | | | | | | ● | | | | |
| 13 | | | | ● | | ● | | | | | | | | | | | | | | | |
| 14 | | | | ● | | ● | | | | | | | | | | | | | | | |
| 15 | | | | ● | ● | | | | | | | | | | | | | | | | |
| 16 | | ● | | | | | | | | | | ● | | | | | | | | | |
| 17 | | ● | | | | | | | | | | | | ● | | | | | | | |
| 18 | ● | | | | | | | ● | | | | | | | | | | | | | |
| 19 | | | | ● | ● | | | | | | | | | | | | | | | | |
| 20 | | | | ● | | | | ● | | | | | | | | | | | | | |
| 21 | | ● | | | | | | | | | ● | | | | | | | | ● | | |
| 22 | | ● | | | | | | | | | | | | | | | | | | | ● |
| 23 | | ● | | | | | | | | | | | | | | | | | | | ● |
| 24 | | | | ● | | | | | | | | | | | | | | | | | ● |
| 25 | | | ● | | | | ● | | | | | | | | | | | | | | ● |
| 26 | | | | | | | | | | ● | | | | | | | | | | | |
| 27 | | | | | ● | | | | | | | | | | | | | | | ● | |
| 28 | | | | | | ● | | | | | | | ● | | | | | | | | |
| 29 | | | | | | | ● | | | | | | | | | | | | | | |
| 30 | | | | | | | | ● | | | | | | | | | ● | | | | |
| 31 | | | ● | | | | | | | | | | | | | | | ● | | | |
| 32 | | | ● | | | ● | | | | | | | | | | | | ● | | | |
| 33 | | | ● | | ● | | | | | | | | | | | | | | | | |
| 34 | | ● | | | | | | | 3 | | | | | | | | | | | | |
| 35 | | | | | | | | | 1 | | | | | | ● | | | | | | |
| 36 | | | | | | | | | 1 | | | | | | ● | | | | | | |
| 37 | | | ● | | ● | ● | | | | | | | | | | | | | | | |
| 38 | | | | | ● | | | | | | | | | | ● | ● | | | | | |
| 39 | | | | | | | | ● | | | | | | | | | | | | | |
| 40 | ● | | | | | | | | | | | | | | ● | | | | | | |
| | 2 | 10 | 6 | 11 | 9 | 7 | 2 | 4 | 5 | 1 | 1 | 1 | 2 | 3 | 6 | 2 | 2 | 3 | 1 | 1 | 4 |

       *b*  follow one-step directions
       *c*  follow steps in sequence
    5  *Specialized skills*
       Can the student do the following?
       *a*  understand the significance of pictorial aids
       *b*  read and interpret graphs
       *c*  read and interpret tables
       *d*  read and interpret charts
       *e*  read and interpret maps
       *f*  read and interpret cartoons
       *g*  read and interpret diagrams
       *h*  read and interpret pictures'

The following comes from the Bullock Report (1975 - see Department of Education and Science, reference under 'Oral language', p.245):

'We believe that in the course of the middle and secondary years pupils should acquire the following and become accustomed to applying them in the various areas of learning:

   (i)   knowledge of available resources (e.g. books, magazines, files, pictures, tapes, cassettes, film), their location, and the way they are organised;

  (ii)   ability to define an area of search by using reference books of various kinds and more specialised publications where necessary;

 (iii)   ability to use subject index, classified catalogues, abstracts, and bibliographies, and to record sources systematically;

  (iv)   ability to survey source material, making an assessment of author, publisher, and content.

... A large number of pupils pass through school without ever learning to make notes efficiently.  One has only to look at much "project" work to see the truth of this.  Unable to read selectively and to summarise the information, most pupils resort to copying verbatim from books they are consulting.'

(paragraph 8.13)

Since middle schools have pupils from eight or nine years of age, the statements above can also apply to the upper primary school.

*Not recommended*

In Fig. 6 (opposite) is a record incorporating a five-point rating scale which uses 'always' and 'never' at either end.  For the reasons given in chapter 4 (p.24),

Fig. 6   Record using five-point scale from 'always' to 'never'

| WHA T WE ARE AIMING FOR<br><br>Name | Always | Usually | Sometimes | Seldom | Never | |
|---|---|---|---|---|---|---|
| 1   Co-operates well with teacher | | | | | | |
| 2   Co-operates well with other pupils | | | | | | |
| 3   Shows interest in work | | | | | | |
| 4   Thinks for himself/herself | | | | | | |
| 5   Is keen to get on with work | | | | | | |
| 6   Contributes to group discussions | | | | | | |
| 7   Works consistently and is not easily distracted | | | | | | |
| 8   Does independent reading | | | | | | |
| 9   Has good recall of knowledge | | | | | | |
| 10  Is efficient at finding out information | | | | | | |
| 11  Presents work in a tidy manner | | | | | | |
| 12  Writes with efficient use of language (for age) | | | | | | |
| 13  Shows originality in creative work | | | | | | |
| 14  Uses information | | | | | | |
| 15  Speaks fluently | | | | | | |
| 16  Is thorough in his/her work | | | | | | |
| 17  Shows an ability to assess his/her work | | | | | | |
| 18  Has made good progress | | | | | | |
| 19  Exercises self-control | | | | | | |
| 20  Listens courteously | | | | | | |
| 21  Participates in group activities | | | | | | |
| 22  Demonstrates thoughtfulness for others | | | | | | |
| 23  Cares for materials and properties | | | | | | |
| 24  Adheres to school rules | | | | | | |
| 25  Comes into school on time | | | | | | |
| 26  Can control his/her body movements | | | | | | |

using a scale as this is of limited value.  However, the same constructs 1-26 could be used with a
modified scale.

# Appendix B
# Taxonomy of educational objectives and aims of primary education

*Taxonomy of educational objectives*

Tables 11-15 (pp.258-66) review the major categories in the cognitive and affective domains, with illustrations of general instructional objectives and behavioural terms for these and for the psychomotor domain. The classification is based on the work of Bloom,[1] Krathwohl[2] and Harrow.[3]

*Aims of primary education*

The list of 72 aims included here (pp.267-72) was developed by the Schools Council Aims of Primary Education project (director P.M.E. Ashton).[4]

*Taxonomy of early childhood education goals*

This section (pp.273-81) incorporates material developed by the Center for the Study of Evaluation, University of California Graduate School of Education, Los Angeles.

*References*

1 B.S. Bloom (ed.), *Taxonomy of Educational Objectives: the Classification of Educational Goals*, Handbook I, *Cognitive Domain*, Longmans, 1956.
2 D.R. Krathwohl *et al.*, *Taxonomy of Educational Objectives: the Classification of Educational Goals*, Handbook II, *Affective Domain*, Longmans, 1964.
3 A.J. Harrow, *A Taxonomy of the Psychomotor Domain: a Guide for Developing Behavioral Objectives*, New York, McKay, 1972.
4 P.M.E. Ashton *et al.*, *The Aims of Primary Education: a Study of Teachers' Opinions* (Schools Council Research Studies), Macmillan Education, 1975.
5 E.J. Simpson, 'The classification of educational objectives in the psychomotor domain', in *The Psychomotor Domain*, vol. 3, Washington, DC: Gryphon House, 1972.

258

Table 11  Major categories in the cognitive domain of the taxonomy of educational objectives[1]*

Descriptions of the major categories in the cognitive domain

1. *Knowledge.* Knowledge is defined as the remembering of previously learned material. This may involve the recall of a wide range of material, from specific facts to complete theories, but all that is required is the bringing to mind of the appropriate information. Knowledge represents the lowest level of learning outcomes in the cognitive domain.

2. *Comprehension.* Comprehension is defined as the ability to grasp the meaning of material. This may be shown by translating material from one form to another (words to numbers), by interpreting material (explaining or summarising), and by estimating future trends (predicting consequences or effects). These learning outcomes go one step beyond the simple remembering of material, and represent the lowest level of understanding.

3. *Application.* Application refers to the ability to use learned material in new and concrete situations. This may include the application of such things as rules, methods, concepts, principles, laws, and theories. Learning outcomes in this area require a higher level of understanding than those under comprehension.

4. *Analysis.* Analysis refers to the ability to break down material into its component parts so that its organizational structure may be understood. This may include the identification of the parts, analysis of the relationships between parts, and recognition of the organizational principles involved. Learning outcomes here represent a higher intellectual level than comprehension and application because they require an understanding of both the content and the structural form of the material.

5. *Synthesis.* Synthesis refers to the ability to put parts together to form a new whole. This may involve the production of a unique communication (theme or speech), a plan of operations (research proposal), or a set of abstract relations (scheme for classifying information). Learning outcomes in this area stress creative behaviors, with major emphasis on the formulation of *new* patterns or structures.

6. *Evaluation.* Evaluation is concerned with the ability to judge the value of material (statement, novel, poem, research report) for a given purpose. The judgements are to be based on definite criteria. These may be internal criteria (organization) or external criteria (relevance to the purpose) and the student may determine the criteria or be given them. Learning outcomes in this area are highest in the cognitive hierarchy because they contain elements of all of the other categories, plus conscious value judgements based on clearly defined criteria.

* Reproduced from N.E. Gronlund, *Stating Behavioral Objectives for Classroom Instruction*, New York: Macmillan (UK: Collier-Macmillan), 2nd ed. 1978, Table II.

Table 12  Examples of general instructional objectives and behavioral terms for the cognitive domain of the taxonomy*

| Illustrative general instructional objectives | Illustrative behavioral terms for stating specific learning outcomes |
|---|---|
| [1] Knows common terms<br>Knows specific facts<br>Knows methods and procedures<br>Knows basic concepts<br>Knows principles | Defines, describes, identifies, labels, lists, matches, names, outlines, reproduces, selects, states |
| [2] Understands facts and principles<br>Interprets verbal material<br>Interprets charts and graphs<br>Translates verbal material to mathematical formulas<br>Estimates future consequences implied in data<br>Justifies methods and procedures | Converts, defends, distinguishes, estimates, explains, extends, generalizes, gives examples, infers, paraphrases, predicts, rewrites, summarizes |
| [3] Applies concepts and principles to new situations<br>Applies laws and theories to practical situations<br>Solves mathematical problems<br>Constructs charts and graphs<br>Demonstrates correct usage of a method or procedure | Changes, computes, demonstrates, discovers, manipulates, modifies, operates, predicts, prepares, produces, relates, shows, solves, uses |
| [4] Recognizes unstated assumptions<br>Recognizes logical fallacies in reasoning<br>Distinguishes between facts and inferences<br>Evaluates the relevancy of data<br>Analyzes the organizational structure of a work (art, music, writing) | Breaks down, diagrams, differentiates, discriminates, distinguishes, identifies, illustrates, infers, outlines, points out, relates, selects, separates, subdivides |

| [5] | Writes a well organized theme<br>Gives a well organized speech<br>Writes a creative short story (or poem, or music)<br>Proposes a plan for an experiment<br>Integrates learning from different areas into a plan for solving a problem<br>Formulates a new scheme for classifying objects (or events, or ideas) | Categorizes, combines, compiles, composes, creates, devises, designs, explains, generates, modifies, organizes, plans, rearranges, reconstructs, relates, reorganizes, revises, rewrites, summarizes, tells, writes |
| [6] | Judges the logical consistency of written material<br>Judges the adequacy with which conclusions are supported by data<br>Judges the value of a work (art, music, writing) by use of internal criteria<br>Judges the value of a work (art, music, writing) by use of external standards of excellence | Appraises, compares, concludes, contrasts, criticizes, describes, discriminates, explains, justifies, interprets, relates, summarizes, supports |

* Reproduced from N.E. Gronlund, *Stating Behavioral Objectives for Classroom Instruction*, New York: Macmillan (UK: Collier-Macmillan), 2nd ed. 1978, Table III.

Table 13  Major categories in the affective domain of the taxonomy of educational objectives[2]*

---

Descriptions of the major categories in the affective domain

---

1. *Receiving*.  Receiving refers to the student's willingness to attend to particular phenomena or stimuli (classroom activities, textbook, music, etc.).  From a teaching standpoint, it is concerned with getting, holding, and directing the student's attention.  Learning outcomes in this area range from the simple awareness that a thing exists to selective attention on the part of the learner.  Receiving represents the lowest level of learning outcomes in the affective domain.

2. *Responding*.  Responding refers to active participation on the part of the student.  At this level he not only attends to a particular phenomenon but also reacts to it in some way.  Learning outcomes in this area may emphasize acquiescence in responding (reads assigned material), willingness to respond (voluntarily reads beyond assignment), or satisfaction in responding (reads for pleasure or enjoyment).  The higher levels of this category include those instructional objectives that are commonly classified under 'interests'; that is, those that stress the seeking out and enjoyment of particular activities.

3. *Valuing*.  Valuing is concerned with the worth or value a student attaches to a particular object, phenomenon, or behavior.  This ranges in degree from the more simple acceptance of a value (desires to improve group skills) to the more complex level of commitment (assumes responsibility for the effective functioning of the group).  Valuing is based on the internalization of a set of specified values, but clues to these values are expressed in the student's overt behavior.  Learning outcomes in this area are concerned with behavior that is consistent and stable enough to make the value clearly identifiable.  Instructional objectives that are commonly classified under 'attitudes' and 'appreciation' would fall into this category.

4. *Organization.* Organization is concerned with bringing together different values, resolving conflicts between them, and beginning the building of an internally consistent value system. Thus the emphasis is on comparing, relating, and synthesizing values. Learning outcomes may be concerned with the conceptualization of a value (**recognizes** the responsibility of each individual for improving human relations) or with the organization of a value system (**develops** a vocational plan that satisfies his need for both economic security and social service). Instructional objectives relating to the development of a philosophy of life would fall into this category.

5. *Characterization by a Value or Value Complex.* At this level of the affective domain, the individual has a value system that has controlled his behavior for a sufficiently long time for him to have developed a characteristic 'life style'. Thus the behavior is pervasive, consistent, and predictable. Learning outcomes at this level cover a broad range of activities, but the major emphasis is on the fact that the behavior is typical or characteristic of the student. Instructional objectives that are concerned with the student's general patterns of adjustment (personal, social, emotional) would be appropriate here.

* Reproduced from N.E. Gronlund, *Stating Behavioral Objectives for Classroom Instruction*, New York: Macmillan (UK: Collier-Macmillan), 2nd ed. 1978, Table IV.

Table 14 Examples of general instructional objectives and behavioral terms for the affective domain of the taxonomy*

| Illustrative general instructional objectives | Illustrative behavioral terms for stating specific learning outcomes |
|---|---|
| [1] Listens attentively<br>Shows awareness of the importance of learning<br>Shows sensitivity to human needs and social problems<br>Accepts differences of race and culture<br>Attends closely to the classroom activities | Asks, chooses, describes, follows, gives, holds, identifies, locates, names, points to, selects, sits erect, replies, uses |
| [2] Completes assigned homework<br>Obeys school rules<br>Participates in class discussion<br>Completes laboratory work<br>Volunteers for special tasks<br>Shows interest in subject<br>Enjoys helping others | Answers, assists, complies, conforms, discusses, greets, helps, labels, performs, practices, presents, reads, recites, reports, selects, tells, writes |
| [3] Demonstrates belief in the democratic process<br>Appreciates good literature (art or music)<br>Appreciates the role of science (or other subjects)<br>in everyday life<br>Shows concern for the welfare of others<br>Demonstrates problem-solving attitude<br>Demonstrates commitment to social improvement | Completes, describes, differentiates, explains, follows, forms, initiates, invites, joins, justifies, proposes, reads, reports, selects, shares, studies, works |

[4] Recognizes the need for balance between freedom and
   responsibility in a democracy
   Recognizes the role of systematic planning in
   solving problems
   Accepts responsibility for his own behavior
   Understands and accepts his own strengths and
   limitations
   Formulates a life plan in harmony with his
   abilities, interests, and beliefs

Adheres, alters, arranges, combines,
compares, completes, defends, explains,
generalizes, identifies, integrates,
modifies, orders, organizes, prepares,
relates, synthesizes

[5] Displays safety consciousness
   Demonstrates self-reliance in working independently
   Practices cooperation in group activities
   Uses objective approach in problem solving
   Demonstrates industry, punctuality and self-
   discipline
   Maintains good health habits

Acts, discriminates, displays, influences, listens, modifies, performs, practices, proposes, qualifies, questions,
revises, serves, solves, uses, verifies

* Reproduced from N.E. Gronlund, *Stating Behavioral Objectives for Classroom Instruction*, New York:
Macmillan (UK: Collier-Macmillan), 2nd ed. 1978, Table V.

Table 15  Examples of general instructional objectives and behavioral terms for the psycho-motor domain of the taxonomy*

| Taxonomy categories | Illustrative general instructional objectives | Illustrative behavioral terms for stating specific learning outcomes |
|---|---|---|
| (See Harrow, A.J. (1972)[3] for one method of classifying psychomotor behaviors) | Writes smoothly and legibly<br>Draws accurate reproduction of a picture (or map, biology specimen, etc.)<br>Sets up laboratory equipment quickly and correctly<br>Types with speed and accuracy<br>Operates a sewing machine skillfully<br>Operates a power saw safely and skillfully<br>Performs skillfully on the violin<br>Performs a dance step correctly<br>Demonstrates correct form in swimming<br>Demonstrates skill in driving an automobile<br>Repairs an electric motor quickly and effectively<br>Creates new ways of performing (creative dance, etc.) | Assembles, builds, calibrates, changes, cleans, composes, connects, constructs, corrects, creates, designs, dismantles, drills, fastens, fixes, follows, grinds, grips, hammers, heats, hooks, identifies, locates, makes, manipulates, mends, mixes, nails, paints, sands, saws, sharpens, sets, sews, sketches, starts, stirs, uses, weighs, wraps |

* Reproduced from N.E. Gronlund, *Stating Behavioral Objectives for Classroom Instruction*, New York: Macmillan (UK: Collier-Macmillan), 1970, Table V. The second (1978) edition of Gronlund's book includes a more elaborate analysis based on the work of E.J. Simpson.[5]

72 AIMS FOR PRIMARY EDUCATION*

**Aims related to intellectual development**

KNOWLEDGE

1. The child should have a wide vocabulary.

2. The child should know the correct spelling of a basic general vocabulary.

3. The child should know the basic grammatical rules of written English

4. The child should have a general knowledge of his local environment in some of the following aspects: historical, geographical, natural, economic, social.

5. The child should have a wide general (not subject-based) knowledge of times and places beyond his immediate experience.

6. The child should have ordered subject knowledge in, for example, history, geography.

(column cont. on next page)

SKILLS

9. The child should know how to convey his meaning clearly and accurately through speech for a variety of purposes; for example, description, explanation, narration.

10. The child should be able to listen with concentration and understanding.

11. The child should be able to read fluently and accurately at a minimum reading age of eleven.

12. The child should be able to read with understanding material appropriate to his age group and interests.

13. The child should know how to write clear and meaningful English appropriate to different formal purposes; for example, factual reports, letters, descriptive accounts.

14. The child should know how to write interestingly and with sensitivity.

15. The child should know how to observe carefully, accurately and with sensitivity

(column cont. on next page)

QUALITIES

22. The child should be developing the ability to make reasoned judgements and choices, based on the interpretation and evaluation of relevant information.

23. The child should be developing a critical and discriminating attitude towards his experiences; for example, of the mass media.

* Reproduced from P.M.E. Ashton *et al.*, *The Aims of Primary Education: a Study of Teachers' Opinions* (Schools Council Research Studies), Macmillan Education, 1975, pp.239-44.

**Aims related to intellectual development—cont.**

KNOWLEDGE

7. The child should know some simple scientific experimental procedures and some basic scientific concepts; for example, properties of materials, the nature and significance of changes in living things.

8. The child should have some understanding of modern technological developments; for example, space travel, telecommunications, automation.

SKILLS

16. The child should be developing the skills of acquiring knowledge and information from written material; for example, summarizing, taking notes accurately, the use of libraries.

17. The child should know how to acquire information other than by reading; for example, by asking questions, by experimenting, from watching television.

18. The child should know how to compute in the four arithmetic rules using his knowledge of, for instance, number, multiplication tables and different units of measurement.

19. The child should know how to think and solve problems mathematically using the appropriate basic concepts of, for example, the number system and place value, shape, spatial relationships, sets, symmetry and the appropriate language.

20. The child should know how to use mathematical techniques in his everyday life; for instance, estimating distances, classifying objects, using money.

21. The child should be able to conduct a simple conversation in a foreign language.

269

## Aims related to physical development

### KNOWLEDGE

24. The child should have an understanding of how his body works.

25. The child should know the basic facts of sex and repro-duction.

### SKILLS

26. The child should have a range of movement and gymnastic skills.

27. The child should know how to play a variety of games; for example, football, skittle-ball, rounders.

28. The child should be able to swim.

29. The child should know how to apply the basic principles of health, hygiene and safety.

### QUALITIES

30. The child should have precise and economic body control for all ordinary physical activities including the handling of tools and equipment.

## Aims related to aesthetic development

### SKILLS

31. The child should know the appropriate techniques of some arts and crafts; for example, how to use paint, clay.

32. The child should have sufficient know-ledge and skill to be able to engage in simple music-making; for example, singing, percussion, home-made instruments.

33. The child should be able to play a musical instrument such as a recorder, violin, guitar.

34. The child should be able to write legibly and know how to present his work attractively.

### QUALITIES

35. The child should be developing a personal appreciation of beauty in some of its forms, both natural and artistic.

36. The child should be able to communicate his feelings through some art forms; for example, painting, music, drama, movement.

37. The child should be able to listen to and enjoy a range of music; for example, pop, folk, classical.

38. The child should be beginning to under-stand aesthetic experiences and should be able to talk about them; for example, looking at pictures and sculpture, listening to poetry and plays.

## Aims related to spiritual/religious development

### KNOWLEDGE

39. The child should have some knowledge of the Bible and Christian beliefs.

40. The child should have some knowledge of the beliefs of the major world religions other than Christianity.

### QUALITIES

41. The child should try to behave in accordance with the ideals of the Christian religion.

42. The child should try to behave in accordance with the ideals of his own religion whether or not this is Christian.

43. The child should be developing an awareness of the spiritual aspects of prayer and worship.

## Aims related to emotional/personal development

### KNOWLEDGE

44. The child should be beginning to understand his own emotions

45. The child should be beginning to realize that he can play an important part in his own development by, for example, recognizing his strengths and limitations and setting his goals accordingly

### SKILLS

46. The child should be developing the ability to control his behaviour and emotions.

47. The child should be developing the ability to plan independent work and organize his own time.

### QUALITIES

48. The child should be an individual, developing in his own way.

49. The child should be developing the capacity to form a considered opinion and to act upon it even if this means rejecting conventional thought and behaviour.

50. The child should be self-confident; he should have a sense of personal adequacy and be able to cope with his environment at an appropriate level.

51. The child should be happy, cheerful and well balanced.

52. The child should be enthusiastic and eager to put his best into all activities.

53. The child should find enjoyment in a variety of aspects of school work and gain satisfaction from his own achievements.

54. The child should be developing his inventiveness and creativity in some fields; for example, painting, music, mechanical things, poetry, movement.

55. The child should be adaptable to changing circumstances and flexible in outlook.

56. The child should have a questioning attitude towards his environment.

57. The child should find enjoyment in some purposeful leisure time interests and activities both on his own and with others.

QUALITIES

65. The child should be kind and considerate; he should, for example, be willing to give personal help to younger or new children, to consider the elderly, the disabled.

66. The child should be developing tolerance: respecting and appreciating others, their feelings, views and capabilities.

(column cont. on next page)

## Aims related to social/moral development

KNOWLEDGE

58. The child should know those moral values, relating to people and property, which are shared by the majority of members of the society.

SKILLS

59. The child should know how to behave appropriately in a variety of situations; for example, talking to visitors, going on outings, answering the telephone.

60. The child should know how to behave with courtesy and good manners both in and out of school.

(column cont. on next page)

272

**Aims related to social/moral development—cont.**

SKILLS

61. The child should be a good mixer; he should be able to make easy social contacts with other children and adults in work and play situations.

62. The child should know how to speak in a clear and fluent manner appropriate to different situations; for example, informal occasions with children and adults, formal occasions.

63. The child should know how to engage in discussion; for example, he should be able to talk about his own and others' opinions in a reasonable way.

64. The child should know what to do in emergencies; for example, fire, sickness, accident.

QUALITIES

67. The child should be beginning to feel community responsibility; for example, he should be loyal to groups such as class and school of which he is a member and, where possible, the wider community, and willing to accept the responsibilities which membership implies.

68. The child should be able to maintain lasting relationships with a few close friends.

69. The child should be careful with and respectful of both his own and other people's property.

70. The child should be beginning to acquire a set of moral values on which to base his own behaviour; for example, honesty, sincerity, personal responsibility.

71. The child should be industrious, persistent and conscientious.

72. The child should be generally obedient to parents, teachers and all reasonable authority.

TAXONOMY OF EARLY CHILDHOOD EDUCATION GOALS*

The purpose of this book is to extend the use of the MEAN test
evaluation system, originally developed by the Center for the
Study of Evaluation and applied to the assessment of elementary
school tests in a previous publication, to commercially available tests for preschool and kindergarten children.  However,
because the stance adopted here is both pragmatic and objective
rather than theoretical, the first step has been to interview a
wide spectrum of practitioners, including teachers, supervisors,
and early childhood specialists, as well as to conduct an exhaustive search of the program and research literature, to obtain as comprehensive a statement as possible of the professed
objectives of preschool and kindergarten education.  No goals
were eliminated merely because they seemed inappropriate in
terms of the ideology or philosophy of any member of the staff
employed in the preparation of the book.  All these goals were
translated into operational definitions of the desired behaviors,
and these descriptors were then grouped together so as to form
the logical taxonomy which follows.

*Taxonomy of goals of preschool-kindergarten education*

The affective domain
  1.  Development of personality
      A.  Shyness-boldness
          Is not excessively modest, seclusive, or reserved;
          does not avoid or withdraw from personal contact;  is
          not overly dominant or boisterous;  avoids excessive
          exhibition or ascendance;  can be a good leader and a
          good follower;  has social poise.

      B.  Neuroticism-adjustment
          Feels generally happy;  tolerates variety and frustra-
          tion;  is not overly moody, irritable, timid, sensitive,
          or somber;  is not excessively anxious, apprehensive,
          fearful, or emotional.

      C.  General activity-lethargy
          Maintains a healthy level of activity and curiosity;
          is not excessively apathetic, lethargic, fatigued, or
          listless;  has a healthy amount of stamina, endurance,
          and energy.
      D.  Dependence-independence
          Becomes increasingly self-responsible, self-sufficient,
          and autonomous;  has a healthy need for affiliation,
          friendship, and love;  does not have an excessive need
          for attention, acceptance, approval, security, or
          succorance.

* Reproduced from R. Hoepfner *et al.*, *Preschool/Kindergarten Test
  Evaluations*, Center for the Study of Evaluation, ECRC, 1971.

E.  Self-esteem
Develops a healthy self-concept, self-esteem, and self-
confidence;  develops a sense of personal worth, self
understanding, and security;  develops an ability to
present self to others with confidence.

2.  Development of social skills
A.  Hostility-friendliness
Strives to be considerate of others, forgiving, friendly, affectionate, and cooperative;  begins to be aware
of needs, feelings, and wishes of others;  is interested in people;  makes and keeps friends;  begins to
develop positive affective means for emotional release;
has a sense of humor;  is not excessively angry,
aggressive, hostile, aloof, or defensive;  is not
selfish or self-centered.

B.  Socialization-rebelliousness
Knows when to conform and the worth of obedience;
avoids excessive rebelliousness;  does not reject
authority or disrespect his country;  is not persistent-
ly disorganized, sloppy, or reckless;  develops a
reasonable and consistent code of behavior;  is capable
of self discipline, is courteous, polite, respectful,
and hospitable;  expects no special privileges or advantages;  respects public and private property;
shares things willingly.

C.  Moral belief and practice
Applies moral precepts to everyday life;  understands
moral doctrines of honesty, fairness, respect, and in-
tegrity;  knows right from wrong.

3.  Development of motivation for learning
A.  School orientation
Develops a favorable attitude toward attending school,
teachers, school administrators, learning, and an interest in academic subjects.

B.  Need achievement
Is reasonably ambitious, persistent, and competitive;
develops reasonable aspirations;  continues direction
in spite of frustration, handicaps, failures, and
difficulties;  has a reasonable need for superiority;
does his best;  recognizes his best efforts;  appreciates the achievements of others;  sets standards for
himself.

C.  Interest areas
Begins to develop a wide variety of interests;  engages
in various indoor and outdoor recreational activities;
enjoys many school subjects and activities;  begins to
develop potential career interests.

4.  Development of aesthetic appreciation
    A.  Appreciation of art
        Responds emotionally to moods and feelings in art; en-
        joys non-directed self expression through the various
        art media; expresses satisfaction and pride in crea-
        tivity and self expression; makes judgments about art
        work, including his own.

    B.  Music appreciation
        Likes different types of music; develops interest in
        music as a part of school and life experiences; appre-
        ciates beauty as expressed through song and dance;
        develops enjoyment of music; uses music and dance as
        a means for self expression.

## The intellectual domain
5.  Cognitive functioning
    A.  Spatial reasoning
        Develops and uses skills in spatial visualization and
        orientation; is able to identify directions, such as
        up, down, over, under, with or without own body as
        reference.

    B.  Classificatory reasoning
        Recognizes and produces superordinate-subordinate rela-
        tionships or class membership based on common proper-
        ties; uses classification schemes consistently; eva-
        luates classification schemes.

    C.  Relational-implicational reasoning
        Recognizes and produces syllogism, analogies, syllo-
        gistic, and analogic reasoning; recognizes and pro-
        duces inferential solutions to problems.

    D.  Systematic reasoning
        Recognizes, produces, and evaluates complex rules and
        relations, including ordering tasks; uses the analytic-
        deductive conceptual style; solves complex problems.

    E.  Attention span
        Develops selective attention; increases overall time
        of concentration; attends to a wider variety of
        stimuli; can easily shift attention as needed.

6.  Creativity
    A.  Fluency
        Develops fluent production and processing of familiar
        information; fluently produces and elaborates upon
        information; fluently produces original information.

    B.  Flexibility
        Recognizes the identity of an object or process seen
        from different viewpoints; produces reinterpretations
        and redefinitions of known information; learns basic

conservation principles, e.g., conservation of volume.

7. Memory
   A. Span and serial memory
      Memorizes series, sequences, and lists by rote.

   B. Meaningful memory
      Remembers meaningful ideas and information, non rote.

   C. Visual memory
      Remembers what things looked like, how they were
      shaped.

   D. Auditory memory
      Repeats spoken series;  listens for specific details;
      imitates sounds and patterns;  repeats oral selections;
      repeats variations in pitch, stress, and punctuation;
      associates letter sounds and forms.

The psychomotor domain
   8. Physical coordination
      A. Eye-hand coordination
         Is able to draw a line;  can copy and trace basic forms;
         learns to use manipulative toys;  aims and throws
         accurately.

      B. Small muscle coordination
         Is able to hold a pencil in a position for writing;
         open a book and turn its pages;  screw nuts on and off
         bolts;  is able to use scissors proficiently;  can
         color within boundaries of lines.

      C. Large muscle and motor coordination
         Learns to move his body at varying speeds and with
         varying means of locomotion;  is able to control ba-
         lance during body movements;  holds and carries objects
         carefully, responds to rhythm with body movements;
         shows controlled walking, running, skipping, jumping,
         and other fundamental actions.

The subject achievement domain
   9. Arts and crafts
      A. Arts and crafts comprehension
         Makes discriminations in types of art;  recognizes the
         various media;  gains awareness of the many things that
         can be made out of common materials;  develops know-
         ledge of art terminology, vocabulary and concepts.

      B. Expressive and representational skill in arts and
         crafts
         Explores, experiments, and produces expressive and re-
         presentational works in various media;  shows crea-
         tivity and originality, communicates ideas and feelings.

10.  Foreign language
    A.  Oral comprehension of a foreign language
        Responds to basic and idiomatic foreign language.

    B.  Speaking fluency in a foreign language
        Speaks basic and idiomatic language in an acceptable
        manner;  develops spontaneous expressiveness;  speaks
        with good pronunciation.

    C.  Interest in and application of a foreign language.
        [Participates] in foreign language activities in
        class and independently.

    D.  Cultural insight through a foreign language
        Understands another culture;  accepts another culture
        due to study of the language.

11.  Function and structure of the human body
    A.  Identification of body parts and positions
        Knows and can identify various external body parts;
        manipulates them on command;  identifies right and left
        body parts.

    B.  Growth and Development
        Begins to understand the process of growing up;  under-
        stands the value of rest and sleep and the value of
        exercise.

    C.  Knowledge of emotional health
        Understands his emotions;  knows how the environment,
        events, and physical well-being can affect the feelings,
        emotions and behaviors;  is aware of how people may act
        when sad, angry, disappointed, hungry, tired, etc.

    D.  Identification of self and surroundings
        Has realistic mental image of his own body;  under-
        stands his relationship to the immediate environment.

12.  Health
    A.  Knowledge of personal hygiene and grooming
        Develops knowledge of cleanliness in relation to health,
        learns table manners;  understands care of teeth and
        the function of food in building and maintaining the
        teeth.

    B.  Practicing personal hygiene and grooming
        Keeps hands and fingernails clean;  learns toilet
        training;  dresses self;  cares for hair;  keeps
        clothes neat and clean;  practices dental health;
        cares for eyes, ears, and nose;  develops good posture
        habits.

    C.  Knowledge of food and nutrition
        Learns the importance of drinking water;  realizes the
        value of milk and dairy products in the diet;  learns

the importance of eating regular meals.

D.  Practicing food and nutrition
    Eats balanced meals;  drinks proper amount of water.

E.  Knowledge of prevention and control of disease
    Learns detection of symptoms of disease;  understands
    the relationship between cleanliness and health;
    learns simple first-aid procedures;  understands the
    purpose of immunization.

F.  Practicing prevention and control of disease
    Treats and avoids colds;  uses simple first-aid proce-
    dures;  sleeps enough;  gets proper amount of exercise
    and activity.

13.  Mathematics
    A.  Counting and operations with integers
        Recites numbers correctly and in order;  relates coun-
        ted numbers to numerosity of things;  adds and subtracts
        whole numbers;  checks answers.

    B.  Comprehension of sets in mathematics
        Recognizes sets and understands set membership;  per-
        forms basic set operations.

    C.  Comprehension of numbers in mathematics
        Identifies and discriminates numbers and numerals;
        knows cardinal and ordinal numbers and the number line;
        knows odd and even numbers.

    D.  Comprehension of equality and inequality in
        mathematics
        Understands basic ideas of numerical equality and in-
        equality;  understands ideas of parts of things and how
        they relate to the whole;  familiarity with fractional
        terminology.

    E.  Arithmetic problem solving
        Solves simple problems of everyday life;  learns names
        of coins and value relationships;  develops an interest
        in problem solving.

    F.  Measurement reading and making
        Understands concepts of length, volume, weight, time,
        and temperature, and how to measure them.

    G.  Geometric vocabulary and recognition
        Recognizes, names, basic geometric shapes and compo-
        nents;  understands the concept of closed figures,
        curved and straight;  makes basic comparisons among
        geometric shapes.

14.  Music
   A.  Aural identification and music knowledge
       Recognizes melodies of familiar songs;  recognizes ob-
       vious changes in tempo, dynamics, rhythm, and harmony;
       learns to listen to identify sounds;  identifies simple
       musical instruments.

   B.  Singing
       Sings in tune and with good tone quality;  begins to
       sing rhythmically;  develops happy, spontaneous group
       singing.

   C.  Instrument playing
       Explores the sounds of percussion instruments and vari-
       ous ways to play them;  learns to play simple patterns
       of tone and rhythm.

   D.  Rhythmic response (dance)
       Keeps time with music;  develops ability to respond to
       music through large body movements;  expresses himself
       freely in dance;  imitates rhythmic movements;  learns
       simple dances.

15.  Oral language skills
   A.  Oral semantic skills
       Utilizes a spoken vocabulary relevant to needs and emo-
       tions, to home and family, to school activities, to
       community and environment.

   B.  Oral phonology skills
       Produces initial, medial, and final consonant sounds;
       consonant blends, and digraph sounds, and long and
       short vowel sounds in spoken words.

   C.  Oral syntactic skills
       Uses complete sentences;  uses determiners, auxiliary
       words, and verb tenses correctly;  constructs substi-
       tutes or parts of speech and transformations.

   D.  Oral morphology skills
       Forms plurals of parts of speech;  constructs and uses
       compounds and contractions;  uses possessives correctly;
       constructs and uses prefixes and suffixes correctly.

16.  Readiness skills
   A.  General readiness skills
       Recognizes spoken word meanings;  understands pictorial
       representations of meanings;  translates between audi-
       tory and pictorial representations of meanings;
       follows directions.

   B.  Visual discrimination and recognition
       Distinguishes and names colors, shapes, sizes, and
       letter forms rapidly and accurately;  reads from left

to right;  has good figure-ground distinction;  develops mental imagery.

C.   Auditory discrimination and recognition
Differentiates among sounds;  identifies gross sounds and common environmental sounds;  differentiates directions of sources of sounds;  distinguishes among sound characteristics;  identifies the number of words in a sentence and the number of syllables in a word;  identifies accented syllables.

D.   Kinesthetic and tactile perception
Kinesthetic and tactile recognition and perception.

17.   Reading and writing
A.   Recognition of word meanings
Has growing reading vocabulary;  recognizes word meanings through context;  recognizes synonyms and opposites.

B.   Understanding ideational complexes
Grasps the thought of short written sentences and paragraphs;  recognizes main ideas of longer written communications.

C.   Oral reading
Reads aloud with smoothness, emphasis, and intonations;  phrases reading correctly by attending to punctuation marks.

D.   Writing
Independently writes name and basic words.

E.   Familiarity with standard children's literature
Is acquainted with a variety of children's classics.

18.   Religion
A.   Religious belief and practice
Applies religious precepts to everyday life;  understands basic religious doctrines;  participates in religious activities and believes in his religion.

19.   Safety
A.   Understanding safety principles
Understanding reasons for practicing safety;  knows common causes of accidents;  has knowledge of safety principles to help prevent accidents;  knows what to do in case of an accident or other emergency.

B.   Practicing safety principles
Puts into practice his safety knowledge to avoid accidents and maximize safety.

20. Science
    A.  Observation and exploration
        Observes and explores the world around him, including
        the earth, matter, environment, and living things.

    B.  Knowledge of scientific facts
        Develops basic science vocabulary; knows of important
        scientists and their discoveries or inventions.

    C.  Appreciation of the scientific approach
        Develops a scientific attitude toward the unknown; de-
        velops an appreciation of nature; acquires techniques
        of scientific procedure; appreciates science's bene-
        fits to man.

    D.  Development and application of scientific attitude
        Develops scientific interests as leisure time activi-
        ties; uses science as a means of problem solving by
        making observations, asking questions, gathering evi-
        dence, and evaluating conclusions.

21. Social studies
    A.  Community health and safety
        Learns about community helpers who protect our health
        and safety; knows how children can help to maintain
        community health and safety.

    B.  Cultural-economic geography
        Becomes aware of people in other countries and appre-
        ciates their contributions; understands relationships
        of home, family, and community; knows roles and values
        of various types of workers, communications, and travel.

    C.  Democratic practices
        Knows about citizenship, national holidays, basic
        rights, and freedoms (flag and other patriotic symbols);
        knows about our government; relates democratic prac-
        tices to his own environment.

    D.  Physical geography
        Knows about nature and the environment; learns way to
        and from school; knows his neighborhood; learns
        simple geographic concepts; understands simple maps;
        learns concepts of distance and direction.

    E.  History
        Develops a sense of the past; acquires simple histori-
        cal facts; understands the meaning of some holidays;
        begins interpreting current events and developing an
        interest in them.

# Appendix C
# What to look for in a standardized test★

*Identifying data*

1. Title of test.
2. Author/s.
3. Publisher.
4. Date of publication.

*General information*

5. Nature and purpose of test.
6. Grade or age levels covered.
7. Scores available.
8. Method of scoring (hand or machine).
9. Administration time.
10. Forms available.
11. Cost (booklet and answer sheet).
12. The test's antecedents, if any (e.g. the Iowa Tests of Basic Skills, 1954, became the Richmond Tests of Basic Skills, 1974).

*Technical features*

13. *Validity:* type of validity and nature of evidence (content, construct, and criterion-related).
14. *Reliability:* type of reliability and nature of evidence (stability, internal consistency, and equivalence of forms).
15. *Norms:* date of standardization, type, adequacy, and appropriateness to local situation.

*Practical features*

16. Ease of administration (procedure and timing).
17. Ease of scoring.
18. Ease of interpretation.
19. Adequacy of test manual and accessory materials.

★ Slightly modified from N.E. Gronlund, *Measurement and Evaluation in Teaching*, New York: Macmillan (UK: Collier-Macmillan), 3rd rev. ed. 1976, pp.366-7.

*General evaluation*

20. Comments of reviewers (e.g. O.K. Buros, *Tests in Print II*, Highland Park, NJ:  Gryphon Press, 1974).
21. Summary of advantages and limitations for local use.

# Appendix D
# Conversion of raw scores to z scores

The purpose of converting raw test scores to $z$ scores
is to put them in standard form. This standard form
is related to a mathematical curve known as the Normal
curve (or Normal distribution curve). It has been
found that, when a large number of observations are
made, the values obtained for many human characteristics - including body measurements, aptitudes and
personality aspects - are distributed according to
this curve. The curve has a characteristic bell shape
and is symmetrical about the central *mean*, or average
for the set of scores. It has several important
mathematical properties, which are used in analysing
test results. Fig. 7 shows one of these properties:
if we divide the curve into *standard deviation* units,
which indicate the general tendency for scores in the
set to deviate from the mean, we find that each sector
contains a fixed proportion of scores from the set.
Thus, about 34% of the set will occur between the mean
and one standard deviation above it.

As Fig. 7 makes clear, the $z$ score is in fact expressing the raw score in terms of standard deviation
units. There are other ways of expressing a raw score
in standard form, two of which are also shown in Fig.
7. The *stanine* system divides the curve into nine
sectors, and the diagram shows the percentage of the
set of scores that occurs in each division. Alterna-
tively, the *percentile* system may be used. Here, a
score is expressed in terms of the percentage of the
set of scores that occurs below the one in question.
More detailed accounts of these and other standardization methods may be found in texts such as Youngman,[1]
Lewis,[2] and Gronlund.[3]

Once a standard score has been obtained, it is
possible to make comparisons and predictions using the
properties of the Normal curve. Most useful for
teachers is the fact that this procedure permits valid
comparisons to be made between results from different
tests.

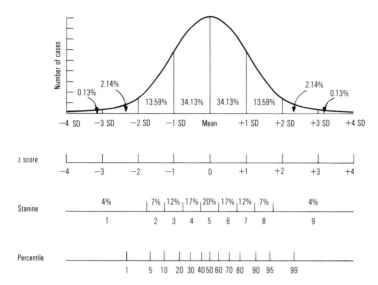

Fig. 7   The Normal curve and some associated standard scores


*Finding the MEAN*

*Step 1:*   Add up all the scores for a particular test.
If we use $X$ to stand for one pupil's score, the
total of all the scores may be written $\Sigma X$.   The
sign $\Sigma$ means 'the sum of'.

*Step 2:*   Divide the total by the number of pupils'
scores ($N$).

$$\text{Mean} = \frac{\Sigma X}{N} \text{ and is often written as } \overline{X}.$$


*Finding the STANDARD DEVIATION (SD)*

Method I
Find the *mean* for the set of test scores (as above).
For each pupil's score perform the following steps.

*Step 1:*   Find the difference ($d$) between each score
and the mean, i.e. ($X - \overline{X}$);   some values will be
positive and some negative, and they will add up
to zero.

*Step 2:* Square each difference ($d^2$) to give positive values throughout.

*Step 3:* Total up all the squared differences to give the sum of squares ($\Sigma d^2$).

*Step 4:* Divide the sum of squared differences ($\Sigma d^2$) by the number of pupils' scores ($N$), i.e.
$$\frac{\Sigma d^2}{N}.$$

*Step 5:* Find the square root of the value for step 4, i.e. $\sqrt{\dfrac{\Sigma d^2}{N}}$.   SD $= \sqrt{\dfrac{\Sigma d^2}{N}}$ and is often denoted by the symbol $\sigma$.

Example calculations

| (1) | (2) | (3) | (4) |
|-----|-----|-----|-----|
| Pupil | Score ($X$) | Difference ($d$) | Squared difference ($d^2$) |
| 1 | 8 | −6 | 36 |
| 2 | 15 | +1 | 1 |
| 3 | 10 | −4 | 16 |
| 4 | 8 | −6 | 36 |
| 5 | 18 | +4 | 16 |
| 6 | 16 | +2 | 4 |
| 7 | 18 | +4 | 16 |
| 8 | 15 | +1 | 1 |
| 9 | 19 | +5 | 25 |
| 10 | 13 | −1 | 1 |
| $N = 10$ | $\Sigma X = 140$ $\overline{X} = 14$ | $\Sigma d = 0$ | $\Sigma d^2 = 152$ |

$$\text{SD} = \sqrt{\frac{152}{10}} = \sqrt{15.2} = 3.89$$

Method II

If you have a calculator with statistical functions, it will be able to give $\Sigma X$ and $\Sigma X^2$ for a series of scores. It is then convenient to use an alternative way of calculating the standard deviation, and some calculators will perform the entire calculation and show the final value. The formula is:

$$\sqrt{\frac{\Sigma X^2 - \dfrac{(\Sigma X)^2}{N}}{N}}$$

*Converting a score to a STANDARDIZED SCORE or z score*

For each pupil's score in the table:    SD = 3.89, mean ($\overline{X}$) = 14.

*Step 1:*    Find the difference between the score and the mean, i.e. $(X - \overline{X})$ or $d$ (column 3 in the table).
*Step 2:*    Divide the obtained value by the standard deviation, i.e.

$$\frac{X - \overline{X}}{SD}.$$

For pupil 1:    score = 8, $\overline{X}$ = 14, SD = 3.89.

$$z \text{ score} = \frac{X - \overline{X}}{SD} = \frac{8 - 14}{3.89} = \frac{-6}{3.89} = -1.54$$

This score indicates that a pupil is placed at a point about 1.5 standard deviations *below* the mean.    A positive value would indicate a similar position *above* the mean.

## REFERENCES

1  M.B. Youngman, *Statistical Strategies* (Rediguide 20), Nottingham University School of Education, 1978.
2  D.G. Lewis, *Statistical Methods in Education*, University of London Press, 1967.
3  N.E. Gronlund, *Measurement and Evaluation in Teaching*, New York:  Macmillan (UK:  Collier-Macmillan), 3rd ed. 1976, part III.

# Appendix E
# Transfer of children's educational and medical records to and from Service Children's schools★

1.  This guide is written for the purpose of explaining in detail the system of transferring pupils' records to and from Service Children's schools. It does not apply to transfers *between* schools and the United Kingdom, as the transfer of records then comes under the jurisdiction of the relevant Local Education Authorities in the UK.

    *Transfer from UK school to Service Children's school overseas*

2.  Service parents who are to be posted overseas from the UK receive with their posting instructions a transfer report (MOD Form 172A) in respect of each of their children of school age. The parent should take this form to the child's UK school for completion by the headteacher. After completion, the transfer report should be collected by the parent and given to the headteacher of the Service Children's school overseas when the child is presented there for the first time.

3.  Headteachers of Service Children's schools overseas should complete and post to SCEA (Schools Branch) an MOD Form 137 in respect of every child arriving at his school from the UK regardless of whether a transfer report is received or not. If a transfer report is not received this fact should be indicated on the MOD Form 137.

4.  On receipt of the completed MOD Form 137, SCEA (Schools Branch) will request the headteacher of the UK school to forward the educational and medical records, enclosing for this purpose two official pre-paid envelopes addressed to the relevant Command Headquarters and naming the Service Children's school as the ultimate addresses. If the medical records are held sepa-

★ Reproduced by permission of the Service Children's Education Authority of the Ministry of Defence.

rately as is often the case please send one of
the pre-paid addressed envelopes, together with
our letter, to the relevant Health Authority.
This enables the documents to be sent from the
UK school directly to the overseas school;  by
air mail to all theatres excepting NW Europe.

5.  If no transfer report has been received from the
UK school via the parent the UK headteacher is
sent a transfer report and, if no documents are
held by the UK school, he is requested to forward it after completion to the overseas headteacher.

6.  If the records are not received by the overseas
school within two months of raising an MOD Form
137 another Form 137 is to be raised marked
'Second Application', underlined in red and forwarded to SCEA (Schools Branch).  On receipt of
the 'Second Application' SCEA (Schools Branch)
will telephone the headteacher of the UK school
requesting that the documents be forwarded to
SCEA for onward transmission to the relevant
Service Children's school.  If for any reason
there is no possibility of obtaining the documents, the headteacher of the overseas school
will be informed.  He should then raise a set of
new records for that child.

*Transfer from Service Children's school
overseas to school in UK*

7.  *Action by overseas headteacher*  Before a child
transfers from an overseas to a UK school the
overseas headteacher should ensure that the
child's parent receives a completed transfer report (MOD Form 460-464) and a partially completed Form 173 to be handed to the UK headteacher
when the child is first presented to the UK
school.

8.  *Action by the UK headteacher*  On receipt of the
partially completed Form 173 the UK headteacher
should complete it and post it, thus requesting
from the overseas headteacher the child's educational and medical records, which the overseas
headteacher on receipt of the card, should forward direct.

9.  *Documents remaining unclaimed*  When no request
for documents has been received at an overseas
school by the end of 3 months *after* that in
which a pupil left the school, the documents
should be forwarded to the Children's Documents
Section.  Before despatch, it is essential that

the BEd 6 (Record Cover) *is completed in full.*

10. *Bulk transfer of documents*  The system of bulk
transfer of documents with the Advance Party when
a unit is posted as a body is to be retained.   In
this case the officer in charge of the bulk
transfer at the despatching end will be instructed to inform the UK or overseas headteachers not
to forward transfer reports and MOD Forms 173 or
137 as the case may be.

11. *Tracing a child's school from unclaimed documents*
In order to trace a child's school it is first
necessary to trace the address of the father's
unit and this is *only possible if the details of
the father* appear clearly and *in full* on the
BEd 6.   By feeding these details to the relevant
Record Office the Children's Document Section
obtain the unit address and can then write to the
unit requesting the address of the child's
school, after receipt of which, the documents can
then be forwarded.

12. *General*  As many thousands of people, world wide,
are engaged in operating this system, there are
obvious difficulties in the way of communications, and for this reason exceptional cases
cannot be catered for within the system.   For the
same reason 'short cuts' and local efforts to
'short circuit' the procedures must be deplored
and discouraged.

# Appendix F
# Suggested frameworks for assessing personal/social and aesthetic development

Of the six curriculum areas originally mentioned by the Assessment of Performance Unit, those concerned with *aesthetic* and *personal/social* development elicited the most response from teachers involved with the project. This was a great surprise to the project team, who felt that, as there had been the greatest manifest activity in the assessment of reading, mathematics and scientific development, the interest of teachers would lie in these three areas. Perhaps it is because so little is known about how to assess the ethical or aesthetic development of children, or indeed whether it is desirable or feasible, that teachers consistently requested more information.

Two stimulus papers were therefore produced for use by the project teachers. Their purpose was to inform the teachers of such theoretical frameworks as existed in this area of the curriculum, in order to help with the evaluation of existing records and the formulation of new ones. These papers were generally well received and are included here for the use of teachers wishing to improve their record keeping in respect of these aspects of children's development.

### PERSONAL/SOCIAL DEVELOPMENT

This aspect of children's development is defined by the APU (see p.21) as: 'The development of the pupil in personal and social relationships. The increase in self-awareness and sensitivity to other people as well as his moral attitude towards his environment.'

Whilst most teachers accept that their responsibilities to children include personal/social development, they also accept its essentially diffuse nature. Aspects of it do appear - sometimes - on the timetable as religious education, or recently as moral education, but generally it is seen as part of the context rather than the content of the curriculum (see p.1). These frameworks are offered as aids to the definition of what might be assessed, hence recorded.

291

*Framework I*

This view of moral development comes from the Farming-
ton Research Trust Unit, which was set up in 1965 to
conduct research into the topic of moral education.
The core research staff included John Wilson (a philo-
sopher), Norman Williams (a psychologist), and Barry
Sugarman (a sociologist).  They put forward a hypo-
thesis of the nature of moral behaviour based on a
number of strands of psychological research and observation.  They identified several component factors
involved in moral behaviour, each best regarded as a
group of similar abilities or an area of activity
rather than a single factor.[1]

  1.  *Cognitive factors*
      (*a*)  'Abilities connected with the formation
             and use of moral concepts', e.g. 'The
             ability to reason morally and to make ra-
             tional judgements:  the cognitive aspects
             of the use and understanding of rules'.
      (*b*)  'Abilities connected with the understand-
             ing of facts and causal relationships',
             e.g. 'Concepts of causality:  the abilities
             to predict consequences ... and to learn
             from one's own or others' experience'.

  2.  *Other ability factors*
      (*c*)  'The ability to relate emotionally to
             others, and ... the ability to identify
             and sympathize with other people'.
      (*d*)  'Ego-controls [self-control], both the
             defence mechanisms ... and other, con-
             scious, means of inhibiting or redirecting
             primitive impulses'.

  3.  *Motivational factors*
      (*e*)  'The super-ego [concern for the self] and
             feelings of guilt'.
      (*f*)  'Social acceptance and feelings of shame'.
      (*g*)  'The ego-ideal and self evaluation'.

Williams argues that, whereas (1) and (2) are concerned with the development of true morality, the motivational factors of moral development in (3) are
not in themselves moral, since behaviour in this case
is entirely motivated 'by the desire to avoid the un-
comfortable feelings, or to have other people approve
of you, or to conform to a self-picture'.[2]
  He adds that there are a number of *preconditions*
which must be met before moral behaviours can arise.

*Preconditions*
'1.  Correct perception:
    (*a*)  of objects and events in the outside
         world;
    (*b*)  of one's own motives, thought and feelings.
  2.  Reality-testing [this term comprises a number
     of activities connected with the boundary
     between self and not-self].
  3.  Intelligence - ... there is a lower level below
     which the idea of rational morality does not
     apply.
  4.  Mental health, or adjustment ... [ditto].'[3]

It could be argued that whereas (1) to (3) are possible starting points for assessment based upon observation, items (1) and (2) of the preconditions for moral behaviour suggested by Wilson, Williams and Sugarman may be used by teachers as an indication of how to approach the task of encouraging mature behaviour (rational morality) in their pupils.

Framework I references
1  J. Wilson, N. Williams, B. Sugarman, *Introduction to Moral Education*, Penguin, 1967, pp.287-8.  See also J. Wilson, *Assessment of Morality*, Slough:  NFER Publishing Co., 1973.
2  Wilson *et al.* (see note 1 above), p.288.
3  Ibid., pp.288-9.

*Framework II*
This view of moral behaviour, in terms of the moral objectives that the core curriculum should incorporate, is principally concerned with the secondary school.  However, it has been included because it gives some idea of a philosophical approach to moral education or development.

'The moral objectives of a uniform curriculum' is an elaboration of the views of J.F. Herbart (1776-1841) by J.P. White (Philosophy Department, University of London Institute of Education).[1]  Its features are as follows.

  1.  *Sympathy with humanity*.  The development of:
    (*a*)  moral attitudes towards individuals;
    (*b*)  imaginative understanding of people's
        points of view in different circumstances
        from one's own.

  2.  *Sympathy with society*.  The development of interest in the welfare of the whole community rather than individuals:

(*a*)   in learning to adopt something like a
'politician's' point of view;

(*b*)   in being equipped with the 'politician's'
knowledge - e.g. complexities of the larger social relationships (e.g. the division of labour) and government and social
institutions.

3.   *Relation of (1) and (2) to the Highest Being*
Raising one's moral insights above ongoing
social and political arrangements to the 'con-
templation of Humanity as a whole and its relationship to the Universe', i.e. the meaning
of life.

Framework II reference
1   J.P. White, 'The moral òbjective of a uniform curriculum',
in M. Taylor (ed.), *Progress and Problems in Moral
Education*, Slough:  NFER Publishing Co., 1975, pp.68-9.


*Framework III*

Some of the most important work in research into moral
development has been carried out by L. Kohlberg, a
developmental psychologist of the Piagetian school.
Although his terms of reference were much wider than
a simple consideration of moral judgement, in that he
hoped to lay bare the sequential stages of moral
thought, most of his conclusions were principally concerned with moral judgements.

Kohlberg deduced that there are six clearly defined
stages of development, each of which depends upon the
level to which the child's moral judgement has
matured.  The last three stages will not apply to the
primary school.

1.   *Pre-moral*
*Stage 1:*  Morality founded on punishment and
its avoidance - no moral obligation, no concept
of the rights of others - no respect for
authority.
*Stage 2:*  Hedonistic morality - centred on the
notion that actions which satisfy needs are
justified for that reason.  Conformity to rules
is for the purpose of gaining favours and re-
wards from others.

2.   *Conventional role conformity.*  Moral value re-
sides in the conformity to the expectation of
others.  It involves understanding and ad-
justing to other people's point of view.

*Stage 3:* 'Good boy' orientation. The right
action is defined by the general consensus and
the motive, to remain accepted by others.
*Stage 4:* Respect for authority. Moral objec-
tion is equated with duty towards social and
religious authority and the motive is to avoid
letting authority down.

3.  *Morality of self-accepted moral principles.*
Morality has now become internalized and auto-
nomous.
*Stage 5:* Morality of contract. The rights of
the individual regardless of status, role,
social importance.
*Stage 6:* Morality of individual principles of
conscience. The universal principles for
guiding conduct.

### Framework III reference

1  L. Kohlberg, 'Development of moral character and ideology',
in M.L. Hoffman and L.W. Hoffman (eds), *Review of Child
Development Research*, vol. 1, New York:  Russell Sage
Foundation, 1964.

*Framework IV*

In his book *Moral Education*,[1] William Kay is concerned
with moral *education* rather than moral *development*.
He sees the task of the educator as to confirm and
inculcate:

1.  the 'preconditions of morality';
2.  the 'primary moral traits';
3.  the 'primary moral attitudes'.

1.  *Preconditions of morality*
        The establishment of:
    (*a*)  sense of identity;
    (*b*)  ability to accept oneself;
    (*c*)  experience of identification;
    (*d*)  development of the informed conscience.
    (*e*)  sustained experience of personal achieve-
           ment.

    All of these are facilitated by the experiences
    of a loving home and familial school.  Kay ar-
    gues that teachers must be aware of the degree
    to which the preconditions of morality have
    been established in every child and furthermore
    make every effort to establish and confirm them
    in their pupils.

2. *Primary moral traits*
   (*a*)  'Moral judgement' - self discipline -
          rational judgements.
   (*b*)  'Moral dynamism and flexibility'.
   (*c*)  'Personality changes' due to moral devel-
          opment.

3. *Primary moral attitudes*
   (*a*)  'Moral autonomy' - an individual can rely
          on the validity of his/her own moral
          judgements.
   (*b*)  'Moral rationality' - the willingness to
          discuss reasonably the moral objectives of
          interpersonal interactions, and the flex-
          ibility to abstract moral principles.
   (*c*)  'Moral altruism' - concern for others.
   (*d*)  'Moral responsibility' - the ability to
          make moral decisions and the willingness
          to accept culpability for one's actions.

**Framework IV reference**
1  W. Kay, *Moral Education*, Allen & Unwin, 1975, ch. 19.

*Framework V*

This derives from suggestions from teachers (from
South Glamorgan - Bridgend group) on frameworks for
recording ethical development based on Dearden's book,
*The Philosophy of Primary Education*,[1] and the Open
University course E283.

   *Ethical development* is concerned with the
   following.
1. Respect and consideration for others, to know
   their feelings and interests.
2. Relationships involving one to one, group,
   class and school situations.  Relationships
   with either sex, adults, peers, etc.
3. Knowledge of oneself.
4. Knowledge of facts relevant to moral choices -
   right, wrong, dangers, etc.
5. Ability to cope with social situations and act
   accordingly.
6. Control over inclinations of aggressiveness,
   greed, intolerance, sexuality.
7. Recognition of positive obligation to others -
   truth telling, promise keeping, co-operation
   in joint enterprises, rendering assistance to
   others in need.
8. Acquisition of concepts of good, bad, worthwhile, desirable, satisfying, happiness, health
   etc.

9. Standards of valuation - respect for property, caring for the environment, etc.
10. Attitudes towards people, objects and situations, opinions and learning.
11. Religion - comparative religions.  People who help us, in need, the world around us.

This could form the basis of a primary record describing the moral or ethical development of pupils.

*Principles of assessment*
1. Assessment could take the form of a profile based on *teacher observation* and knowledge gained from talking to the child, his/her parents and other teachers.
2. It should be used solely within the school, i.e. not handed over on transfer - (this principle was questioned by the group).
3. It should be made with consideration of possible accessibility to other teachers, parents and outside welfare agencies.
4. It should be made with particular concern for objectivity, justifiability and continual updating and reassessment.
5. Possible disparities between moral standards in the home and at school should be taken into account.
6. In the case of 'abnormal' behaviour on the part of the pupils, e.g. signs of maladjustment, unsocial behaviour or aggression, diagnostic tests may be administered either by the teacher or the school psychological service, leading to possible diagnosis of the cause.

Framework V reference
1   R.F. Dearden, *The Philosophy of Primary Education:  an Introduction*, Routledge, 1968, chapter 8.

AESTHETIC DEVELOPMENT

The APU defines aesthetic development (see p.21) as: 'The pupil's appreciation of form, colour, texture, sound.  His affective response to his environment and respect for quality.  "The capacity to harness imagination and feeling in creative work."'
As with personal/social development, this aspect of children's development is diffuse, permeating the whole of the school curriculum and is concerned essentially with *feelings* rather than knowledge. Several other definitions are offered below.

Penguin English Dictionary
*Aesthetics:* 'study of beauty and ugliness; the philosophy of *taste*'.
*Aesthetic, adj.:* 'pertaining to appreciation of
beauty especially in art; keenly appreciating beauty'.

Chambers Twentieth Century Dictionary
*Aesthetic, adj.:* 'relating to perception by the
senses: generally relating to possessing, or preten-
ding to, a sense of beauty'.

Concise Oxford Dictionary
*Aesthetic, adj.:* 'belonging to the appreciation of
the beautiful; having such appreciation; in accordance with principles of good taste'.

Encyclopaedia Britannica
'Aesthetic studies include all the arts including
music and literature, theatre, dance and film as well
as painting, sculpture, architecture, landscape design and town planning. [The subject] deals with the
"useful" as well as the "fine" arts insofar as they
appeal to aesthetic taste'.

These frameworks are offered as aids towards objectivity of assessment and recording

*Framework VI*

   (i)   How does one measure appreciation of form,
         colour, texture and sound?
   (ii)  What are the aims of education with reference
         to aesthetics?

A committee report written in 1899 listed the following aims of art education.

'1. To offer a consistent development in the faculty of sight.
 2. To develop an appreciation of the beautiful.
 3. To acquire the ability to represent.
 4. To develop the creative impulse.
 5. To prepare pupils for manual industry is purely accidental.
 6. The development of professional artists is in no sense the
    aim of art education in the public [i.e. state] schools.'[1]

The last two are indirect and negative in some respect. An analysis of the first four aims may be
worth pursuing.

## 1.  *To develop visual perception*

'Visual training increases the wealth of material the children
have to work with.  If visual training becomes rigid and authoritarian it may inhibit creative activity, but if it is used
to motivate visual curiosity and exploration it should widen
the range of creative students.  Much more effect of light and
colour, of form and line will become available for children to
use.  They will go beyond "cognitive" categorizing and see more
details and significant relations as they respond to their
environment, both visually and cognitively.'[2]

The child progresses from a subconscious use of
art values in the primary school to a conscious use
of them in secondary school.

'Aesthetic values are best learned through personal experience,
rather than through general concepts;  they should be discovered
through activity, not dictated through principles.  The art
experience is more emotional than intellectual, especially at
the lower age levels.'[3]

## 2.  *To develop an appreciation*
How does one recognize a person who appreciates something?

'If we say a person has a *favourable attitude* toward classical
music, it means we predict he will say favourable things about
it, that he will put himself into the presence of that kind of
stimulus, and that he will stay in the presence of that kind of
stimulus as long as he can ...
    If we say that a person has a *negative attitude* toward tele-
vision, it means we are predicting that if he is put into the
presence of a TV set he will try to get away as best he can,
and that he is not likely to bestir himself very·often to put
himself into the presence of that kind of stimulus.'[4]

Two kinds of responses can be observed:

(*a*)  approach - or 'moving toward' behaviours;
(*b*)  avoidance - or 'moving away from' behaviours.

The degree of approach or avoidance behaviours can be
observed informally often without a pupil's knowledge.
A questionnaire or attitude scale could in certain
instances be devised and used, but the user must be
wary of possible distortions.  What one says may be
quite different from what one does.
    Attitudes may be described on a more systematic
basis by using a framework such as the categories of
the 'affective domain'.[5]  This five-category system

is set out to enable the user to describe a pupil's
level of commitment to the task under surveillance.

*Level 1, Receiving*   (passive state of
attending to a situation)
 Awareness;   willing to receive;   selected attention.

*Level 2, Responding*   (active attention to an activity)
 (*a*) Acquiescence in responding (obedience or com-
   pliance).
 (*b*) Willingness to respond (volunteers to carry
   out activity).
 (*c*) Satisfaction in response (enjoys volunteering).

*Level 3, Valuing*   (committed to completing
the preferred task)
 (*a*) Acceptance of a value (shows consistency of
   commitment).
 (*b*) Preference for a value (actively seeks out an
   activity).
 (*c*) Commitment (loyality;   convictionally motivated;   deepening one's involvement in an
   activity).

*Level 4, Organization*   (conceptualizing and
internalizing conflicting values)
 (*a*) Conceptualizing a value (compares own values
   with others).
 (*b*) Organization of a value system (re-ordering
   of one's values to take into account the
   values of others;   developing a philosophy).

*Level 5, Characterization*   (behavioural
characteristics of a person)
 (*a*) Generalized set (a predisposition to act in
   a certain way).
 (*b*) Characterization (develops a consistent philosophy of life).

These categories are arranged from the lowest level,
'receiving', to the highest level, 'characterization'.
The categories 1 to 3 are more likely to be applied
to primary school children than 4 and 5, as the
latter depend on a longer period of experience of
life.
 In analysing this second aim - to develop an
appreciation of the beautiful - the concept of what
is 'beautiful' may pose a greater difficulty than the
identification of 'appreciation'.   Herbert Read
suggests that there are three stages in the development of a sense of beauty:

'... first, the mere perception of material qualities - colours, sounds, gestures, and many more complex and undefined physical reactions;  second, the arrangement of such perceptions into pleasing shapes and patterns.  The aesthetic sense may be said to end with these two processes, but there may be a third stage which comes when such an arrangement of perceptions is made to correspond with a previously existing state of emotion or feeling.  Then we say that the emotion or feeling is given *expression*.'[6]

He goes on later to say:  'Aesthetics, or the science of perception, is only concerned with the first two processes;  art may involve something beyond these values of an emotional kind.'[7]
    The first two stages suggested here would seem to form the basis of the third aim - to acquire the ability to represent.  The skills required to achieve this aim can be categorized under abilities in the 'psychomotor domain';  in particular the sections dealing with 'perceptual abilities' and 'skilled movements'.[8]

## Framework VI references

1   Committee of Ten on Drawing organized by the National Education Association, USA.  Quoted in B.S. Bloom, J.T. Hastings, G.F. Madaus (eds), *Handbook on Formative and Summative Evaluation of Student Learning*, New York:  McGraw-Hill, 1971, p.501.
2   J.K. McFee, *Preparation for Art*, Belmont, Calif.:  Wadsworth, 1961, p.63.
3   V. D'Amico, *Creative Teaching in Art*, Scranton, Pa:  International Textbook Co., 1953, p.49.
4   R.F. Mager, *Developing Attitude toward Learning*, Palo Alto, Calif.:  Fearon, 1968, p.15.
5   D.R. Krathwohl *et al.*, *Taxonomy of Educational Objectives: the Classification of Educational Goals*, Handbook 2, *Affective Domain*, Longmans, 1964.
6   H. Read, *The Meaning of Art*, Faber, 1969 printing, p.20.
7   Ibid., p.20.
8   See Figure 5 in A. Harrow, *A Taxonomy of the Psychomotor Domain:  a Guide for Developing Behavioral Objectives*, New York:  McKay, 1972.  Psychomotor behaviours in industrial education are discussed by T.S. Baldwin's 'Evaluation of learning in industrial education', chapter 23 in Bloom *et al.* (see note 1).

*Framework VII*

This framework considers creativity. Jackson and Messick[1] argue that there are four major main components of creativity.

- (i)   novelty and unusualness (as compared with that in children of similar age);
- (ii)  appropriateness - must make sense;
- (iii) transformation power - the transformation of material and ideas to overcome conventional constraints - involves creation of new forms;
- (iv)  condensation - products which have intensity and concentration. Both (iii) and (iv) are more difficult to judge than (i) and (ii).

This analysis of creativity could be adapted to provide a framework for record keeping using aims/objectives procedures.

*1.  Aims*
To produce in pupils:
- (*a*)  originality → work that is → unusual;
- (*b*)  sensitivity → work that is → appropriate;
- (*c*)  flexibility → work that is → perceptive;
- (*d*)  poetry       → work that is → poetic, condensed.

*2.  Teaching style*
To elicit:
- (*a*)  originality → tolerance of incongruity, inconsistency;
- (*b*)  sensitivity → analytic and intuitive behaviours;
- (*c*)  flexibility → open mindedness;
- (*d*)  intensity, poetic response → reflective and spontaneous behaviours.

*3.  Evaluation*
Creative products may be assessed in the following way.

| Creative responses | Standards against which judgements are made | Criteria upon which judgements are made |
| --- | --- | --- |
| Originality | norms | likely to evoke surprise |
| Appropriateness | context | likely to evoke satisfaction |
| Transforming power | constraints | likely to evoke stimulation |
| Intensity, poetry | summary | likely to evoke savouring |

## Framework VII reference

1  P.W. Jackson and S. Messick, The person, the product, and the response:  conceptual problems in the assessment of creativity', *J. Personality* 33, 1965, 309-29.

*Framework VIII*

This uses a *cognitive-developmental* approach to aesthetic development,[1] similar to Piaget's theory of moral development.

Stage I (i.e. before about 8 years of age)
Use of notion of 'favourites', whereby children identify the attractiveness of objects directly to themselves, e.g. 'I like it therefore it is good'.  They tend to ignore the opinions of others.  Judgements and preferences are heavily idiosyncratic.

Stage II:  Primary (i.e. 8 to 11+)
Use of rules and conventions.  'The theory of "favourites" is abandoned, we may suppose, because it begins to conflict with the facts of perception and of social life.'  In its place comes the idea that 'what really counts about a work of art is to what extent it satisfies a certain kind of rule. The attraction of the object lies in this satisfaction and hence anyone can see it.'
    There are three categories of rules at this stage.

1.  Rules of *realism:*  '... an implicit set of rules' is formulated, 'to which paintings are expected to conform'.  They must be recognizable.
2.  Rules of *form:*  Children of primary school age 'tend to comment increasingly on formal matters:  questions of balance, harmony, contrast, repetition, grouping and so on'.
3.  Rules of *subject-matter:*  '... expectations concerning aesthetic subject-matter are more conventional and less whimsical than at the earlier stage ...  In general they include the pretty, the picturesque, the nostalgic, the magnificent;  the most general praise word becomes the "beautiful".'

Stage III:  beginning at pre-adolescent
It is now realized that there may be alternative sets of rules by which works can be judged, rather than 'realism' alone.  'The expressive qualities of art become central to response, contrasting with the rather formal approach of the previous stage', which was mainly concerned with technique and skill.

Stage IV (post adolescent)
'I take this stage to be the end point of development because it marks the end of the decentering
process, by locating aesthetic qualities firmly in
the aesthetic object itself and not in some more
egocentric relation.'

Framework VIII reference
1   Based on M.J. Parsons, 'A suggestion concerning the
    development of aesthetic experiences by children',
    *J. Aesthetics and Art Criticism*, 1976, 305-14.

*Framework IX*

A further framework for recording aesthetic development is suggested by Robert Witkin in his book *The
Intelligence of Feeling*.[1] Though his ideas derive
from research on the traditional arts curriculum at
secondary level and are, for the most part, highly
complex and heavily theoretical, the importance of
his ideas lies in the fact that Witkin attempts to
throw light on the connexion between art education
and the development of sensations and feelings in the
young.

He sees the arts curriculum as being primarily
concerned with 'the emotional development of the
child through creative self-expression' and the role
of the teacher as developer of the *intelligence of
feeling* in the pupil. In brief, he defines the intelligence of feeling as the way the individual comes
to understand the world of his or her own feelings
and emotions. This clearly differs from the traditional role of education, which is principally concerned with giving pupils knowledge and skills of the
world of objects.

Witkin suggests a tentative outline for the
classification of *sensate experience*, i.e. senses or
disturbances within the individual. Whereas there is
no attempt to define specific stages of sensate development, Witkin identifies eight operations in
terms of which the ordering of sensate experience may
be described. This has a general applicability to
all of the creative arts, e.g. literature, drama,
art, music, etc.

Pre-adolescent stages
*Level 1, 'Contrasts':* Understanding distinctive fea-
    tures by virtue of contrast, e.g. contrasts in
    shape and colour.

*Level 2, 'Semblances':*  Recognizing similarities, e.g. bright yellow may bring to mind bright red.

*Level 3, 'Harmonies':*  Recognition of the way in which some sensates blend together, e.g. musical chords.

*Level 4, 'Discords':*  Recognition of the way in which certain sensates conflict, e.g. colours that clash.

Adolescent and post-adolescent stages
*Level 5, 'Polarities':*  Recognition of a continuum of contrast.
*Level 6, 'Identities':*  Recognition of a continuum of similarities.

*Level 7, 'Synthesis':*  Where individual sensations or sensate events can be blended into a whole.

*Level 8, 'Dialectics':*  Where sensate contradictions and divisions blend into a whole.

It is difficult to see how the above analysis can be used in the formulation of a record.  However, it does reveal the conceptual complexity involved when we as teachers try to influence the personal or aesthetic development of our pupils by offering them situations designed specifically for 'creative self-expression'.  What do we really mean?  Are we seriously concerned, as Witkin is, to develop intelligence of feeling, *or* do we organize our lessons hoping in a vague fashion that our pupils will become more 'creative', *or* is 'creative self-expression' a term used as a smoke-screen when teachers are not quite sure what precisely they are trying to achieve?

Framework IX reference
1   R.W. Witkin, *The Intelligence of Feeling*, Heinemann Educational Books, 1974, chapter 8.

*Framework X*

This last framework is based on classroom practice. Rather than looking towards academic theory to provide frameworks for recording aesthetic development, it may prove more fruitful to start at classroom level.  Teachers have suggested that careful recording of aesthetic *experience*, in the form of *materials used*, is preferable to the class teacher's subjective assessment of the aesthetic development of each pupil. Many primary teachers attempt to provide for their pupils a number of widely varying craft techniques which may then be used in lessons other than the traditional 'art' or 'art and craft' lesson.  It would be useful, therefore, if teachers with new classes could be informed of the craft techniques which their pupils have already experienced. Such a record would perhaps look like Fig. 8. Where a pupil has used a certain medium, the date would then be put in the appropriate box. The number of entries would indicate the regularity of use of a particular craft technique and possible pupil expertise.

Fig. 8 Suggested record for craft experiences

MATERIALS USED IN CRAFT ACTIVITIES

Name ............................

| | Date | | | | | | | | | | | | |
|---|---|---|---|---|---|---|---|---|---|---|---|---|---|
| Painting | | | | | | | | | | | | | |
| Powder paint | | | | | | | | | | | | | |
| Poster paint | | | | | | | | | | | | | |
| Oil paint | | | | | | | | | | | | | |
| Other | | | | | | | | | | | | | |
| Wax crayon | | | | | | | | | | | | | |
| For drawing | | | | | | | | | | | | | |
| Wax-resist printing | | | | | | | | | | | | | |
| Oil pastels | | | | | | | | | | | | | |
| 3 dimensional construction | | | | | | | | | | | | | |
| Clay | | | | | | | | | | | | | |
| Plasticine | | | | | | | | | | | | | |
| Plaster of Paris | | | | | | | | | | | | | |
| (etc.) | | | | | | | | | | | | | |

Although art education has been regarded as 'particularly concerned with fostering the growth of imagination'[1] and not with the accumulation of specific craft skills, a record such as the aforementioned may provide important data for teachers who are considering their future curriculum programme.

Framework X reference

1 Department of Education and Science, *Art in Schools*, (Education Survey 11), HMSO, 1971, p.93.

*Addendum*

Can the school influence the creative power of its
pupils - is it desirable?  This is a description of a
'creative' scientist:

'He was the first born child of a middle-class family, the son
of a professional man.  He is likely to have been a sickly
child or to have lost a parent at an early age.  He has a very
high I.Q. and in boyhood began to do a great deal of reading.
He tended to feel lonely and 'different' and to be shy and
aloof from his classmates.  He had only a moderate interest in
girls and did not begin dating them until college.  He married
late (at 27), has two children and finds security in family
life;  his marriage is more stable than the average.  Not until
his junior or senior year in college did he decide on his vocation as a scientist.  What decided him (almost invariably) was
a college project in which he had occasion to do some independent research - to find out things for himself.  Once he discovered the pleasure of this kind of work, he never turned
back.  He is completely satisfied with his chosen vocation.
(Only one of the 64 eminent scientists - a Nobel prize winner -
says he would have preferred to do something else:  he wanted
to be a farmer, but could not make a living at it.)  He works
hard and devotedly in his laboratory, often seven days a week.
He says his work is his life, and he has few recreations, those
being restricted to fishing, sailing, walking or some other
individualistic activity.  The movies bore him.  He avoids
social affairs and political activity, and religion plays no
part in his life or thinking.  Better than any other interest
or activity, scientific research seems to meet the inner need
of his nature.'[1]

and:

'My own suspicion is that progressive schools do make most
children happier than authoritarian ones;  but that they with-
draw from children the cutting edge that insecurity, competi-
tion, and resentment supply.  Here the progressive dream comes
home to roost.  If we adjust children to themselves and each
other, we may remove from them the springs of their intellectual and artistic productivity.'[2]

Researchers suggest that eminently creative people
tend to (be):

1.  original, unconventional, inventive;
2.  perceptive;
3.  insightful;
4.  independent in judgement, self-sufficient;
5.  open to new experience, open-minded, flexible;
6.  sceptical;

7.  verbally facile;
8.  humorous;
9.  tolerant of ambiguity, delighting in para-
    doxes, preferring complexity;
10. wide-ranging in interest;
11. less interested in small details;
12. interested in the practical and concrete
    rather than in theoretical ideas and symbolic
    transformation;
13. ambitious;
14. achievement-oriented, determined;
15. dominant;
16. have a sense of destiny about themselves;
17. emotionally mature;
18. venturesome, displaying playfulness;
19. emotionally and aesthetically sensitive;
20. industrious;
21. introspective;
22. have greater femininity;
23. self-centred;
24. exhibitionistic;
25. prone to retreat to the role of observer.

Is this a checklist which could be used in the classroom for identifying potentially creative individuals
or for marking out children's development in creativity?

Addendum references
1   A. Roe, 'A psychologist examines 64 eminent scientists',
    *Scientific American* 187 (5), November 1952, p.22.
2   L. Hudson, *Contrary Imaginations: a Psychological Study
    of the English Schoolboy*, Methuen, 1966, p.114.